LO GOD

& EVERYTHING

"Predicated on the truths of quantum physics, Nicolya Christi's bold and exciting synthesis weaves modern energy field science, including the powerful influence of astronomy, with ancient spiritual insights to reveal the vibrational fabric composing the Universe. Nicolya's heroic intention is to awaken a sense of cosmic consciousness that will facilitate the survival of human civilization and all life on Earth. Her inclusive insights offer a pathway out of a world in chaos by enabling readers to evolve from passive victims to responsible co-creators of their life experiences. *Love, God, and Everything* provides a bold and hopeful vision of the next 'holistic' stage of human civilization—and how each of us can fully participate as co-creators of the world to come. Nicolya Christi offers readers a remarkable opportunity to move beyond misperceived limitations and write new empowering stories for themselves, their children, and the world."

BRUCE LIPTON, PH.D., AUTHOR OF *THE BIOLOGY OF BELIEF*

"Nicolya Christi has reached a level of spiritual development that is nearly unmatched in the contemporary world. To read what she has written is to catch a glimpse of the reality that lies below the surface and makes us who we are: beings that come from love, are love, and to love will return. To fail to benefit from and to live Nicolya's message is a crime against humanity—and against us, as intelligent and responsible members of humanity."

ERVIN LASZLO, PHILOSOPHER AND AUTHOR OF *SCIENCE AND THE AKASHIC FIELD*

"Part memoir, part spiritual primer, this book takes us on a revelatory journey throughout multi-dimensions and our own ancient history all at the same time. Thorough, unique, and profound, Nicolya's wise voice comforts, reassures, and enlightens us. The feeling one is pervaded with when reading this sagacious work is one of having a visionary and trusted friend and guide accompany you on a sacred inner journey. If you are ready to dig deep, you will not be disappointed, but know that you just might find yourself getting so joyfully lost in this marvelous, magical, and mystical book, you might never want to come back out!"

PATRICE KARST, AUTHOR OF THE *THE INVISIBLE STRING*

"I've known Nicolya for a long time, and it has been extraordinary to witness her loving and empowering message for humanity expand to all those who are ready and willing to receive it. In her new book, Nicolya continues to bring to the world her miraculous gifts of awakening. She leads the reader on a journey to self-discovery and into the heart of the very meaning and purpose of life. If you enjoy reading books that provide life-changing teachings and insights, you will want this one in your collection."

EMMANUEL DAGHER, AUTHOR OF
EASY BREEZY MIRACLE

"Momentous—a book for our times. This remarkable work illuminates the great evolutionary transition we are undergoing as a species. Christi's phenomenal experiences on the other side of this evolutionary shift give us hope, direction, and guidance for who we are becoming and what we are destined to do. Thus, the next dimensions of reality can be guided and illuminated by her profound life's work, which is so clearly written for all to see and understand."

BARBARA MARX HUBBARD (1929–2019), FUTURIST,
VISIONARY, AND COFOUNDER AND PRESIDENT
OF THE FOUNDATION FOR CONSCIOUS EVOLUTION

"Nicolya Christi guides humanity to a place of transformation and empowers the love that resides within us all. This perspicacious book propels us into a phenomenal exploration of who we really are and where we are really from and more fully connects us to the divine spark that resides within each one of us. I see Christi as a leader who brings great hope and shines the light of realization on a world that is evolving fast, a world we can co-create together, and one in which all can live side by side in greater peace and understanding."

MASAMI SAIONJI, GLOBAL PEACE ACTIVIST AND
AUTHOR OF *YOU ARE THE UNIVERSE*

"This is one of a very small handful of especially important books I have read in more than fifty-five years of professional reading. It is a book that may well shake you to your roots and what you believed to be firmly established knowledge. At the same time it could bring you great peace, as it did to me, through its strong conviction that we are not directing the incredible show that has been running for millions of years on this planet but that there is a Higher Intelligence that appears to have quite a clear idea of where we are really going, even if we do not."

PIERRE PRADERVAND, AUTHOR OF
THE GENTLE ART OF BLESSING

LOVE, GOD
& EVERYTHING

Awakening from the Long, Dark Night of the Collective Soul

NICOLYA CHRISTI

Bear & Company
Rochester, Vermont

Bear & Company
One Park Street
Rochester, Vermont 05767
www.BearandCompanyBooks.com

Text stock is SFI certified

Bear & Company is a division of Inner Traditions International

Cataloging-in-Publication Data for this title is available from the Library of Congress

ISBN 978-1-59143-421-4 (print)
ISBN 978-1-59143-422-1 (ebook)

Printed and bound in the United States by Lake Book Manufacturing, Inc.
The text stock is SFI certified. The Sustainable Forestry Initiative® program
promotes sustainable forest management.

10 9 8 7 6 5 4 3 2 1

Text design and layout by Virginia Scott Bowman
This book was typeset in Garamond Premier Pro, Legacy Sans, and Gill Sans with
Fnord Forty and Goudy Oldstyle used as display typeface

To send correspondence to the author of this book, mail a first-class letter to the
author c/o Inner Traditions • Bear & Company, One Park Street, Rochester, VT
05767, and we will forward the communication, or contact the author directly at
https://nicolyachristi.love.

Contents

Foreword

Ervin Laszlo

To write a foreword to *Love, God, and Everything* is a curious sensation for me: it is like writing a foreword to my own unwritten book. This book has remained unwritten by me not because I did not want to write it, but because I could not write it—not in the form in which Nicolya Christi has written it.

This book conveys the experience of a mind-boggling reality, beyond the everyday world. I could not have written any part of this book myself—nobody could but Nicolya. This is not a book that was thought out and planned; it is a book that has been lived and is communicated as lived. Its spirit is inclusive: it embraces the experience of our species, embedded in the experience of all life in the biosphere.

It appears that there comes a time in the history of a conscious species when it becomes necessary for that species to become conscious of its own existence—of what unites it with other forms of life, what distinguishes it in its unique individuality, and why it exists in the first place. Such a time has dawned for our species. Recognizing who we are, what the world is, and why we are in the world has become a precondition of our continued presence on this planet. This recognition is not something we can achieve by logic and reasoning, although logic and reasoning can support it. This is a spontaneous happening—a happening that Nicolya and other spiritually advanced persons call "awakening." It appears that Nicolya was born with the ability to achieve the fullness of awakening. The insights that mark the way stations of this stupendous process are reflected in her spontaneous, deep, and extraordinary experiences.

In my case, the corresponding recognition has been reached by surveying what I and science in general know of life and the Universe and of the nature of Consciousness. The way we have reached our "awakening" has differed, but its substance has been the same. It would be both presumptuous and unnecessary for me to try to describe or characterize Nicolya's experiences as she recounts them in this book. Her experiences are real and meaningful and need to be grasped in the way she communicates them.

But what can we or do we need to do on reading these experiences? I can answer this with two words: *listen* and *remember*. Here *listen* means to read and be open to what you read. Then you will absorb the meaning and make it your own. And when the meaning becomes yours, you will *remember*. *Remembrance* as Nicolya calls it, in company with Plato and scores of insightful individuals, is basic to a meaningful life. We are speaking of *re*-membrance because this is not the first time we have encountered the meaning communicated here; it has been intuitively present throughout our life. What is unique in this book is the direct vivid experiencing of the insights that carry this meaning. We need to listen; we will then absorb, and we will then *remember*. There is nothing simpler and more important in our life than this.

A few years ago, Nicolya wrote a book called *2012: A Clarion Call*. Now she has written another book proclaiming the same crucial Call. She is uniquely privileged to live the Call she proclaims: In her experience, it is a multidimensional super-Technicolor feature presentation of our being and the being of our world. She is fortunate in living it and being able to communicate it. And we are fortunate in receiving it from her. This is a stroke of fortune, because while the hour to wake up is late, perhaps, just perhaps, it is not *too* late.

We need to pick up Nicolya's real-life Call to the Soul and to the World and absorb its meaning. We will not be the same person ever after.

It has always been my hope to contribute to a call for a timely global awakening, and now I can join Nicolya in doing so by reissuing her call. Receiving and responding to it is not an academic exercise but a spontaneous life-transforming experience. For all our sakes, I can only wish that this transformation will spread throughout the world.

Nicolya is a true visionary, thinker, and thought leader, and her insights are profound and unique and merit vast public readership and recognition across the board. Her book reveals the substance of her vision and how this connects with what I have contributed all these years in terms of the new paradigm in science, and I value it, indeed I think it is essential reading. Her "tome" conveys the wisdom that comes through a direct experience of the Intelligence that lies at the heart of the Universe.

ERVIN LASZLO is a philosopher and systems scientist. Twice nominated for the Nobel Peace Prize, he has published more than seventy-five books and over four hundred articles and research papers. The subject of the one-hour PBS special *Life of a Modern-Day Genius*, Laszlo is the founder and president of the prestigious Laszlo Institute of New Paradigm Research. The winner of the 2017 Luxembourg Peace Prize, he lives in Tuscany. In 2019, Ervin Laszlo was cited as one of the "100 Most Spiritually Influential Living People in the World" according to *Watkins Mind Body Spirit* magazine.

Acknowledgments

The journey this book has taken to arrive in your hands has been a lengthy and eventful one. I would like to thank the following Soul friends and colleagues for their invaluable advice or support along the way.

Firstly, I bow to my mother's spirit, for the writing of this book began while sitting right next to her sickbed as she prepared for her own journey **HOME**,* a process that began in June 2013 and ended in June 2017. As we sat in silence, for she was unable to talk as she lay between worlds, I was often struck by a powerful sense that her Soul was "out there" facilitating a Higher-Dimensional connection in support of bringing through some of the unique metaphysical insights I share. I would also like to thank her spirit for consenting to include *our experience* of her final moments in this world. I know she offers this as her own legacy, in terms of what she wished to convey regarding what really happens when we leave this mortal body. You are always with me mum, and I with you. I love you.

Secondly, I would like to thank my editor, who also happens to be one of my closest friends, Cherry Williams. Together, we have traveled this path for over eleven years and it is, and has always been, a deeply respectful, harmonious, and effortless dance of communication and

---

*See the glossary at the back of the book for my expanded and deeper meaning of this word.

communion. Thank you, Cherry. This book would not be the quality of read that it is without you. LOVE and Namaste.

The next wave of inexpressible gratitude goes to Jon Graham, acquisitions editor at Inner Traditions. From the moment Jon first read the manuscript in January 2019 he championed its publication. It was a long and arduous road to finally securing a contract, yet Jon persevered as he felt the book had something special, and after eighteen months of advocating for it he was finally given a yes in June 2020. Without his efforts this book would not be in your hands. Thank you from the depths of my heart and Soul for making this possible Jon. Namaste and LOVE.

A special thank you to my project editor, Meghan MacLean, for ensuring that the raw manuscript achieved its final perfected state ready for publishing with grace and in an effortless flow, for listening deeply, and for always communicating in a positive and respectful manner. Thank you again, Meghan, for making this final stage of the labor a beautiful memory. Namaste and LOVE.

Another special thank you to my publicist, Manzanita Carpenter, for always being so consistently respectful and responsive, so accommodating, so present, and so understanding and encouraging. Namaste and LOVE.

I would also like to express gratitude to another heart friend, Patricia McCurry, who painstakingly pored over the final manuscript with the necessary and uncompromisingly critical eye it needed for its final draft. She also reproduced a perfect interpretation of the rudimentary scribbles and sketches I had sent her regarding the illustrated models I wished to include. Patricia, thank you. Namaste and LOVE.

My sincere appreciation also to John Hayes, sales director at Inner Traditions, who supported the ongoing efforts to secure a publishing contract. John, thank you so much. Namaste and LOVE.

My deepest appreciation and gratitude to my agent, Bill Gladstone, who utterly believed in the manuscript and remained diligently present and supportive in the interim between submitting it and my publisher ultimately taking it on. Thank you for holding the faith, Bill. Namaste and LOVE.

Finally, I would like to thank my endorsers: the genius cellular biologist and spiritual voice for a movement that is Bruce Lipton; the philosopher extraordinaire that is Jean Houston; the incomparable visionary and futurist that was/is the late Barbara Marx Hubbard; the twice Nobel Peace Prize nominee and world-leading quantum scientist and systems theorist that is Ervin Laszlo; the award-winning global peace activist, spiritual teacher, and author that is Masami Saionji; the bestselling author and renowned spiritual teacher that is Emmanuel Dagher; the bestselling author and inspirational healer of children through the written word that is Patrice Karst; and the deeply spiritual and pure example of unconditional love that is the bestselling author and spiritual teacher Pierre Pradervand. Thank you, thank you, thank you, for your precious words that reflect so well the overall message of this book. Namaste and LOVE.

Note to the Reader
Regarding a Glossary of Terms

Several important or unusual terms have been outlined in the glossary at the back of the book for easy reference. These terms are denoted in bold and with a * symbol at first use.

INTRODUCTION

Messages from the Heart of the Cosmos

A Story of the Soul and the World

This is essentially a book about LOVE and CONSCIOUSNESS. Born out of a lifetime of direct spiritual and extraordinary metaphysical experience, it conveys the wisdom and insights that have led to my personal philosophy of truth, and all that I have come to realize about the spirit and Soul, the metaphysical and mystical, and the **psychospiritual*** and physical. It is an offering to our collective exploration as to the meaning and purpose of Life and Love on Earth and Beyond. The content and words combine to create a powerful energetic transmission, and while the information may inspire, it may also challenge, as it amplifies all that may block our journey of psychospiritual healing, integration, and awakening.

This book also aims to convey the profundity and truth of a higher-dimensional reality. Within its pages I share publicly, for the first time, the extensive catalogue of extraordinary metaphysical and **out-of-body experiences (OBEs)*** I have personally undergone since early childhood. These include a "conscious dying" experience that occurred in 2002 and a "moment of **enlightenment***" in 2009 that ultimately transformed my entire understanding of life on this Earth. I share highly metaphysical and spiritual insights inspired by my personal mystical experiences for the purpose of informing, enlightening, and accompanying you,

1

the reader, on an exploratory journey that addresses some of the most **existential*** questions about life on Earth and life beyond the physical human experience.

Within these pages, I also revisit some of the passages I originally presented in my first book *2012: A Clarion Call—Your Soul's Purpose in Conscious Evolution*. I have edited and integrated the most essential elements of information that remains highly relevant to the critical times in which we are now living. Echoes of the voices of ancient wise ones from long ago support the spiritual and metaphysical insights I share and confirm how a Conscious humanity *can* cocreate a visionary, enlightened, and harmonious world.

The book also focuses on the psychological, biological, technological, and cosmological, aspects of a new Conscious paradigm. It explores the origins of consumerism within the context of **epigenetics*** and how this relates to conscious evolution. It touches on major astrological events in the coming years that will exert a defining evolutionary influence on individual and **collective consciousness*** and support the conscious awakening of the world. An in-depth overview of a new age in health, wellness, and regeneration is presented in the appendix, along with glimpses of some of the key elements of a new Conscious world.

A note on language: Throughout the book you will come across specific words that are presented in three ways: lowercased, capitalized, or in all capitals—for example, consciousness, Consciousness, and CONSCIOUSNESS. This is purposeful and explained in the upcoming chapters. You will also encounter various terms in all caps such as LOVE, CONSCIOUSNESS, GOD, THE DIVINE, THE BELOVED, and SOURCE, all of which are interchangeable for they describe the same thing: the Origin and Ultimate Reality of the incarnate Soul in human form.

This is a book that invites you to explore, consider, and meditate on the hypotheses of *transcendence* presented herein. It addresses some of the most fundamental questions about this life and life after this life; questions that philosophy, religion, mysticism, and spirituality have been contemplating for millennia. It will take you on an evolutionary journey and through the "veil" that marks the threshold between this mortal realm and the Infinite Reality that exists beyond it.

Fundamentally, it will lead you on a journey of discovery, of the *more than* you are, the *more than* of life as you may know it, and the *more than* that is the Ultimate Reality of Life beyond this physical domain. As you move through the pages allow the book to take you gently by the hand and accompany you into the very depths of your heart and Soul and into the limitlessness and boundlessness that is the Heart of the Cosmos and Beyond.

Read this book with an open mind for you will encounter unique concepts and theories in regard to key existential questions including, Who are we? Why are we really here? Where are we really from? and Where do we go when we "die"? Much of what I share originated from my lifelong communication and communion with the Higher Realms as well as my extensive and ongoing metaphysical experiences that brought about many of the profound spiritual realizations and conclusions that are included here.

The abstract source of the metaphysical, spiritual, and philosophical material is numinous and therefore not possible to prove, disprove, or substantiate factually. Yet, remember the ancient Gnostics who had direct metaphysical and spiritual experiences and **gnosis***—*to know yet not know how we know, we just know*—and wrote a treatise about them to be circulated within the wider community. Others would then share their own gnosis in the light of this Work and each commentary would build upon and complement the original treatise.

The book also focuses on the phenomenal and enlightening ancient wisdom teachings and prophecies that have been handed down to humanity throughout millennia by the most sagacious and prophetic visionaries and cultures. This sacred wisdom has now arrived at its ultimate destination—these modern times—and speaks of the unparalleled crises confronting humanity and Nature, yet, also of prophecy that foretells of an unprecedented and extraordinary transformation of our world.

The material explores the emergence of a New Conscious Eon, which is potentially the most significant event to ever have occurred on the evolutionary timeline of humanity. It highlights what we need to do to bring an end to the old dysfunctional **paradigm*** that has its roots in the love of power and to co-manifest an enlightened new epoch founded upon the Power of Love.

The aim of this book is to present the most pressing and pertinent information that can support a consciously awakening/awakened humanity to safely and successfully navigate through and out the other side of the long dark night of the collective Soul. It seeks to explain just how and why it is that we have arrived at the exact moment prophesied by the ancient wise elders: the time of humanity's ultimate rise or fall. They spoke of the following two potential outcomes: (1) planet-wide destruction on an irreversible scale that would ultimately lead to extinction and (2) complete global regeneration and the birth of an enlightened new age.

The outcome is ultimately dependent upon one critical factor: *Remembrance*—remembering who we really are and why we are really here and that we are spirits incarnate in human form who have chosen to be in the world at this crucial but auspicious time to cocreate a sweeping new age, a Lotus Eon.

The book also strives to convey an evolutionary truth: collectively, we seem to understand that the imperative is to position ourselves in Unity Consciousness and refuse to be part of any expression that supports even an iota of separation. What remains essential is the need to work together, to align in Oneness and Greater Purpose. The time is now upon us to commit to supporting and being part of the cocreation of a new Conscious paradigm and to remember that as nearly eight billion people, we are not the "insignificant" microcosm but the influential and effectual macrocosm. When we join together as enlightened Consciousness, we can move mountains to manifest peace in the world.

No force is mightier than an awakened, unified, visionary, and empowered humanity that is rooted in uncompromising, unwavering, and unequivocal Love, Wisdom, and Truth.

Life is a miracle, and it is my deepest wish that *Love, God, and Everything* will transpire to create a miracle in your life. May experiencing it guide you to new inspired levels of awakening and remembrance. This may be a physical book, but its essence is that of Spiritual Revelation, a divinely timed affirmation of the awe-inspiring reality of the miracle we each are, the reality that is Life on Gaia, and the reality of LIFE beyond this earthly realm.

1

Direct Metaphysical Experiences and Spiritual Insights

We are LOVE, we are from LOVE, and to LOVE we shall return.

NICOLYA CHRISTI

I have chosen to open this book with an in-depth account of my own extensive metaphysical and spiritual experiences, which transpired to answer the myriad existential questions I have been reflecting upon since I was a young girl: *Who are we? Why are we really here? Where are we really from? And, where do we go when we "die"?* The ultimate realization I have arrived at is that *we are LOVE, we are from LOVE, and to LOVE we return* when it is our time to take leave of this mortal world.

The following chapter presents just some of the metaphysical and otherworldly happenings that have taken place during my life that led to the profound spiritual insights presented throughout this book. Everything I share has been sourced from the entirely natural and spontaneous. I have never taken mind-altering substances of any kind and, except for one "experiment" with alcohol when I was sixteen, have remained completely teetotal.

During the five years of OBEs that I share later in the chapter, I sought the advice of conventional medical doctors and consultants to ascertain if there might be a physical cause that was triggering them.

One neurologist suggested I was suffering from narcolepsy, a condition that causes one to fall asleep on the spot!

I requested that my GP investigate further, which resulted in my being sent to a leading neurologist, a Professor Parker, whose practice was located near central London. Following a detailed interview, she proceeded to fix dozens of wires in numerous positions on my head and face. The tests and analysis lasted for approximately one hour at which point some results were available, including the one that had most astonished her. She explained in basic layman's terms that there is a portion of the brain that relates to "spiritual activity" and that my tests indicated something of an "extraordinary nature." She told me that this area of my brain was developed to an astounding degree, one that she had never observed before. Suffice to say, further results yielded no diagnostic insights as to why the OBEs were occurring, and I stopped any further medical investigations.

So, let us begin our journey into Love, Life, and Everything by starting with my childhood . . . when it all began.

DIRECT METAPHYSICAL EXPERIENCES AND SPIRITUAL INSIGHTS

THE PRESENCE OF THE "OTHERWORLDLY" IN MY EARLY CHILDHOOD

As I mentioned earlier, the questions *Who Am I? Why Am I Here? Where Am I Really From?* have preoccupied me since I was seventeen years old. As a young child, I was subject to otherworldly events, encounters, and occurrences that began at the age of six, when I underwent what is known as a "**psychic attack***"—my first, but by no means my last.

These attacks continued for a couple of years and always followed the same theme: I would be tucked up in bed when suddenly the covers would be pulled over my head and held so tightly that I could barely breathe, let alone move. It felt as if I was suffocating, and I would thrash around trying to free myself but to no avail, as I was completely pinned down. I would scream for help until my parents would rush up the stairs and into my bedroom only to find me in tears as I tried to explain what had occurred. Each time they would respond by pointing out that my bedclothes were exactly as they had been when they had said goodnight earlier that evening. I would look at the blankets only to find them neat and tidy and fully tucked in. Bewildered, I would protest again and again, repeating what had happened but my parents simply did not believe me. Later throughout my early adulthood I would experience similar attacks when in bed and in a hypnogogic state, only instead of the covers being held over my head, my arms would be pinned down by some invisible force rendering me unable to move.

A Less-Than-Well-Intentioned Presence

For years, a less-than-benign presence dominated my childhood. It seemed intent on upsetting me. For example, I would find myself at the bedroom window with an urge to jump. This was not coming from my own thoughts for although I was an extremely sensitive child I was also blessed with a sunny, optimistic, and happy-go-lucky nature. Even then, I recognized it to be an outside force and often wondered if there was a malevolent resident "ghost" in the family home.

At other times a random and obscure thought about something would suddenly pop into my mind only for it to manifest moments later. For example, on one occasion a bee was flying around the living room. Sitting on the sofa with my shoes off I suddenly heard a discarnate voice state, "What would you do if that bee flew into your shoe and stung your big toe?" Later that afternoon, having forgotten this, I proceeded to put on my shoes only to scream in shock and pain. I quickly kicked off a shoe to discover I had been stung on my big toe. I was particularly distressed because the bee having used its sting had died. Even though I was aware of a mildly malevolent presence, I was also aware of an extraordinarily benevolent one too.

While spirituality and religion were absent in my childhood

home, I would regularly pray to a higher force that I seemed to know, or *gno* (a word originating from the Greek *gnosis,* meaning "an inner knowing arising from a deep intuitive recognition") existed, especially when I was having these experiences and would feel afraid. Why was I having such experiences at that early age? In my understanding there were two reasons: The first of these was due to my tender years. "Dark" energies are inclined to target the very young, those who are acutely sensitive, and those who are vulnerable, unprotected, traumatized, or unwell.

Dark energies are drawn like moths to a flame to adults who experience depression, have been diagnosed with another mental illness or substance disorder, undergo a general anesthetic for an operation, or frequent hospitals or residential medical centers. Another reason why such attacks may occur is that the "dark" seeks to extinguish the "light" and is set upon blocking the path of particular individuals who are in the world to help awaken humanity. It recognizes those who emit a specific light and **frequency*** or who play a significant role in the evolution of humankind. It will often target such individuals from one timeline to the next.

Many whose Soul agenda is to be of service to humanity and the Earth reincarnate in order that they may complete what they were unable to fulfill in a previous life. Dark forces follow them to prevent the fulfillment of an altruistic mission. The subject of reincarnation is still a debatable one for many, yet I believe it is a real phenomenon because of personally having experienced vivid past timeline memories several times.

A Message from Mr. Yamamoto

Mr. Yamamoto was a neighbor who lived directly opposite the house I grew up in. One day, unexpectedly, he knocked on our front door. My parents opened it to find him in a state of considerable distress having returned from work to discover his beloved wife had passed away at home in her chair.

Mr. and Mrs. Yamamoto were a World War Two love story. When they first encountered each other in pre-war London, he was a handsome young Japanese man, and she was an English rose. They met, fell deeply in love, married, and settled in London. They remained childless and lived only for each other.

Before the day Mr. Yamamoto turned up on our doorstep, I had never seen him or his wife. Yet, for most of the nights throughout the months that followed his wife's passing either my parents or my brother John and I would take turns going to his house to sit with him. My mum felt that he was too distraught to be left alone after he returned home from work at the end of each day. So each evening she ensured that Mr. Yamamoto had company. My brother and I could not have been more than eight or nine, but we would try to make small talk with this humble, gentle, and intelligent man, who to us appeared ancient although he was most likely in his late fifties. He was always so kind and would greet us each time at his front door, saying in his gentle but strongly accented voice "Crisp? Lemonade?"

And so it was that every other evening my brother and I would sit with a packet of cheese and onion crisps and a glass of lemonade keeping Mr. Yamamoto company and trying to distract him with thoughts of something other than the loss of his wife, even if only for a couple of hours.

Several months later, the time had come for our annual family holiday. My mum implored Mr. Yamamoto to come with us but he graciously declined, and so she worried terribly. She knew he wanted to join his beloved wife and was concerned that he might attempt to do so while we were away. Nevertheless, she hoped this feeling was no more than her own anxiety, and we set off on our two-week summer holiday.

Immediately upon our return my mum asked my brother and I to go and buy some milk from the local store. Upon arriving back home with it we were confronted by her attempts to hide the fact that she had been crying. She explained to us that Mr. Yamamoto had died while we were away. It was reported that he had been standing at the exit point on a London bus and had deliberately stepped off while it was turning a corner in the middle of the city center. By all accounts it had appeared to be a "purposeful" act on his part.

My mother was distraught, and the house was filled with an air of solemnity. Mr. Yamamoto's death hit her very hard as she had always sensed that were he to be left alone he would end his life, which is why we had taken it in turns to sit with him each evening. That night, I went to bed and fell asleep and had a profoundly vivid "dream" just before waking, the content of which I still clearly remember to this day.

I was with my brother, and we were walking back to our house after going to get the milk my mother had sent us to buy when we first returned home from our holiday. I realized that she already knew about Mr. Yamamoto's passing before she sent us out and had needed some space to process the news and to compose herself and think about how she was going to break it to us. We turned onto our road and began to walk toward home. It was a beautiful summer's day. Then everything unfolded in slow motion. As we neared our house, my brother went ahead and straight indoors; I, however, had become distracted.

Mr. Yamamoto was at his garden gate in a wheelchair. His head was dressed with a fresh clean white bandage. Standing behind him with her hands on his shoulders was his wife. Mrs. Yamamoto appeared serene and content. I had never seen her when she was alive so this was my first encounter with her. She was smiling gently. Mr. Yamamoto then lovingly said to me, "Please tell your mum that I am fine and that I am with my wife and that we are very happy. Please tell her not to worry about me anymore because I am happy again." I smiled and reassured him that I would pass on his message.

At that point I woke up. I got out of bed and skipped down the stairs to find my mum busy in the kitchen. I told her about my "dream" and what Mr. Yamamoto had asked me to convey to her. She said something like, "Oh, that was a nice dream" and continued with her tasks. Whether she accepted it as real I do not know, but I sensed it gave her some comfort. The meeting with Mr. and Mrs. Yamamoto was as real to me as was my mum standing in the kitchen.

A Light at the End of the Tunnel

Throughout my early teenage years, as is often the case, spirit activity, or at least my awareness of it, stopped. However, at the age of seventeen, it began again. The first event happened unexpectedly in a public place when I fainted twice on the same occasion. Both times I experienced myself hurtling down a long dark tunnel with a light at the end of it. All I recall of those two moments was traveling at great speed, the deafening sound, and then coming to just before reaching the light. I was taken to a hospital where no medical explanation could account for what had occurred. It never happened again.

The following morning, I woke up agoraphobic, claustrophobic, and sociophobic and battled with these conditions for the next twenty years until I finally overcame them. Overnight, I had literally changed from a carefree, confident, fun-loving, outgoing, vivacious, and spirited extrovert to a deeply sensitive and quiet introvert. I became excruciatingly shy and awkward and was terrified of the world. Years later, when looking back at that fateful day, I came to realize what a catalyst it had been for the unfolding of an extraordinary journey of psychological healing, conscious evolution, and spiritual awakening.

My seventeenth year also proved to be quite profound because it was just weeks after the fainting episodes that I discovered Carl Jung, Mahatma Gandhi, and Omraam Mikhael Aivanhov, in that order. Hindsight is a wonderful thing, and it became evident to me that these three new influences were also spirit mentors for my future Work, which is now founded on psychological integration (Jung), conscious evolution (Gandhi), and spiritual awakening (Omraam).

The Luminous Ones

As I progressed into my early twenties, I experienced endless vibrant inner-psychic states as my brow and crown **chakras*** began to open and become active. I started to see small brilliant violet orbs along with various other colored ectoplasmic shapes and forms. I recognized these as manifestations of spirit guides, the energy of highly evolved benevolent beings, or loved ones who had passed over. I saw energy fields and colors around people and all too often felt their experiences as if they were my own.

This was also the period when I first encountered the beings I refer to as the **Luminous Ones***—a group of formless energies of **Light*** who have since accompanied me throughout my life. I have lost count of the times I found myself floating in another realm surrounded by my higher-dimensional luminous friends who would draw me to them to heal and rebalance my energy body and soothe my human **Self***. From 2002 until 2009 I rarely saw them. Then in March 2009 they returned at the exact time I was guided to write my first book *2012: A Clarion Call*. I make several references to them in that book as they undoubtedly influenced its overall message and content.

Lucid Astral Traveling

At the age of twenty-one, on a powerful full moon, I participated in my first **sweat lodge*** ceremony. After completing the nine rounds of ritual and emerging from the lodge to sit in silence around the great outdoor fire, I recall closing my eyes and on the "inner screen" of my brow chakra experiencing myself flying. I was soaring toward the Sun and winging my way across vast continents and magnificent landscapes. Nature had never appeared more breathtaking and vibrant; it was as if I were seeing her in full technicolor. My senses were dramatically heightened and with my fears and inhibitions gone, I had my first experience of the *more than* I am, that we all truly are. Such was the intensity of the full moon that the moonstone I was holding up to it left a scorch mark in the palm of my hand.

The sweat lodges that I attended in my early twenties exposed me to an entirely new experience of the world, and, most importantly, myself, for they gave me a glimpse of a Healed, Balanced, Evolved, Awakened, Realized, Actualized, and Transcended Self. This vision brought a feeling of total freedom and connected me to the mystical and to the **Great Mystery***.

A Friend in Spirit Dancing at Her Own Funeral

In 2001, I attended the memorial of a friend and colleague, Emma, who had passed away from cancer at the age of twenty-seven. As the tributes and recollections of her life were being shared at the front of the auditorium, I found myself distracted by her spirit, which had appeared on the podium. I observed her dancing with great joy and she seemed to be ecstatically happy.

Later, after the service had finished, her loved ones and friends joined together for an intimate celebration of her life. I was talking with a mutual friend and proceeded to explain to her that during the memorial service I had "seen" Emma dancing barefoot in a long white dress with her hair flowing loosely around her shoulders. My friend's face paled, and she insisted that I relay this to Emma's husband whom I had never met. I asked her if there was a particular reason for doing so, and she told me that Emma had asked her husband to bury her in her favorite long white dress, to keep her feet bare, and to make sure her hair was loose around her shoulders. The friend also shared that Emma had promised her husband that she would *dance at her funeral.*

A Brief Message from the Spirit of the Mother of a Friend

On another occasion, the mother of a student friend was very ill. Having spent time with the friend that day, much later that night I awoke in the early hours to see her mother's spirit present in my room. She conveyed to me that she had passed into the Light. The following day, I entered the student hall to notice my friend in tears. As I went to comfort her, she proceeded to tell me that her mum had left this world the previous night. I shared with her that her mother had visited me to prove that even though she had passed from this world she was still very much alive.

A Walk in the Upper Realms

Many years ago, I recall being extremely concerned about a close friend I had grown up with who seemed set on a course of self-destruction. I did all that I could to help him, but he was not really open to receiving any support. At one point my concern reached a peak, and I retired to bed quite distraught at the thought of what was to become of him. During that night I had a **lucid dream*** in which I was accompanying him through a sublimely peaceful and beautiful meadow.

> The atmosphere was warm and golden. We were walking together and gently talking. The usual tension on his face had disappeared. He was relaxed, centered, and peaceful. His voice, which was usually coarse, forceful, peppered with expletives, tense, and emotionally charged, was soft and calm. What struck me most about him was his easy manner and graceful physical appearance. Ordinarily overweight and looking unhealthy, here he was slim, vibrant, and radiant. He was "all knowing" and conveyed an air of deep understanding. I was aware that we were walking in the upper realms, just as we had done on many occasions prior to this lifetime, and just as we would do again after transitioning our earthly lives.

Upon waking, I knew that I no longer needed to worry about him in the same way. This lucid dream had blessed me with a direct experience of seeing the *more than* that he was then/is now, the *more than* that I am, that each of us is. To this day, I am able to view him as a peaceful Soul living the life he is meant to be experiencing in the world, his personality healing and refining, his Soul ever-perfect, ever-joyful, ever-divine.

Kundalini Awakening: Out of Body Experiences

In June 1997, I attended a Kundalini Yoga class in central London. The session began with deep and rapid breathing exercises. Later, we all assumed yoga postures to further facilitate the breathwork, and vice versa. Finally, we were instructed to lie on our yoga mats, faces toward the ceiling with our eyes closed.

An intense silence pervaded the atmosphere. I was drifting into another realm, going deeper and deeper, when suddenly, and shockingly, I became aware of a deafening sound that was so loud I thought a plane was about to crash into the building. The vibration shook not only our bodies but also the objects and chairs in the room. I sat bolt upright only to see everyone else calmly receiving what transpired to be the sound waves of an enormous gong. I lay down once more and surrendered.

At the end of the class, I bowed silently to the teacher expressing my gratitude and then made my way out of the building to my car. On the drive home, I was aware of being in a slightly altered state. It felt as if every cell in my body was tingling and my life force felt unusually strong. The combination of rapid breathing, yoga postures, and the gong had left a powerful impact. Something had occurred during and because of that class—a kundalini awakening—and I was about to find out just what and *why*.

Two days later, in the early morning hours, I awoke from a profound "dream" in which I had received a telephone call informing me that my mother had passed away. I recall standing with the telephone in my hand and at the moment I was given the news suddenly rising up and out of my body and floating toward the ceiling. At that point I woke up. As I lay with my eyes open processing the dream, I became aware of a highly charged atmosphere pervading the room. I had the distinct impression that something out of the ordinary was about to happen.

It was approximately 6:00 a.m. and just as I was waking and still in a hypnogogic state when I heard a loud *whooshing* noise circling around my head. Within moments it had entered my left ear, and I began to convulse. Although I was awake and conscious, I had no control over what was going on. It felt as if I was plugged into an electric generator of a city; ten thousand volts of electricity were surging through my body and mind. My senses felt heightened, my skin tingled all over, and there was an intense buzzing in my body. I was unable to physically move, and even though I was conscious and awake I could not open my eyes. My face was contorting, and there was an unbearable pressure on my base chakra.

I was aware of an excruciating and unbearable pain in the area of my base chakra, and at one point it felt as if my pelvis was going to burst open. It was at this moment that the energy began to wane and continued to do so until the final residue exited out of my toes. The room was silent, and I lay in shock as my body continued to buzz and tingle to a lesser degree. Cautiously, I arose from the bed to look at myself in a mirror: I was flushed and the pupils of my eyes were dilated. The buzzing sensation remained for another couple of hours. Later, I telephoned a few psychic friends, but not one could offer an explanation for this experience.

The next day the incident reoccurred and then happened again each morning for an entire week at which point it stopped. These events took place around the same time each day (between 6:00 a.m. and 8:00 a.m.) and with the same intensity. During the last episode in that first week I distinctly heard a voice say, "We will return exactly a month to the day,"—and "they" kept their promise.

The next round of experiences was the same only this time the excruciating pain I had felt in my base chakra had moved up to the sacral center. During month three, the same experience occurred again, and then again a month later, and soon thereafter almost daily. The OBEs always followed the same pattern with the unbearable pressure moving up through the lower chakras. Month five brought the same overwhelmingly intense voltage surging through my body, only this time no chakras were involved.

During some of the OBEs, I would find myself on the Earth looking up at the heavens to see them part and open to a myriad of swirling constellations that I could reach toward and almost touch. On other occasions, I would rise up and travel at great speed through the stars and gateways and **portals*** to other **dimensions***. The experiences were always cryptic and intensely surreal. On one occasion I was visited by an otherworldly being who shared with me something of my future.

I became accustomed to **astral traveling***, and the experience of being conscious and awake while in a trance. I began to accept (without fear) the moments when my **astral body*** (the nonphysical counterpart of the human body) would begin levitating in the room or traveling far out into hyperspace. Nothing I was shown or experienced was ever threatening or frightening. I would always know in advance when the energy was approaching because I would hear that intensely hypnotic *whooshing* sound. After a couple of years, an even more powerful buzzing and sensation replaced this, but I knew I could choose to stop an episode from happening. I could do this by sitting up and forcing my eyes to stay open, but it was never easy as the buzzing sound was so overwhelmingly hypnotic.

The energy that coursed through me was indescribable. It was as if a powerful voltage of currents was pulsing through my body like an electrical tsunami. The closest I have come to seeing anything similar to this was in a scene from the movie *Phenomenon,* where the main character is struck by a heavenly beam of light and knocked to the floor, twisting and vibrating in an uncontrollable manner. Unsure of what was happening to me I endeavored to contact numerous mediums and psychic organizations. I even consulted doctors and specialists but to no avail.

No one understood what I was talking about. I wondered if I was having early morning fits and, at my request, a doctor referred me to a neurologist. The specialist sat perplexed as I shared it all with him, but he suggested that I was suffering from narcolepsy, a condition where people fall asleep on the spot, day or night. Of course, this was far from the case as I could now control what was happening, remain awake throughout, and was none the worse for the experience. In fact, I would feel quite energized and well following these almost daily episodes.

These experiences continued for five more years until I made a conscious decision to stop them. Each event would catapult me out of my body. Often, I would find myself floating high above the building I was living in and over the town. I would rise higher and higher soaring over vast landscapes and oceans. I would see, hear, and sense the presence of "spirit beings" as I journeyed my way through the Universe. I would pass through portals and gateways, often defined by intricate sacred geometric patterns and symbols.

In 2000, during one particular OBE, I was told of a constellation called "ophicus," a "new constellation to come into human awareness that would represent a significant turning point for the awakening of humanity." Never having heard of it before, I wrote down the name on a piece of paper and later spoke to an eminent astronomer/astrologer friend who confirmed that my spelling of "Ophicus" was in fact the constellation Ophiuchus. Nine years later, having given this experience no further thought, I suddenly found myself researching Ophiuchus for my first book, *2012: A Clarion Call.*

Sometimes during these experiences I would levitate. On one occasion when a friend was staying with me and sharing my room, I was lifted off my bed while she still slept in hers. I was moved around the room to be placed directly alongside her. I spent a short time gazing at her sleeping face before being lifted and returned to my own bed.

On another occasion, I was flying over vast oceans before arriving at a beach. I indicated telepathically that I would like to be set down upon the sand and this automatically happened. I recall standing on that beautiful beach, whether it was on this Earth or in an otherworldly paradise, and feeling the warmth of the sand beneath my bare feet. All at once, without any thought, I lifted my arms directly in front of me and immediately began to fly into a great ray of light that was shining from the Sun. I was also aware of other beneficent beings accompanying me from behind and at either side.

At another time, I recollect being far out in space looking back at the Earth. It was a profound moment similar perhaps to what astronauts have described. An experience such as this changes something deep within one's consciousness. During another event, I was visited by an extradimensional being that appeared on my bed and proceeded to talk about my future. He seemed to be half human and half extraterrestrial but not what we might commonly refer to as "alien." He had dark weathered skin and brilliant sapphire eyes.

Many times, I found myself hurtling through space until I was in infinite pitch blackness far from the Earth. I would begin to panic, only to return swiftly to my body whereupon I would open my eyes and be back in my bed. These OBEs were terrifying with respect to the intensity of the voltage rushing through my body, yet fascinating because of what I was experiencing.

Often my out-of-body journeys of the previous night would be confirmed the following day. For example, the day after my experience of gazing back at the Earth, I was attending a course and confronted by exactly the same vision only in the form of an image on the inside of a door in the building where the event was taking place. Another time, after catapulting through hyperspace the night before, I returned the following morning to a stall I was managing at an alternative fair and the people on the opposite stand were erecting a giant poster of Leonardo da Vinci's "Vitruvian Man." Only hours had passed since I had hurtled through the very center of this original sacred geometric symbol in the vast starry heavens.

Between Life and Death

Back in early 1997, around the time of the fateful Kundalini Yoga class, I had begun to pray in earnest to the heavenly realms, offering myself as a channel through which they could work for the greater good of the world. Unbeknownst to me at the time, in order to do so I would be required to literally undergo a death and rebirth experience.

The OBE episodes continued until March 16, 2002, a date I will never forget for it is when I collapsed with a mysterious condition that threatened my life. That morning as I got out of bed, my legs gave way and I remained bedridden for three months after. I could not walk unaided or withstand any sensory stimulation such as television, music, or light. I remained in my bedroom in complete silence unable to do anything and feeling as if I were dying. I was barely able to speak more than a few words. I could not sit as my body would not hold me up, and for one twenty-four-hour period, I was unable to open my eyes at all, as I simply did not have the energy or life force to do so. Nothing mattered to me anymore, not the books, the clothes, or any of the objects in the room. Everything was slipping away.

I lost all interest in the world and lay alone suspended between life and death. Two weeks later, in March on Easter Sunday 2002, I underwent the process of dying. The conscious experience of this is unlike any other. To be conscious as the body dies and feeling each nuance of it at a physical level is incomprehensible. I was losing consciousness and became aware of rapidly aging to the point of being around eighty-five and skeletal, with long platinum hair splayed out behind me, and lying crumpled and lifeless on a bed at the point of death. This is the moment when I died to the life I had incarnated into.

I aged decades in seconds as I underwent my own death half a century ahead of time. In that moment, I reincarnated skipping the stages of growth from birth to young adulthood to arrive in my thirties as my Future Self. This was made possible because of the relentless path of Self-awareness and Self-realization I had been on for my entire adult life, which allowed me to mostly complete what I had come here to work through at a personal level. While out of my body, I was given the choice to remain in the spirit world or to return as a new incarnate aspect of my Soul that was already residing in a future world. I chose to return as a being from the future to work with thousands of others who are also here to anchor and establish a new more enlightened template for the Earth.

From Easter 2002, I began to anchor my Future Self more fully, a process that took seven grueling years as the higher **vibration*** of this is vastly different, and my physical body needed time to adjust and align with this new frequency.

Four years later in October 2006, I was inextricably struck down with extreme dizziness that persisted for twenty-four hours a day, seven days a week, for nearly two years, but the experience continued in total for six years. In the first year, the symptoms were constant day and night and were severely debilitating. By the second year, though ever-present, they were less intense; and by the end of that year I was able to stand and move around, although the dizziness was still present. I was unable to lie down, however, until December 2012 because of the spinning and accompanying nausea. Six long years of being upright took their toll, and I was grateful when this process came to an end. I had heard through several sources that in October 2006 the Earth's **etheric*** poles had reversed. Being hypersensitive, I believe it was this energetic phenomenon that caused such a reversal of energy within me. As the etheric stabilized so too did the dizziness, as my body had adjusted, rebalanced, and realigned itself.

Suffice to say, my life has irrevocably changed. Even though in many ways I am the same Nicolya, I am infinitely different from the former expression of myself. When I look back on my life as a child, adolescent, and young adult, it is as if I am viewing a past timeline, which, in fact, I am. Undoubtedly, the five years of incoming energy followed by seven years of harrowing illness enabled a transmutation to occur at every level of my being. During the OBEs, I experienced the sublime, the extraordinary, the inconceivable, and the unbelievable, and I received extraordinary insights, visions, and futuristic information. This form of **hypercommunication*** works differently for me now in that it flows through my energy body and its "receptors" (think of satellite dishes across the body of the Earth receiving information from space). These translate the incoming data, which is then picked up by my mind instead of coming directly into my physical body.

Seven Years to the Month: March 2002–March 2009

The OBEs came to a halt in 2002, except for two other (final) occasions when the energy reappeared directly after my collapse in March 2002 and then again in November of that same year. I was too unwell to allow it access, and my vibration was so low that I knew I was at risk of succumbing to psychic attack, which is exactly what occurred. For the first time since I was six years old, I experienced a terrifying psychic attack. The March episode involved a deathly white vampire-like entity that had a bright red mouth and was clad in black. It was laughing hideously while pinning me to the floor with its hands around my throat trying to strangle me.

The second attack in the November of that year involved two of these types of entities doing the exact same thing. I realized that I needed to raise my vibration in order to free myself. I managed to do this by reciting sacred mantras, at which point they released me and disappeared. I promised myself then that I would never allow such energies near me again and that if spirits of an evolved nature wished to work through me then they needed to respect my boundaries, and this they have done.

The hypnotic buzzing visits me occasionally but almost immediately disappears when I state a firm no, and in that I feel respected. In stating a categorical no because of the episodes with the dark entities, I also had to say a reluctant but necessary no to the remarkable encounters I had been having for five years. I decided that only when I was fully well again would I reconsider opening that channel.

Trip and the Heavenly Waiting Room

In the summer of 2009, a good friend, Ursula, a prolific healer, called to tell me she was about to work with someone called Trip who was in Torbay Hospital in Torquay. Due to coughing as a result of a virus he had broken his ninth left rib. His local GP had determined that it was a "pulled muscle." However, infection set in and then pneumonia of the left lung, which then spread to the right. He was rushed into the hospital and put straight into the ICU where he remained at death's door for more than five weeks.

I immediately felt an overwhelming need to accompany her. I mentioned this to Ursula and she instantly agreed. I had known her for almost ten years and had never worked with her on any of her clients, but this felt especially important.

Our intention was to spiritually and energetically assist this young man so he could either return fully to this world or take leave of it. A point worth noting is that a healer must always remain neutral and recognize that the outcome of any healing, or energy support work, depends on the destiny of each individual Soul.

We arrived at the ICU and took a seat in the waiting room until Trip's partner appeared and explained that only two people were allowed at his bedside at any one time. As she left, we entered the room to begin our Work. Once inside, the thick pungent smell of death hung in the air so intensely that after a few minutes I was almost heaving and had to step outside for some fresh air. I knew the situation was very grave as my body was shaking from head to toe and the nausea that had overwhelmed me started to abate when I was away from his bedside. I wondered how I was going to be able to be present for Trip when I was unable to tolerate the deathly odor in the room. Ursula, also realizing the gravity of the situation, then joined me. We looked at each other in quiet despair, both recognizing that his situation was far from promising. I spoke with my luminous friends in the Higher Realms and asked them for support so that I could fulfill my reason for being there.

After taking a few deep breaths we made our way back to his room. Ursula stood on one side of the bed and I stood on the other. Trip was attached to many devices, and his bare torso was covered with an array of wires. Beneath these I could see several symbolic tattoos that gave an indication of the spiritual person he was in his everyday life. The smell of death was still all-pervading, and I knew that he was not long for this world if it was his destiny to depart.

As I gazed down at Trip, I was struck by the sense that his personality was no longer present and the space it would normally occupy was now filled purely with his Soul. It was a unique experience to be with someone whose personality was absent for it allowed a direct access to his true being. A great peace, beauty, and purity emanated from him, and there was no trace of the emotional and mental stories that would otherwise be part of his normal day-to-day life.

We began to work on him with the intention that we were there only in service of his highest good and at the bidding of his Soul. If he was preparing to leave, then we were there to assist him and if he was going to stay, then we were there to hold a specific space and support his life force to fully return to his body so he could become well once again.

The first day we worked on him for a couple of hours, laying our hands on his body while telepathically communicating with his Soul. I had taken notes of his "sats" (oxygen saturation levels/blood pressure/pulse) before we started, and these had all slightly improved by the end of the session.

Later that evening when I arrived home, and then more vividly when I went to bed, I had a clear image of Trip sitting in a Heavenly White Waiting Room that was full of Light. He was dressed all in white, perfectly well, and sat alone on a white bench. Periodically, he would look across the other side of the room at a white door. I knew he was waiting for an answer. I also understood that he was meant to transition at this point in time but the deep love between him and his partner, along with his love for life, had compelled him to ask the Higher Realms if he could remain. My sense was that the "jury was out" and so he waited, suspended between two worlds.

As I entered the room on the second day, I observed that the stench of death had reduced by 50 percent. His sats, however, had taken a downward turn. On looking at his medical notes at the end of the bed a chill ran down my spine: "This patient is not expected to live." Still, Ursula and I rolled up our sleeves and began working in earnest for the best outcome. Once again, we laid our hands on his body and telepathically communicated with his Soul.

Two hours went by and when we were finished, his sats had once again slightly improved. Later that night in bed, I tuned in to the Heavenly White Waiting Room and immediately found Trip sitting as before, still waiting for an answer.

By the third day the smell of death was almost gone, but Trip's sats had taken a downward turn. We worked with him for just over an hour. His partner had informed us before we entered the ICU that the doctors had told her the life-support machine would be switched off in the next forty-eight hours, as in five weeks he had showed no medical signs of improvement. No one except for his partner, Ursula, and me believed he was likely to survive, and the doctors had given him just a 5 percent chance of living.

We gave our all to Trip in that last hour of tending him. Before I took my leave for the final time, I held his hand and whispered into his ear explaining exactly what was going to occur within the next forty-eight hours. I conveyed to him, several times and in no uncertain terms, that if he were coming back, he would need to do so NOW or it would be too late. Ursula and I knew that this was to be our last healing session with Trip, so we left his bedside and could only wait. Later that day he was given the last rites.

That night in bed I took myself back to the Heavenly White Waiting Room only to find that the white bench was empty, and Trip was gone. I brought my awareness back into my room and lay there wondering what had occurred. Had he passed over? Or had he received a divine dispensation to return to this life and his beloved? I could not feel which one it was.

Early the following morning I messaged Ursula but there was no news. Then a couple of hours later she called me to exclaim that all of his sats had registered as normal overnight, so he was to be brought out of the induced coma that day. And the news just got better and better: he had woken, and he was hungry! Within a day he was transferred to a normal ward, and just four days later he was fully recovered and so discharged.

That was the last I heard of Trip, except for just one update from Ursula shortly after he had gone home. It transpired that he and his beloved had married on the wild moors of Devon surrounded and celebrated by family and friends.

Psychic Goings On in Tuscany

In 2011, I found myself staying at a colleague's house in Tuscany for the weekend because of a meeting with mutual associates. During the first night as I lay awake unable to sleep, I became aware of his dog, Tykie, climbing onto my bed. Being the animal lover that I am, I enjoyed this great lump lounging all over me as it was lovely to have his company. However, pushed to the edge of the bed, I barely slept a wink, while Tykie slept very well!

The next day, I joked with my colleague about having had little sleep owing to his dog taking up most of the bed. He stated that Tykie had been with him and his wife all night as usual, and that their bedroom door had been shut. He then shared that they once had another Rhodesian Ridgeback who had passed before Tykie came along. It was at this point that I realized it had been the spirit of his former dog who had spent the night with me! The following night was also interesting but for different reasons. Throughout its entirety, I walked in the Higher Realms with my host talking of cosmology, ecology, philosophy, and the current trajectory of humanity.

A WW2 Life: A Future Story to Tell

On three separate occasions during the first two weeks following my **Conscious Dying Experience*** (CDE), while in a lucid dream state during which I experiencing the familiar unbearable voltage coursing through my body, I was shown four dramatic, chronological, and unforgettable scenes from a past timeline I appear to have lived in Europe at the time of the Second World War. The story that unfolded was so extraordinarily powerful that to this day, eighteen years later, I can still clearly visualize and recall it all. The message conveyed is important for humanity now, and will be shared in a fiction, based-on-fact novel that I am currently writing.

A Trinity of LOVE

I will now share three extraordinary and otherworldly experiences of SOURCE LOVE that took place between 1997 and 2008.

An Encounter with Yeshua

The first of these experiences occurred when I lived in Totnes in Devon. I had bid farewell to an ongoing psychotherapy client following a breakthrough session in which he had come to a profound realization. There were no more clients booked on that particular day, so I walked back into my practice room to close the space down. However, the atmosphere was unusually sublime so I sat on the floor and shut my eyes to experience it.

Almost immediately a feeling of *extraordinary* LOVE began to fill the room. I opened my eyes to observe the space saturated in gold. I began to feel a profound sense of calm, euphoria, ecstasy, and intoxication, and was, literally, drunk on LOVE. The atmosphere, the feeling, and the golden energy intensified to such a degree that I completely merged with it. My eyes remained open and my awareness and whole being became permeated with an all-encompassing energetic impression of Y E S H U A. At this point, the feeling magnified exponentially, and I knew then how it is possible to be driven mad with LOVE. I fully understood how such a HIGH frequency could fry a mere mortal, no matter how evolved or advanced.

The energy was *so* intense and *so* close that it was too much to bear. Just at the point I thought I would disintegrate entirely, the energy began to pull back and lessen until it had almost gone. The room was still lit up, and the energy was still present, only now it was far gentler. I sat quietly for a couple of hours trying to process what had just occurred.

Here for the Many, Not the One

The second of the Trinity experiences occurred in the summer of 2008 when I was living in Godney just outside of Glastonbury. I was driving along a quiet country lane when all of a sudden I became totally overwhelmed by an all-permeating sense of LOVE that came out of nowhere. It filled my being with its intensity and purity. The feeling was so strong that I was temporarily unable to drive and had to pull into a layby. Tears began to flow as my heart, my body, my entire being was bursting with LOVE. I remained calm and breathed slowly and deeply in an attempt to manage the enormity of what was occurring. After a while, I received the distinct and unmistakable impression, as if a voice was talking directly to me: "The LOVE that I AM, that I carry within me, is too great for just one and is for the world."

An Experience of Enlightenment

The third of the Trinity experiences occurred in October 2009, shortly after I had traveled to Rennes-le-Château in southern France, for the first time following a powerful *call* to go there. The trip was amazing, and the energy of the region so sublime and extraordinary that it is difficult to put into words. It had been seven years since my last OBE, and apart from the occasional (and respectful) hypnotic *whooshing* sound that I was able to resist, I barely gave the experiences a second thought.

Clearly, I had needed space and time to integrate the enormity of all that had taken place between June 1997 and March 2002. However, on the night of my return from France on October 13, 2009, I went to bed and at around 4:00 a.m. was woken by the familiar *whooshing,* only this time it was insistent, and I was unable to resist. All at once, I experienced the extreme voltage surging through me and the next thing I was aware of was being out of my body. I found myself walking along a familiar street in broad daylight somewhere in southern Europe, possibly France. I was heading toward a secret gathering and seemed to know exactly where I was going. I turned into a mews at the end of which stood an impressive looking building that other people were entering. I did the same and instinctively walked down some steps until I came to a great set of ancient solid oak doors. As I stood before them, I heard the sound of the bolts from the inside releasing as they were opened. Familiar Souls that were unknown to me in this timeline greeted me in a loving and knowing silence.

I stepped into what resembled an enormous "operations room" similar to the type used in the Second World War. The room itself was more like a great hall. It was long and wide with an expansive ceiling that reached up toward the heavens. Although it was busy with concentrated activity it was also immensely calm. The people within it were focused on tasks that seemed to revolve around a large circular table in the center of the room upon which I could see a vast network of brilliant lights overlaying a map of the Earth. The table appeared to be a live portal, a living, breathing, pulsing, and toning Grid of Light. The sounds emitting from it were sublime, and clusters of lights flashed over specific areas, whereas other groups of lights remained static. What was taking place on the table seemed to be instrumental to the purpose of the people gathered around it because it was linked to the future of humanity.

In an instant, I registered everything that was occurring in the environment. Initially I was standing alone observing the scene but then all of a sudden everyone turned toward me. The atmosphere was pervaded by a sense of *knowing* who I was and why I was there. They began to approach me in a manner of reverence. I knew them to be friends, family, and collaborators from other places and other times. I seemed to be of particular importance to the "mission" they were engaged in.

One male, who appeared to be the leader, stated, "We have been waiting for you." When these words were spoken the voltage that had been a constant presence in my body began to dramatically intensify. In the next moment my Consciousness was leaving through my crown while, at the same time, the voltage coursing through me began to magnify to such a degree that my ears were filled with a deafening rushing sound.

I was rising higher and higher toward the domed ceiling and looking down at the people who had gathered to watch what was happening. They were calm and all knowing. The "ceiling" appeared to be limitless and as I rose higher and higher, I transcended my human emotions and all thoughts dissolved. At this point I stopped rising and was floating in midair.

To have transcended all emotions and mind and to have reached an enlightened state while still in the physical body is rare and ordinarily only possible when a mortal life comes to an end. This was *the* most extraordinary experience of all the OBEs, indeed of my life, and an absolute validation of the deepest wisdom and most profound insights that have been shared by some of the greatest mystics and holy men and women to have walked the Earth—all of whom have spoken of the reality of the enlightened state and the ultimate liberation that comes when one has transcended the emotions and mind.

What was I aware of? *Only* of all-pervading and all-encompassing LOVE. I was LOVE and *only* LOVE. It was *the* most exalted, ascended, and mystical state that a human being can experience, an absolute embodiment of higher-dimensional LOVE, and an ultimate state of **Self-transcendence***. A LOVE that poured through my eyes, my smile, my very Being and that defined me completely.

It was pure Enlightenment and confirmed what all the most sacred of scriptures, profound philosophical theories, purest metaphysical ideals, and most ancient of wisdom prophecies have known for millennia: we are LOVE, we are from LOVE, we are here to BE LOVE, and to LOVE we shall return.

Slowly, I began to descend and as I did so my capacity for thought and emotion started to return. As my feet touched the ground my legs gave way, and I found myself lying on the floor looking upward. The energy was still surging through me with the same extreme intensity. A circle of faces gazed down at me with respect and love. I became aware of my physical body, which felt somehow different and strangely odd. As I moved a hand to touch it, I could feel it was covered from head to toe in a hard and prickly casing. The "leader," who was positioned closest to me, conveyed that I was covered in "pine cones" and that these were a "holy symbol" and for my "protection."

The next moment, I found myself back in my bedroom with eyes wide open and the voltage gone. My body was still tingling. A voltmeter would have most likely recorded a very high reading. I went into the bathroom and looked in the mirror to see that my pupils were dilated, and my usual heavy and glossy hair was full of static. It was hard to think because I was still in the space I had just returned from. The physical aftermath of this OBE remained for three days, and the information I received along with the experience of no-emotions-no-mind has profoundly influenced my understanding of who we really are and will remain with me for the rest of this life.

Subsequently, I researched pine cones and discovered a paragraph written by Carl Weiseth on the Third Eye Pinecones website, which stated the following: "Throughout the span of recorded human history, Pinecones have served as a symbolic representation of Human Enlightenment, the Third Eye and the Pineal Gland." Further research led me to author, researcher, and filmmaker, Richard Cassaro, who wrote the following:

> The pine cone alludes to the highest degree of spiritual illumination possible. The symbol can be found in the ruins of the Indonesians, Babylonians, Egyptians, Greeks, Romans, and Christians, to name a few. It also appears in the drawings of esoteric traditions like Theosophy, Gnosticism, and esoteric Christianity.

2012: A Clarion Call—A Wake-Up Call for Humanity

Back in 2002, following the two psychic attacks, I informed my friends in Spirit that the OBEs were no longer to be part of my life and that if they wished to continue working with and through me then they were going to have to find another way to do so—and they did.

It appeared that I had been left to rest and to fully recover from the collapse in March 2002, and the CDE of that Easter. Then, in March 2009, almost seven years to the day of the collapse and seemingly out of nowhere, a title dropped into my awareness in big bold capital letters: **2012: A CLARION CALL—A WAKE-UP CALL FOR HUMANITY**. I immediately intuited it was to be a book and that I was to write it. I had no clue how to do so, yet I sensed that Spirit had found another way to work with and through me via the written word, and it must have been clear that seven years later, I was ready to respond to their new *call*.

Will I ever allow the energy that coursed through my body and catalyzed the OBEs to enter me again? Occasionally it still does when I am asleep and always brings with it some kind of message. For example, in the early hours following the conclusion of a booklet I recently put together and will shortly publish titled, "The New Earth & Future Earth," I experienced the energy again. As is always the case when it comes in this way, I began to lucid dream, and here is what occurred:

I was standing with a friend in an apartment by a great, wide, and fast-flowing river. I walked over to the window for a better view, and as I did so the powerful tide of the river changed direction and began to move and swell toward me. The familiar intense buzzing was coursing through my body (a sign that confirms something otherworldly is happening), and as I stared at the surging water the first of three giant elephants, with the two others directly behind, rose up from beneath the river and fixed its eyes firmly on my own. Immediately, the two other giants did the same. The buzzing intensified as they moved closer toward me without averting their gaze. I felt no fear, only a deep sense of gno-ing/knowing. Then, the all-pervading inner buzzing sensation took external form as billions of "atoms" streaming from the heavens to create a vast column of LIGHT. I told my friend not to be concerned for me and warned her that I might faint and that if I did it was okay because I would be fine. At this point I awoke.

As I lay in the aftermath of that lucid dream with my body still tingling from the voltage that had been coursing through it, I immediately understood that the three giant elephants had represented the three Earths that I had been writing about the night before. Often, after having experienced an altered state with the accompanying visions, something in my waking life will confirm this the following day. However, this time it was my writings of the previous day that had been verified by a lucid dream.

Spiritually and psychologically elephants are said to represent wisdom, strength, stability, tenacity, honor, fortune, protection, longevity, cooperation, sovereignty, loyalty, moderation, and eternity. Were these giant majestic Beings wishing to convey that these are the foundation stones that underpin the New and Future Earths? I believe so. And, what of the great column of LIGHT that was streaming from the heavens? My sense is that it represented the higher-dimensional vibration and frequency that defines both the New and Future Earths, revealing the degree to which each is connected to the Higher Realms and a Higher Intelligence.

I remain curious about what I might experience now, twenty-one years after the initial OBE, if I were to consciously engage with this phenomenon again. So much has changed within me during these past two decades in terms of evolution, awakening, integration, and transformation. I do believe that I will invite these events in the future, but only when I feel ready to do so.

Letting Go into LOVE

Just before I conclude with a final story that is the most personal of all, I will share here one of my first ever OBEs. I found myself driving up a long and ascending road that was flanked on either side by the most beautiful open countryside without a building in sight. In the distance to my left, a great golden mist was descending and moving in my direction. I sensed that when it reached me, I would enter a full OBE. Slowly but surely it approached and then engulfed me. I was immediately catapulted out of my body. During this OBE, I received the distinct impression that my mother had just passed away. Then I came back into the bedroom with my eyes wide open and filled with the familiar post-experience tingling throughout my body.

Since then, I have always known that one day I would find myself driving along that very road and when that time came my mother's transition would be imminent. As it happened, the end of 2013 cast a long shadow over her life, and it became clear that her passing would take place within the next few years. I also remained aware that when it was time for her to "leave" I would know because I would find myself driving along *that* road.

In August 2015, given the extreme deterioration of her health, my mum was moved to a residential medical facility where she could receive twenty-four-hour care. I spent most of my time with her and even though it often appeared she would not make it through the week, still I remained aware I had not driven along that road. In the summer of 2016, I was told that my mum needed to be moved to an advanced medical facility, and in July, she was relocated there.

The move went smoothly, and I just *knew* that this would be where my mum's Soul would leave her body. One day, while on the way to see her it was as if a bolt of lightning shot through my heart when I suddenly realized I was driving along *that* road. The views out of the windows to my right and left were exactly the same as I had seen in the OBE twenty years prior. As for the golden mist that had appeared from the left during that experience, in real time it represented the left turn I would take when traveling to see her on the final part of the journey. I realized I was reliving that OBE because it portended my mother's imminent passing.

As I sit writing this final story in August 2017, it is still as fresh in my mind as if it occurred just moments ago. It is a story that really began in June 2013, but I only wish to speak here of the final few hours, which were the most profound of all. I find it almost impossible to put this experience into words, and I hope that what I am about to convey will in some way do justice to the depth and magnitude of what took place.

In essence, the mother I adored was terminally ill from November 2012 until June 2017. She was severely afflicted with a neurological disease that, ultimately, rendered her physically disabled yet of sound mind. Such was the bond between us that I all but gave up my own life to remain by her side and care for her throughout her illness.

Over the course of four years she continued to deteriorate until the last months of her life had become unbearable. Her condition caused her to be catatonically exhausted and whether awake or sleeping her eyes remained closed for most of the time. She was also unable to speak during the final two years of her life, other than to whisper the occasional word or to indicate yes or no.

The beginning of the end came on Wednesday, June 14, 2017, when, to save her from choking to death, I and the team of specialists assigned to her care made the heartbreaking decision to stop giving her any pureed food or thickened fluids. I knew then that it was only a matter of time. I was usually with her during the day but from that moment on I ensured I was there 24/7. I stayed by her side remaining awake day and night in order to love and support her all the way HOME.

Back in June 2013 I had made a promise to myself, and silently to her, that I would walk her all the way to the threshold, and this I was determined to do. In the last two days of her life she lay peaceful and still, yet never again opened her eyes. But I was able to tell when she could hear me, when she was asleep, or if she was somewhere else beyond this earthly realm.

At 11:00 p.m. on Sunday June 18, I noticed that the rhythm of her breathing had changed. I breathed with her in order to understand just what was occurring. It was clear that she had begun the final part of her life's journey. All night long, I sat by her side, loving her, holding her hand, stroking her hair, gently talking to her, reminiscing, reassuring, and helping to support and prepare her to leave her body. Throughout it all, her eyes remain cast down, almost closed with a fixed stare. When

I leaned across her to look up at her face, I could see the lower part of her pupils, which were their usual color of vivid blue. Yet, when sitting at her side her eyes appeared to be completely closed.

Three times during the early morning hours of June 19 my mum spontaneously heaved, remaining seemingly unaware. We administered three anti-nausea injections, and the effect of each lasted a couple of hours. Her breathing was fast and while not noticeably loud, it began to sound a little obstructed. At 7:13, I gently pushed down on the pillow where her mouth was to make more space for her to breathe, and it was at this point that I heard just how shallow her breathing had become.

All of a sudden, she heaved again, and I understood that her body was attempting to push her spirit out. I realized that each time she had done this her extremities were becoming colder and beginning to resemble white marble. The hand that I was holding was also beginning to lose heat yet her face and head remained consistently warm. Immediately following her last bout of heaving her mouth began to open wide, close again, and then open even wider. As this was happening, she suddenly and purposely turned her face toward me, opened her eyes, and stared directly into my own. It would be more accurate to say that her very Soul was blazing into my entire being.

What I witnessed was astonishing. It was pure Soul-to-Soul contact. I could see her true sovereign essence, no emotions or mind, just pure Consciousness boring into my Soul. Her gaze was so absolute, focused, and intense that I knew she was communicating with me before fully leaving her body. I gazed into her eyes encouraging her to let go into LOVE and the LIGHT. With her eyes still locked and blazing into my own she began to open her mouth wider and wider, and I knew she was about to go. I watched her eyes change color from their usual vivid blue to a darker blue and then to a slate grey, at which point a veil seemed to move across them. The pupils then dilated, and she was gone.

Her eyes then returned to being almost fully closed except for a glimpse of just the lower part of the iris that had returned to its familiar shade of light blue. The entire experience must have lasted no more than a couple of minutes yet conveyed not only lifetimes of Love but also the reality of Eternity, the Immortal Soul, Spirit, and Source. I believe that my mum wanted to show me her Soul and to express to me the following: "The mother, the wife, the daughter and daughter-in-law, the grandmother and granddaughter, the sister and sister-in-law, the aunt and niece, and the friend, colleague, and woman that I have been, is not *who I really AM*."

When I gazed into her eyes, there was no fear or pain, no emotion or sadness, no personality, no trace of the woman that she had been or echoes of the human life she was leaving behind. The Being that was revealed was pure Consciousness and, in that one moment, I fully understood and experienced the reality of us all being equal as Souls—no matter who we have been or what we have done, fundamentally we are all One.

It is astonishing to me that my mum, whose eyes had remained closed for most of the last two years of her life, and who was unresponsive for the two days and most certainly during her final hours, was able to move her head, turn her face directly toward me, open her eyes and lock onto my own, gazing unflinchingly at me while she left her body. The strength, presence, magnificence, and majesty of her Soul were breathtaking. It was a transcendental, mystical, blessed, exalted moment both in and out of time.

I sense that in those last precious seconds of her life she gifted me with the sublime understanding and proof that the Soul is enduring and truly does move on. I have undergone the most profound other-worldly experiences, but this . . . this was in *real* time, human time, Earth time. What my mum showed me in those last two minutes of her life will remain with me forever.

Since her transition, I find myself deeply contemplating what else may have taken place during that *moment* between us; what exchange, download of information, and/or transmission might have been passed from her Soul to mine during that experience of Pure Divine Grace that took place between 7:13 and 7:15 on June 19, 2017.

2

Consciousness *Is*

Even though I have this body, I am not my body; Even though I have these emotions, I am not my emotions; Even though I have this mind, I am not my mind. I AM—Pure LOVE.

ADAPTED FROM ROBERTO ASSAGIOLI

This chapter takes us deeper into the phenomenon of **CONSCIOUSNESS*** and explores each of its three variants, or levels—consciousness/Consciousness/CONSCIOUSNESS, which can be thought of as divine emanations of CONSCIOUSNESS, GOD-SOURCE. Here is an at-a-glance list of the psychospiritual expressions of CONSCIOUSNESS and their corresponding meanings.

CONSCIOUSNESS—GOD, SOURCE, THE DIVINE, THE BELOVED, ALL THAT IS, THE BEYOND, INFINITY, ETERNITY, GREAT SPIRIT, SOUL, LIGHT, LOVE, which is Self-actualized, Self-transcendent, Multidimensional, Mystical, and Enlightened

Consciousness*—Self, Authentic Self, Conscious Self, Integrated Self, Psychospiritual Self, Spiritually Awakened Self, Realized Self, Love

consciousness*—**self***, psychospiritually unawakened self, unconscious self, adapted self, consciously unawakened self,

unintegrated ego, adapted self, historically/psychologically
wounded self, wounded inner child, love

unconscious mind*—self, psychospiritually asleep self, psychospiritually unaware self

Conscious Mind*—Self, Psychospiritually Awake Self,
Psychospiritually Aware Self

Superconscious Mind*—**Higher Self***, Psychospiritually Evolved
Self, Metaphysical Self

Unconscious*—The vast compendium of the sum total of all personal experience throughout all timelines; an encyclopedia of all
collective experience on Earth.

THE UNFATHOMABLE THAT IS CONSCIOUSNESS

The most brilliant minds have long been preoccupied with the question of CONSCIOUSNESS and the greatest philosophers, scientists,
and spiritual teachers have sought to define just what it is. For millennia, mystics, prophets, seers, artists, writers, and the most highly evolved
individuals have brought us to the shorelines of CONSCIOUSNESS,
but we have yet to plumb the very depths and reach the very heights in
our understanding of this phenomenon.

We may comprehend, perceive, conceive, know, and gno (gnosis)
that an actualized or transcended human Consciousness is but a mirror of the incomprehensible reality that is CONSCIOUSNESS. We
are all sparks of CONSCIOUSNESS, and each of us holds a deep gnosis that we are part of something vast, unfathomable, and boundlessly
indefinable that we refer to as SOURCE, GOD, or THE DIVINE.
Our deepest Calling is to remember that *we are* CONSCIOUSNESS
and to fully recognize ourselves as Beings of Light incarnate in
human form.

THE REVELATIONS OF GNOSIS

The reductionist mind, which originates from the left hemisphere of the brain, seeks to qualify, quantify, verify, calculate, evaluate, measure, assess, and categorize; whereas the abstract mind of the brain's right hemisphere has an unquestionable capacity for gnosis and so strives to pierce the veils of what it intuits is an Ultimate Reality existing far beyond the human realm.

The reductionist mind would define Consciousness as a never ceasing repetition of cognitive thought and observation that is part of the neurological function of the brain. It would consider the abstract mind to be inferior and therefore limited in its ability and capacity to grasp the indeterminable magnitude that is CONSCIOUSNESS. Yet, this mind has little concept of such an Ultimate Reality because it is preoccupied with the concrete and the physically tangible.

Even the abstract or gnostic mind is barely able to perceive CONSCIOUSNESS as a multidimensional phenomenon that is present throughout all Space and Time, although its origins are beyond both. It is within and around all life-forms, whether plant, animal, human, galactic, or cosmic.

Whether it is a question of the concrete or abstract mind, the left or right hemisphere of the brain, or of consciousness (self), Consciousness (Self), or CONSCIOUSNESS (SOUL, SPIRIT, SOURCE), the interconnectedness of everything needs to be deeply understood at a collective level.

In recent times, modern physics has been expanding its mechanistic horizons to include a more holistic and ecological viewpoint and science has become increasingly inclined toward the exploration of CONSCIOUSNESS. As a result, the distance between science and spirituality is beginning to close. It is within the meeting zone of opposites that we truly discover the intrinsic connection that transcends Space and Time, and links All Things in the Universe and Beyond, a "zone" that invites us to explore the following question: Is humanity psychospiritually prepared to more fully comprehend what may potentially exist beyond the Field of CONSCIOUSNESS itself?

ALTERED STATES AND CONSCIOUSNESS

Many people have experienced transcendent states of Consciousnes that touch upon or take them into the deeper realms of CONSCIOUSNESS. Yet, these can all too soon disappear into the archives of memory because of the practical demands of day-to-day life.

Experiencing an altered state of mind is not uncommon and can be life changing. Sometimes this is induced naturally, but it may also occur as a result of ingesting specific substances. The extent to which an individual is evolved and awakened will determine not only the experience itself but also the degree to which it becomes an integrated part of their everyday life. However, in one who remains consciously unawakened this may not be the case. Many experiences are profound while others can be frightening, yet all leave a lasting conscious or unconscious impression. Positive experiences may serve as initiatory gateways for evolving and awakening the Self.

THE UNCONSCIOUS

Within the container of CONSCIOUSNESS is held The Unconscious, and its role is unique for it amounts to a vast, infinite alchemical realm of sacred mystery, creative genius, and human potential. Metaphorically, the Unconscious could be likened to the subterranean expanse that researchers of ancient civilizations have referred to as the "inner earth." Access to The Unconscious is not exclusive to those who are psychospiritually evolved, as is evident in the great works of art, music, philosophy, science, mathematics, and literature, alongside the inventions and innovations that have so often been produced by those who were (or are) far from Self-realized.

Like the mystical meaning of the whale, which the First Nations

People consider to be the Record Keeper of the Earth, the Unconscious is a great sweeping library for individual and collective Consciousness, a vast compendium of human memory and experience. Contained within it are humanity's past, present, and future across all timelines as well as the answers to all questions pertaining to the human journey on Gaia (Earth).

Carl Jung was a master of penetrating and interpreting the mysteries of the Unconscious. Journeying into its depths is to directly tap into otherwise imperceptible echoes and wave fields of SOURCE/CONSCIOUSNESS, and this enables sublime communion with the Soul of the Earth.

The Unconscious contains all human evolutionary blueprints and templates, all records for the Earth; more of her mysteries are revealed under the spotlight of a Conscious humanity seeking greater insight into the meaning and purpose of life and our world. Those who are able to Consciously penetrate its depths are the visionaries, philosophers, pioneers, futurists, and artists of a Conscious new world.

LEVELS OF CONSCIOUSNESS

The human mind can be viewed as a system composed of three particular levels: the unconscious, the Conscious, and the Superconscious. This system can be likened to a three-story house, with the unconscious situated in the basement, the Conscious positioned on the ground level, and the Superconscious located on the top floor.

Unconscious Mind

The unconscious mind is an extensive memory bank that records our every thought, feeling, action, and experience. Most of the contents within it originate from one's personal history (past/present/ancestral/karmic). It includes all conditioning imposed upon us by other individuals, our local community, and society as a whole, and this can blind us to our true identity.

Root trauma exerts an inestimable influence on us for better or worse. Trauma imprinting occurs when we experience something deeply disturbing and distressing. This can happen at any time from infancy through adulthood. When trauma remains unprocessed, unhealed, and unintegrated, similar stories will continue to play out in our everyday lives. We unconsciously recreate the theme of an original trauma in an attempt to heal it. By remaining *unconscious* of these patterns we will draw to ourselves the same themes again and again, until we have discovered the root of their cause. Only by healing the original story can we transcend suffering, but if we fail to do this these themes will remain with us throughout our current life and, perhaps, even into our next incarnation on Earth.

We need to recognize the capacity of the unconscious mind to lock us into self-sabotaging behaviors that keep us maintaining cycles and block the way to inner peace and fulfillment. It is time to rewrite the stories that leave us feeling insignificant and disempowered—*Change the story, Change your life, Change the world.*

The Conscious Mind

To return to the metaphor of a three-story house now, if the unconscious mind is located in the basement, then the Conscious Mind is found on the ground floor, and this is the level most responsible for the physical, emotional, and mental experiences of our daily lives. Metaphorically, this floor consists of a series of data processors that filter, interpret, and act upon information received from both the unconscious and Superconscious minds. The ground level (Conscious Mind) is wired up to the basement (unconscious mind), from which it receives most of its input. As a result, life continues to be lived in a structured, safe, and familiar way, albeit directed and influenced by either positive or negative messages. The unconscious mind also stores valuable information that can guide us to make choices that are life serving and life transforming.

Essentially, the Conscious Mind is creative and is able to process multistreams of incoming data. If someone is unevolved, it is because there is minimal Conscious connection with the unconscious and Superconscious minds. If however, a person is connected, and therefore able to Consciously explore and integrate unconscious material, then a natural and open relationship develops with both minds, and one lives a more illumined life that flows even in the shadow of everyday struggles and challenges.

We could understand this better by imagining the Conscious Mind as an international airport, with planes taking off and arriving from all over the world representing incoming and outgoing data, the passengers on them the minutia of the unconscious mind, and the skies representing the Superconscious. Metaphorically speaking, the Conscious Mind is a busy juncture serving both the unconscious and the Superconscious. It has its own independent function, which is to distill, process, assimilate, translate, and transmit the messages it receives.

The Conscious Mind is the unifying and aligning principle of all three minds. It is a receiver and transmitter and an overall *experiencer,* which continually strives to integrate and balance. Its ultimate function is to synchronize and synthesize all three levels of mind as a coherent holistic system operating as an integrated whole.

The Superconscious Mind

The Superconscious Mind is found on the top floor of our metaphoric house. We could imagine this immense space to be a sacred temple that holds the original blueprint for our true sovereign selves. It equates to a vast expanse of supra-intelligence and energy and is both local and nonlocal. It is without boundaries in its connection to Spirit yet has boundaries imposed upon it by unawakened human consciousness.

The Superconscious Mind is a realm within us where we can touch the DIVINE. It is a bridge between Consciousness and CONSCIOUSNESS itself. It remains mostly dormant until the magnitude of psychological and karmic clutter is cleared from the unconscious. As we heal, integrate, and transcend the psychological processes of the unconscious mind, we begin to more fully engage with the imagination (*the Soul in action*) as well as experience the reverential and sacred within our own hearts (the heart being the seat of the Soul). The Superconscious Mind is the domain of prayer, meditation, and contemplation, inspired creativity, visioning, and dreaming. Just as the unconscious mind is preoccupied with the past, and the Conscious Mind with the present, the focus of the Superconscious Mind is on the future.

It is through the Superconscious Mind that we have a more direct experience of CONSCIOUSNESS. It is the link to the Conscious Mind. The Superconscious Mind is the realm of genius and illumination, and, as a direct channel to SOURCE, it inspires the greatest visionaries and evolutionary pioneers. It is within the dominion of enlightened Consciousness that we access the higher purpose of the Soul and discover the truth of *who we really are, why we are really here,* and *where we are really from.*

Returning now to the top floor of our metaphoric house where the Superconscious Mind is located, we find many wires here, each extending to a bank of data processors situated on the ground floor or the Conscious Mind. When disconnected, the Conscious Mind is unable to receive the futuristic vision and revelatory insights of the Superconscious. However, when both levels are connected, a whole new dimension is revealed that enriches and illumines the Conscious Mind and enables a direct encounter with the Soul

CONSCIOUSNESS AND THE HUMAN BRAIN

There is a popular belief that the human brain uses only 10 percent of its potential. In a recent communication, the biologist Bruce Lipton suggested to me that the brain is capable of being "100 percent active all of the time." He went on to share that "90 percent of the brain is comprised of connective and supporting tissue known as 'glial cells,' while the remaining 10 percent is composed of neurons."

Lipton further explained that "glial cells are instrumental in the overall neural function of the brain and can inhibit, activate, and control the activity of the neurons they connect to." In the past, these cells have been considered by science to be passive yet are now recognized to play an essential role in brain function. Glial cells are an integral part of all neuron activity, and according to Lipton, "90 percent of glial cells and 10 percent of neurons create a brain that has the potential to be fully and permanently active." Yet, as he shares, "it is rare that all 90 percent of glial cells would interact with all 10 percent of neurons. Access to all of our brain capacity all of the time is limited because our overriding habits, routines, patterns, and preferences dominate our thoughts and therefore keep us locked in maintaining cycles and the same neuronal pathways."

Lipton advises that it is possible to achieve greater access to our brain function through awakened and higher states of Consciousness, mindfulness, holistic thinking, and hemispheric (left and right brain) exercises. He shared how these practices "have the ability to reshape our lives and that by remaining caught in the loop of habitual behaviors, patterns and beliefs we have limited access to the neural pathways that are available to us."

HEMISPHERIC SYNCHRONIZATION

The human experience is one of interconnected hemispheres: Spirit and Matter, Heaven and Earth, Human and Divine, Consciousness and consciousness, masculine and feminine, concrete and abstract, and left and right brain.

In regard to the brain, the ideal scenario is one in which both hemispheres are equally and simultaneously engaged. This is known as *hemispheric synchronization,* a brain state that also facilitates hyperlearning and a sense of calm and centeredness. The integration of the body and nervous system through hemispheric balancing exercises, such as crossing the arms or the legs and ankles when resting or using the opposite hand to the one that would ordinarily carry out everyday tasks, can facilitate whole-brain synchronization and enable superneural functioning.

When not engaged in such activities the brain is in a modus operandi that scientists call brain dominance (i.e., when one hemisphere of the brain is dominant over the other). A hemispherically synchronized brain has unprecedented potential for whole system (human and global) transformation. Imagine, for example, what nearly eight billion hemispherically synchronized brains could achieve! It is possible for a unified population living as awakened Consciousness to cocreate a Conscious and enlightened society and a peaceful and sustainable world.

The evolutionary lens through which we view the world is focused within and outside of ourselves. When we consider the current state of the collective consciousness, we might well wonder if it is the destiny of humanity to destroy itself. It is the quest of those who are **Consciously awakened*** to support the emergence of a Conscious world. When Consciousness is located within the heart then the emotions are transcended and we live from a place of feeling—of unconditional giving, loving, receiving, doing, and BEing.

So, how to affect a Consciousness shift to such an extent that it could birth a new Conscious world? The revered saint, Anandamayi Ma, also considered an **avatar***, has an answer: "The supreme calling of every human being is to aspire to Self-realization. All other obligations are secondary." This indeed is our Call to Consciousness—to evolve along the psychospiritual trajectory from Self-awareness to Self-integration, Self-realization to Self-actualization, and, ultimately, to Self-transcendence.

CONSCIOUSNESS: INFINITY AND ETERNITY

Futurist and seer Nikola Tesla spoke of the phenomenon that is CONSCIOUSNESS when he said that the human mind simply cannot comprehend Infinity and Eternity. An unawakened mind is an uninspired mind and one that views life through a lens of separation. The human being operating from the lower mind is unable to perceive the Self, or the Higher Self.

With its propensity to be informed by concrete, intellectual, and academic data the unawakened mind simply cannot grasp the scope, meaning, and reality of CONSCIOUSNESS let alone the fact that it *is* CONSCIOUSNESS. In the same way that a computer is only able to receive a program when "online," a human being only receives downloads of CONSCIOUSNESS if it is sufficiently evolved and awakened.

It is not only humanity that is on an evolutionary trajectory, our planet is too. The world is confronted by enormous Earth changes, some of which are engineered, but many can be attributed directly to evolution. As we consider these ecological and environmental changes alongside the sociopolitical unrest across the globe, we can sense that a shift is occurring and that the world is in the midst of *breaking down in order to break through.* This evolutionary phenomenon is also reflected in the personal lives of many individuals.

As humanity slowly begins to Consciously awaken, it will start to witness unparalleled evolutionary change that will impact both the individual and the collective physically, emotionally, mentally, psychologically, intellectually, psychically, energetically, and spiritually.

CONSCIOUSNESS:
SOURCE, SPIRITUAL ESSENCE, AND THE PSYCHE

In the arena of **metaphysics***, one often encounters terms such as *SOURCE, Spiritual Essence,* and *Psyche,* so I thought I would present some thoughts on what these terms suggest:

SOURCE
SOURCE equates to our very BEing, to EXISTENCE ITSELF, ALL THAT IS, GOD, THE CREATOR, THE BELOVED, THE DIVINE. The origin of individual, collective, galactic, and cosmic

Consciousness, SOURCE is our spiritual HOME. It is LOVE, LIGHT, and THE ABSOLUTE. Indefinable, indeterminable, and utterly incomprehensible, SOURCE is where we are truly from.

Spiritual Essence

Spiritual Essence may be defined as the spiritual *fragrance* of the Soul, a personal energetic signature and pure etheric substance that emanates from the core of our very being. Essence is the Light of who we are transmitted as a pure and invisible illumined radiance that exists within every human being. It conveys an incorporeal impression of the Soul, which is intangibly present within the energetic realms of a human form. When one is *living their Essence,* they are directly expressing the pure true beauty of their Soul.

The Psyche

The Psyche and the Soul are independent phenomena yet are intricately associated and intrinsically linked. There are various interpretations of the term *psyche.* Jung spoke of it as "the totality of all psychic processes, conscious as well as unconscious."

Psyche is of the Soul. It equates to an invisible, visceral, biospiritual phenomenon, both present within and beyond the physical body. It is attached to a human being via a luminous cord and remains so throughout a lifetime. The Psyche can be likened to a psychic processing hub and dwells within and beyond the mind. Ethereal by nature yet more energetically tangible than Essence, it is present in the energy bodies that extend beyond the human form.

The Psyche translates the language of matter and light through the lower (unconscious), middle (Conscious), and higher (Superconscious) minds. It permeates all levels of one's being and, like water, acts as a conductor. It is an observer, initiator, and processor of all aspects of a human life ranging from the physical, emotional, mental, intellectual, and psychological to the energetic, intuitive, metaphysical, and spiritual. It assesses, assimilates, and evaluates through its capacity for the perceptual and perpetual, the perceptible and nonperceptible.

CONSCIOUSNESS is where we are truly from, and the Psyche and Essence dissolve at the point the Soul takes permanent leave of the physical body.

As c/Consciousness evolves, we become passionate about and committed to understanding where we are going as an individual and as a global community and recognize how our presence in the world can exert a significant influence on the cocreation of an evolved New Paradigm. The self, Self, and Higher Self become increasingly aligned to Soul, Spirit, and SOURCE, the heart and mind undergo a radical transformation, and we rediscover the truth of *who we really are* and *where we are really from.*

3

The Principal
Spiritual Dimensions

*The truth is: the world is not three- or four-dimensional—
it is multidimensional. But no number of dimensions,
however high, will ever be able to define or even approach
the spiritual nature of God and of the Self. Even an
infinite number of dimensions would still be a prison for
the eternal Self. The eternal spiritual nature of the Self lies
beyond any logic or dualistic perception. The destination
of our life and everything beyond is this: To achieve this
eternal spiritual nature of the Self in relation to the
whole and to God; and to leave the world of conditional
perception and conditional action behind.*

ALBERT EINSTEIN

This chapter offers further insights into the questions of *who we
really are* and *where we are really from* in the context of what I
perceive to be the principal spiritual dimensions, levels of Existence,
or CONSCIOUSNESS. I have gained profound and revelatory metaphysical and spiritual insights from and about these dimensions
through decades of existential contemplation informed by the extensive metaphysical and OBEs I have personally undergone throughout
my life.

CONCENTRIC CIRCLES, DIMENSIONS, AND GRAND SWEEPING AGES

To commence our exploration of the dimensions and begin to gain a better understanding of the evolutionary continuum of an incarnate Soul in human form, let us contemplate the psychospiritual model that I developed in 2013 called the Concentric Circles of CONSCIOUSNESS (CCC), which is shown in figure 1 below.

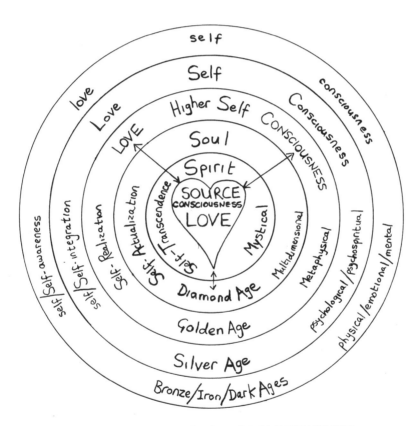

Figure 1. Concentric Circles of CONSCIOUSNESS

This model is a psychospiritual continuum for the psychological integration, conscious evolution, and spiritual awakening of both the individual and the collective. It is made up of five circles, one of which is a central heart symbolizing CONSCIOUSNESS, which, as we have already established, is simply another word for LOVE, GOD, SOURCE, or EXISTENCE, and the ultimate spiritual dimension. The self, being furthest from the inner circle, equates to the least awakened state of human consciousness. Positioned within each circle are various maps and models that chart the trajectories of psychological integration, conscious evolution, and spiritual awakening.

Correlating States and Circles

Figure 1 shows that the c/Consciousness state of an individual (or that of the Collective when referring to the Grand Sweeping Ages) is located within its correlating circle. When the lessons associated with the furthest outer circle of self are learned, and thus integrated and transcended, the individual moves into the next circle of Self to learn the lessons associated with that level, and so it continues.

From the circle of the Self, one is propelled toward the circle of the Higher Self and the embodiment of that. And from there, the phenomenal experiences of the metaphysical, mystical, and transcendental, for example, can be initiated and catalyzed by the energies and frequencies of the circles of Soul, Spirit, and SOURCE, respectively. Because consciousness is either evolving or devolving, a person can move from an outer circle to an inner one or vice versa. The movement from one circle to another can take millennia.

This consciousness/Consciousness/CONSCIOUSNESS trajectory of the self, Self, Higher Self, Soul, Spirit, and SOURCE can also be viewed in a more linear way similar to how we looked at consciousness in chapter 2, from the most outer circle (the self) to the inner circle (closest to the center/SOURCE) as follows:

self—consciousness (unconscious/unawakened self); physical/
emotional/mental self/self-awareness; love (conditional love)
Self—Consciousness (Self-awareness/Self-realization/

Self-actualization); psychological/psychospiritual;
self/Self-integration; Love (Unconditional Love)
Higher Self—CONSCIOUSNESS (LOVE/SOURCE);
Metaphysical; Self-realization
Soul—CONSCIOUSNESS (LOVE/SOURCE);
Multidimensional; Self-actualization
Spirit—CONSCIOUSNESS (LOVE/SOURCE); Mystical;
Self-transcendence
SOURCE—CONSCIOUSNESS/LOVE

We might also superimpose the four levels of Mind discussed in chapter 2: the unconscious would appear in the outermost circle of self, Conscious in the circle of Self, Superconscious in the circle of Higher Self, and the Unconscious (relating to both the personal and collective) in the circle of Soul.

It is important to note that even when one's consciousness is located in the circle of self, the greater energy of an inner circle such as that of the Soul remains a strong influence. Imagine that an individual who is on a path of self-destruction has a dream about a heavenly being or a dearly departed loved one who offers a message of love, of hope, to protect the individual or catalyze a healing. Someone else may have an important premonition, while another might undergo an out-of-body or a **near-death experience*** (NDE). All such examples serve to awaken the psychospiritually slumbering self. Without intervention, be it human or divine, the self is less compelled to heal and evolve into the next sequential circle.

If we were to superimpose the current state of the collective onto the Concentric Circles, we might observe that from the perspective of conscious evolution the outer circle reflects the global crisis that is now confronting humankind. Transcending the circle of self frees an individual and the collective from the conditioned mentality of the **matrix***, so they can ascend into the higher octave of the awakening/awakened Self.

An Extra Word on the Circle of the Self

It is the circle of Self that brings a sense of remembrance in regard to the *more than* we truly are. It compels us to seek and embrace our true vocational calling. We make more loving and mindful choices, and we become more discerning in terms of the people we closely connect with, the environments we choose to live in, and our everyday relationships. At the heart of our focus is an evolutionary drive to discover more of who we really are. We gravitate toward creativity and spirituality, and this is often reflected in our social and vocational fields as well as our living environments. We are inspired to serve not only our immediate communities but also the whole of humanity. We begin to manifest the ideals that are alive within our heart and Soul.

As Consciousness evolves, the self integrates with the Self, which then becomes increasingly aligned to the Soul, Spirit, and SOURCE. As this occurs, the mind undergoes a radical transformation and the heart begins to open more fully. The truth of who we really are and why we are really here becomes increasingly apparent and an unparalleled passion and sense of compassion move us to inspired and visionary actions as the true cocreators we are. Our presence in the world begins to exert an influence, for, as we begin to more fully conceive of where we are really from, *everything changes*.

The Four Great Sweeping Ages

Within the CCC model the Great Sweeping Ages of humanity correspond to the circles of s/Self as follows:

Bronze/Iron/Dark Ages—self
Silver Age—Self
Golden Age—Higher Self
Diamond Age—Soul and Spirit

The Golden Age was the first Age of the world—an untroubled, prosperous, and ideal era during which people lived in perfect harmony.

It was the age when we had our greatest connection to SOURCE (the very BEINGNESS of GOD) and an era when meditation, wisdom, and communion with Spirit held special importance. In the Satya **Yuga***, the average life expectancy of a human being was believed to be about four hundred years. People practiced only loving-kindness, and humanity lived in harmony with the Earth.

The Silver Age was the time when darkness entered human consciousness, and we became more separated from Spirit. And during the Bronze Age an even greater spiritual darkness descended upon humankind that resulted in further disconnection from SOURCE.

The Iron Age/Dark Age is the present age we live in, when darkness has almost completely diminished spiritual Light. However, we are on the verge of entering another major Age—a new Golden Age—that brings the promise of the Hopi prophesy that foretells of "a thousand years of peace." The Mahabharata, one of two major Sanskrit ancient epics, described the last Golden Age as follows: "There were no poor and no rich; there was no disease. There was no lessening with the years; there was no hatred or vanity, or evil thought whatsoever; no sorrow, no fear." The Golden Age is one in which all beings will prosper and know fulfilment and joy. It is the age in which we will experience our greatest connection to SOURCE (the very BEingness of God); where Love, wisdom, peace, and communion with Spirit will be the foundations upon which our world is built. It is an age where goodness, kindness, purity of intent, and harmony are centrifugal forces that source and sustain all experiences for all life-forms.

In the future, during the Diamond Age, an Exalted Race of Beings will arrive on fifth-dimensional Earth. These multidimensional, multifaceted bringers of pure Consciousness and diamond technology will mark the most auspicious epoch yet on the timeline of humanity. The Diamond Age will be defined by a highly evolved and advanced COLLECTIVE CONSCIOUSNESS and will be a truly Great Age for humanity and the planet. The arrival of the Diamond Age remains solely dependent upon the maturational state of the Collective Consciousness.

THE AKASHIC FIELD

We can imagine that SOURCE/GOD/LOVE is effectively a portal into the vast Beyond, the boundless "FIELD" within which the CCC resides. This FIELD has many names: the SOURCE FIELD, the GOD FIELD, the LIGHT FIELD, the FIELD of CONSCIOUSNESS, the FIELD of LOVE, or the FIELD of EXISTENCE ITSELF, all of which as we are already aware, are names for that which humanity has termed as GOD. But perhaps one of the most familiar names for it is the **AKASHIC FIELD***.

The AKASHIC FIELD equates to the underlying unified SOURCE REALITY that *IS*—beyond Space and Time and from which All Things and All Realities manifest. It is the SOURCE of all material manifestation, including the Cosmos, as well as this Universe and others.

Within the AKASHIC FIELD are the **Akashic Records***, which are what people have described as the information that resides within SOURCE REALITY. When a person is accessing the Records, they are also accessing SOURCE. In fact, like fish in the sea, we are, all of us, already within the AKASHIC FIELD/CONSCIOUSNESS FIELD— how can we not be, for it is what we manifest from and remain embedded in. The Records we can retrieve from this SOURCE/FIELD are particular informational aspects of it but are not independent of it— nothing is. As noted in Wikipedia: "In theosophy and anthroposophy, the Akashic Records are a compendium of all human events, thoughts, words, emotions, and intent ever to have occurred in the past, present, or future. They are believed by theosophists to be encoded in a non-physical plane of existence." Like the AKASHIC FIELD, we could superimpose the Akashic Records directly beneath the Grand Sweeping Ages present within the CCC.

DIMENSIONS IN RELATION TO HUMAN CONSCIOUSNESS

One often hears spiritual people referring to "higher and lower vibration and frequency." This does not refer to a hierarchy but instead to the density and speed at which atoms and energy vibrate. As the ancient Chinese philosopher Lao Tzu once stated, "The key to growth is the introduction of higher dimensions of consciousness into our awareness."

Although mystics and scientists have spoken of the existence of thirteen dimensions, in 2008 I intuited that there could well be twenty-six. Recently, I researched "twenty-six dimensions," curious to explore if anyone else had written about this. I came across something called superstring theory that proposes that there are at least ten dimensions. In further research, however, I discovered bosonic string theory, which appears to have identified twenty-six dimensions.

THIRTEEN: THE BASIC STRUCTURAL CODE

Thirteen represents a basic structural unit within Nature. It is the magnetic center around which all elements gravitate and gather. This sacred number can be seen in religion, myth, science, and biology and often appears as a pattern of twelve "parts" surrounding a thirteenth. Below are some examples:

Christ had twelve disciples (1 + 12 = 13)

King Arthur had twelve knights.

Our solar system has thirteen constellations.

The zodiac has twelve signs and a thirteenth sign—Ophiuchus—that is hidden.

Our bodies have thirteen joints: two ankles, knees, hips, wrists, elbows, and shoulders plus the neck, all of which enable us to experience physical movement.

For over 5,526 years, the Maya, Incas, Druids, Egyptians, and Essenes all followed a thirteen Moon calendar, which is still used today by those who align with a galactic system of time. In 1933, the League of Nations voted for this calendar to be the new world standard due to its reliability and continuity. The thirteenth month was to be called Tricember, but the bill was never passed.

The December Solstice Sun of 2012 was in alignment with the thirteenth constellation of Ophiuchus, the sign known as the Serpent Healer because it is represented by a heavenly male figure holding a serpent. The ancient Maya predicted a future serpent race who would be known as the Thirteenth Rainbow Tribe.

All thirteen December Solstices since the 1999 Total Solar Eclipse (on the August 11 at 11:13 UTC) were in alignment with the **Galactic Plane*** and the thirteenth constellation (Ophiuchus).

Research in sound frequency recently discovered a thirteenth tone in Western music that has always been part of the music of the East.

The ancient Maya suggest there are thirteen crystal skulls in the etheric and, according to biologist Japp van Etten, these are positioned at thirteen different sacred or powerful sites around the globe, including Peru, Sedona, Mount Shasta, Arizona, Mount Kilimanjaro, and Rennes le Chateau commune.

TWENTY-SIX: THE COMPLETION DIGIT CODE

Twenty-six is also a sacred and significant numerical digit. The sacred **Mayan calendar*** is 260 days long. The Maya were aware that the Sun's equator rotates in twenty-six days and that ten of these cycles are pivotal to yet more solar cycles, including the greater twenty-six-thousand-year cycle of **precession***. The number 260 equates to the root of the entire Mayan mathematical system (both thirteen and twenty-six are harmonically linked to this sacred number). The pivotal years for humanity between 1999 to the beginning of 2012 contained twenty-six solstices.

I propose that there are twenty-six dimensions of which thirteen are currently accessible to humankind and that human consciousness is on the cusp of an evolutionary leap into a higher fifth-dimensional status. Collective consciousness is currently located within the **third dimension*** and predominantly experienced through the left brain. As people begin to attain a more fifth-dimensional awareness, an increase in right-brain activity will automatically occur. The fourth dimension is the first nonphysical dimension, a bridge between our world and the higher dimensions. Some refer to it as the astral or the realm of the human collective mind and feelings, a place of archetypal patterns. I sense it is a transitional dimension as the Consciousness leaves the Earth Plane and begins to adjust to less dense frequencies. We drop our human selves/human consciousness as we ascend beyond this third-dimensional world. There are many levels within the fourth dimension. Those locked into third-dimensional (consciously unawakened) will spend "time" in the lower realms of the astral before ascending to the fifth-dimension or reincarnating back into this world to resume the ascension process. Those already attuned to fifth-dimensional Consciousness here on Earth, will pass straight into the upper regions of the fourth, and continue the Soul experience at that level and beyond.

SHIFTING HEMISPHERES: ONCE EVERY THIRTEEN THOUSAND YEARS

Each year the December Solstice Sun aligns with the equator mid-line of the **Milky Way***. To gain a perspective on this, imagine the Earth's equator forming a division between the Northern and Southern Hemispheres. Astronomically, the December Solstice Sun has been pointing into the Southern Galactic Hemisphere for the past thirteen thousand years. During the Galactic Alignment process (see chapter 8), the December Solstice Sun will be reoriented to point toward the Northern Galactic Hemisphere and will continue to do so for the next thirteen thousand years.

As we approached perfect alignment with the Galactic Equator in December 2016, the window of the thirty-six-year Galactic Alignment process concluded. Imagine subtly realigning a satellite dish to pick up new channels, humanity is now aligning to pick up new and advanced sources of information because of the shift into a new galactic hemisphere.

This astronomical fact is of momentous importance because the collective consciousness has moved from one thirteen-thousand-year cycle into another, and it is here that we observe the significance and relationship of the digits 13 and 26: 13+13=26. The shift into a new galactic hemisphere will induce unprecedented leaps in Consciousness and set humanity on an accelerated path of conscious evolution and spiritual awakening.

Spiritual texts often suggest that there are twelve dimensional levels, yet human Consciousness spans twenty-six, the thirteenth of which is the initiation point for enlightenment and thus an enlightened world. The reorientation of the December Solstice Sun through its crossing of a thirteen-thousand-year threshold, heralds the thirteenth dimensional level about to be brought into human awareness. The twenty-six dimensions are divided into two hemispheres and span the full spectrum of human Consciousness. One through thirteen represent the aspect of Soul embodied in human form and thirteen through twenty-six represent the transcended Soul expressing as SOURCE CONSCIOUSNESS.

At the time of the December Solstice of 2021, supra-advanced galactic codes will anchor into the planetary heart grid to further accelerate the evolutionary awakening of humankind. These codes will be specific to the frequency of thirteen, the numerical digit that represents the Mysteries.

AWAKENING CONSCIOUSNESS

For millennia, the collective consciousness determined the third-dimensional status of the human experience on Earth. Slowly but surely, however, a fifth-dimensional wave of Consciousness is spreading across the globe as more and more individuals begin to awaken and evolve.

The Earth, as Mother, is also part of a Greater Plan, and she understands that to initiate a dimensional shift for humanity too soon would endanger the unawakened global mind because of its current inability to withstand a sudden evolutionary upgrade. For this reason, a third-dimensional consciousness prevails, yet an amplification of vibration and Light is occurring and this is being transmitted by those who are resonating at a higher, fifth-dimensional frequency.

CONSCIOUSNESS AND HEMISPHERIC SYNCHRONIZATION

As mentioned earlier, the third-dimensional level of consciousness is predominantly expressed through the left hemisphere of the brain but in the not-so-distant future, as humans align more fully with the **fifth dimension***, a significant increase in activity will occur within the right brain. **Fifth-dimensional Consciousness*** will rapidly facilitate an acceleration of spiritual awakening and those human Souls who respond to this will begin preparing for alignment with the sixth dimension.

Fifth-dimensional Consciousness brings the left and right hemispheres of the brain into equilibrium, and, as a consequence, the Eastern and Western hemispheres of the globe also begin to unify.

The majority of incarnate Souls are here to heal, integrate, awaken, and evolve. A few, however, are here to guide, teach, lead, and inspire to the extent that they become the forerunners and initiators of a New Conscious Paradigm. Because of the metaphysical reality of nonlinear "time," Souls reincarnate into the human world in order to resolve and transcend unintegrated residues of other timelines. The same applies to future lives, which run concurrently with our present timeline and exert a significant influence on the *here and now,* thus determining and shaping our day-to-day experiences.

A purpose of the evolutionary journey of the Consciously awakened Self is to embody more of the Higher Self. This brings an extradimensional blueprint to the individual and to the world as a whole, as well as a radically enhanced capacity for the attainment of Self-realization and Self-actualization.

Ultimately, the most enlightened state of embodied Consciousness is Self-transcendence—a fully manifested state of *being in but not of the world.* A rare person with such a high vibration appears to be anchored on the Earth but has the ability to move through multidimensions simultaneously in order to sow new seeds of Consciousness and activate previously dormant codes within humanity. In this way a new type of human emerges and a new world evolves.

In the wise words of the poet T. S. Eliot: "We shall not cease from exploration, and the end of all our exploring will be to arrive where we started and know the place for the first time."

4

The Four
Existential Questions

*Here at the end of an age, we finally have an opportunity
to discover not only what we have done, but also who we
really are.*

Sharron Rose, *Timewave 2013*

As we weave our way through this journey into the very fabric of
LIFE and EXISTENCE, we find ourselves revisiting the four
fundamental questions again and again: Who are we? Why are we here?
Where are we really from? Where do we go when we "die"? These are
existential questions that have preoccupied the most brilliant of minds
of the greatest philosophers, thinkers, cosmologists, quantum scientists,
astrophysicists, existentialists, metaphysicists, theosophists, psychics,
spiritualists, mystics, seers, prophets, and spiritual guides, all of whom
have sought to discover definitive answers.

What has been established in the fields of both science and metaphysics is that there are limitless higher-dimensional realities and
parallel Universes. Yet all of our searching and delving; probing and
analyzing; theorizing and hypothesizing; contemplating, meditating,
exploring, and investigating has revealed the barest of insights into the
unfathomable phenomena that are metadimensional realities.

MATTER IS SPIRIT FALLEN
INTO A STATE OF SELF-OTHERNESS.

Thousands of years of religious, philosophical, and spiritual studies as well as a multitude of recorded cases pertaining to direct experience (OBEs, NDEs, CDEs) have determined that there does appear to be an indefinable phenomenon that many have termed *Spirit*. Ancient texts throughout the world point to the idea that human beings are Spirit incarnate in physical form and that *we are not human beings having a spiritual experience but spiritual beings having a human experience*. The original author of this quote remains uncertain but it is often credited to French Jesuit priest, paleontologist, and philosopher Pierre Teilhard de Chardin. Others have attributed it to Greco-Armenian mystic and spiritual teacher George Ivanovich Gurdjieff. However, it is most likely to have heralded from German philosopher Georg Wilhelm Friedrich Hegel's dictum, which goes something like: matter is spirit fallen into a state of self-otherness.

Such simple yet profound statements bid us to accept that we may after all herald from the stars and that we might just be visitors to Earth who are in but not of this world. It was the prophet and seer Nikola Tesla who encouraged humanity to "do everything that any day, any moment, if possible, not to forget who we are and why we are on Earth."

THE SOUL'S JOURNEY
IN THE HUMAN REALM

The Soul, like Time, is Eternal; like Space, is Infinite; like Spirit, is Immortal; like LOVE, is Boundless, Unending.

Our spirit expresses through our Soul, which in turn acts as a bridge between our spirit and Higher Self. The Higher Self is a bridge between the Soul and the Self, the latter of which is the bridge between the *integrated* self and the Higher Self.

The Soul is a hologram of ALL THAT IS and therefore remains

forever perfect and pure. Memories recorded within it may be in need of healing, but the Soul itself is not for it remains eternally whole and incorruptible. It is multidimensional and experiences multiexistences simultaneously. Contained within it is the blueprint of SOURCE.

ON EARTH AS IT IS IN HEAVEN

Fundamentally, we are here to create Heaven on Earth. On this earthly plane the Soul has a unique opportunity to express as specific aspects of CONSCIOUSNESS and to experience the human phenomena of mind and emotions and life in a physical body.

What registers as most important when we finally return HOME to the Higher Dimensions is what we freely and generously gave from our heart—the seat of the incarnate aspect of Soul. It is not merely how much we loved or gave to others but the pure intention, motive, and unconditional love that was present in each exchange. How we lived our lives and how our presence benefited others, humanity, all sentient beings and life-forms, and the Earth herself are paramount.

The Soul can return again and again to life on Earth until the purpose of its sojourn in this realm feels completed. At this point it ascends as Love into LOVE to continue its journey in other forms and in other Planes of Existence.

This blue-green planet plays host to an eclectic mix of unique human characteristics. The least evolved expression of consciousness can be considered to be a *survival level of being,* whereas a more evolved state equates to a more *awakened level of being.*

To be human is to be immersed in a series of fundamental states that range from fear, suffering, darkness, sadness, and pain to love, bliss, harmony, peace, joy, beauty, ecstasy, happiness, and Light. The animal world also appears to experience similar states, such as sadness, depression, suffering, and pain but also playfulness, happiness, peace, contentment, and even ecstasy. Science has now established that the plant world experiences "feelings" too, and that these can range from fear and pain to equilibrium and well-being. But it is humans that have access to the full spectrum of feeling, emotion, and thought, which can cast the greatest shadow across our world or bring to it the greatest Light.

Life is essentially a multifaceted and multidimensional myriad of realities that the Soul is engaged in at any given time. Even though only one aspect of the Soul may be incarnate in a human body in this world, simultaneous experiences in any number of other dimensional realities are likely to be occurring. Just as the Cosmos consists of billions of stars, so too can the Soul express through multiple forms in multiple dimensions from moment to moment.

The Earth currently vibrates at a third-dimensional frequency as it has done for millennia. This phenomenon facilitates the fundamental physical, emotional, and mental experiences required by the earthbound aspect of the Soul. Many Souls will incarnate with a higher frequency as "way-showers" for humankind who are here to catalyze the New Paradigm. Such individuals are often referred to as "**Light Workers***" and all have the potential to access higher levels of Consciousness. In some, this level of Consciousness is predominant while in others it is more in the background as they begin to awaken within the third dimension to the reality of who they really are. Ultimately, human Consciousness spans twenty-six dimensions as we discussed in the previous chapter, and from this perspective the majority of humans are still at the kindergarten level in terms of their psychospiritual maturity.

PERCEIVED SEPARATION

Our deepest psychological wound is said to be our *perceived* separation from SOURCE. The reality is, however, that we are only ever separate from ourselves. Yet many have forgotten the truth of who they really are and where they are really from, and so every experience of "separation" that plays out in the human realm taps into that "original" wound. Some of these experiences whether they involve a dearly beloved, a community, the world, and/or ourselves, can feel overwhelming and too much to bear, as the source of the separation can become the central theme in the story of our lives.

This can then lead to existential depression, although separation is rarely recognized as a significant factor/root of this condition. When we experience loss through separation it is not ourselves who are lost for we can never be so. The degree to which we experience pain through separation and the duration we experience it reflects the degree to which we have become separate (unconsciously) from the truth of who we really are and where we are really from.

When we have a remembrance of our spiritual origins and are able to remain profoundly connected to this on a day-to-day basis through our spiritual practice (i.e., meditation, prayer, contemplation, unconditional love, kindness, and goodness, connection to the Earth and the Higher Realms), then the pain that accompanies the human experience of separation dissipates within a short period of time. What remains, however, is a *sweet pain,* as we bless and honor the teachings of whatever the circumstances were that led to this particular experience. We know/gno that GOD/LOVE/SPIRIT/CONSCIOUSNESS remains our guiding light and principle.

THE EXISTENTIAL SPOTLIGHT

The perceived separation from SOURCE is a keenly felt experience that plays out at a conscious and unconscious level, and the resultant depressive states can cause day-to-day human life to come under the spotlight of the *existential* (that which relates to *existence*).

Most people are striving to create meaningful lives and often turn to key areas such as relationships, health, and work to attain this. Many are fulfilled in at least one of these areas to a greater or lesser degree, yet it is rare to encounter one who is totally fulfilled in all aspects of their physical, emotional, and material lives. And even if our relationships are wonderful, our health good, and our work inspired, many of us still have a sense that something is missing. Perhaps we deeply long for that which cannot be explained in words or for something that remains just out of our grasp in terms of the intangible that we cannot put a name to.

In our modern world, no matter what our life circumstances, whether we are happy or sad, rich or poor, healthy or unwell, this experience seems to be the same. A crisis of meaning (unconscious or Conscious) is often felt at the heart of our very being—a gnosis that something remains elusive irrespective of our relationships, our job, or our material-financial conditions.

Many people are in the midst of some kind of ongoing existential crisis and unconsciously or consciously search here, there, and almost everywhere for that *something more than* that an innate felt-sense informs them is missing. Recently, I came across a post on social media that deeply moved me because of its courageous transparency and unashamed expression of unrequited longing for heart-to-heart connection and a much-wished-for loving community. It was written by the bestselling author Patrice Karst, and I share it here unedited with her gracious consent:

No sooner could I process my Peru experience, when I got very sick and have been not well for the past 12 days. . . . Some kind of super nasty cold/flu god-knows-what-bug and on its way out. . . . But when you lay in bed for almost 2 weeks sick and you live alone and you already weren't in great mental shape (long challenging incarnation) when you left to go to Peru (oh yeah Alone!), and then you had all that wild experience and then immediately to get sick, well let's just say it's messed with my head something fierce. As in a white-knuckling . . . emotional ride.

What's true for me in this moment is that I know that it's all "within" . . . yet what is also true is that outside I sooooo want to live somewhere safe and beautiful, with people that love me and that I love back. I want to create a family, a village, a tribe. I want to wake up in the morning and have other loving human beings nearby ready to break bread, ready to share truths and hugs and ears and shoulders, when needed. I want to be 100% safe to be who I am, and especially when I feel sad and scared (which I feel a lot). I want a life that feels rich and organic, meaning I'm not running around out there searching for my fun and activities and ways to fill up my time, nor sitting all alone in my four walled prettily decorated prison for more years on end.

By "organic," I mean that my life is happening naturally all around me, I'm part of something bigger than me and I'm with my people. I feel "home."

I'm 59 and I want to be adopted by a big loving family who will take me in and let me rest and stroke me and feed me and love me and listen to me and then share all their stories with me so that I might feel woven together with them, through our deep sharing.

I want my life to finally feel right. I want to find my king that will have my back and my heart, and me his . . . I've slayed too many dragons by myself for too many years.

I feel sad, I feel tired, I feel lost, I feel honest; I feel like I've been wandering in the desert for 40 years and I'm ready for the wandering to be over.

Ironically, the very same medium by which I'm reaching out is the very same technology by which I feel crazy being plugged into, like we're all just too plugged in to our devices, like it's just not right.

The only thing I know how to do with absolute authenticity is to be myself—so this is myself in 2019, on a Monday morning in February.

How many of us can relate to part, if not all, of such Soul-searing transparency. Patrice has a successful career, a stable and lovely coastal home in a beautiful part of the world, good health, financial security, and a deep sense of direction and purpose, and yet her experience is that *something is still missing,* and, what is more, she is able to name just what that is.

A Paradise Way of BEing

A friend recently sent me a piece she had read in the *Earth Pathways Diary 2019*. It was written by Uther Miraiam, a writer and Earthhut/Roundhut builder. Coincidentally, I just happened to be penning this part of the book when she first mentioned it to me in February 2019. It immediately struck a chord because it speaks, in part, of the *something more* that is missing, which Miraiam appears to have found. It reveals how someone was able to experience fulfillment at a fundamental level because of the lengths he was prepared to go to create an ideal life scenario for himself in the midst of our modern world. I have a sense that his words may touch something deep inside others too, so I share what he wrote here:

> In 2014, I entered a three-year retreat deep in the woods of west Wales, stepping quite fully out of modernity and into a more paradise way of being. During these years, I built a simple round hut using natural materials and lived there without electricity, mains water, fossil fuels, digital technology, or the internet. It was a radical journey of descent and reconnection to the earth in her raw elemental aliveness and beauty. . . . It was a process of purification. It was an arduous struggle at times, to step so far outside the comforts and cultural norms of the modern Western society in which I grew up, and it was incredibly healing and empowering, to detox from the technological matrix, the mainstream media, and the consumer nightmare, and to plug back into sources of natural inspiration, well-being, and abundance.
>
> Many times, I dropped into a paradise state, feeling profound wonder and joy at simply being alive and part of the miracle of life on Earth. This experience has shown me that it is not only possible to choose to return to a life lived very simply upon the Earth, but that this choice is also deeply healing, nourishing, and wildly magical.

Miraiam found paradise by deeply connecting and communing with Nature, by unhooking from "modernity," and by committing more fully to the Earth. Could this be significant in relation to what we are missing as a modern global society—a deep and intimate relationship with Mother Earth? Is this where we may find that something missing or at least a part of it? It is an interesting question.

For many people this may be true, yet is living in this way going to fulfill us on a permanent basis? Is it ultimately enough? For others the answer may be found in their experience of the Higher Dimensions and their connection to SOURCE. But can the deepest fulfillment be found in either, or perhaps both, or could there still be *something more?*

What Sustains Us from the Inside When All Else Falls Away?

As I see it, there is a felt-sense relationship between three distinct elements that transforms the *something missing* into a deeper ongoing sense of fulfillment. It is a deeply felt connection between the earth (soil), our Spirit (Soul), and our heart (Self) that equates to the very essence of loving and living. Figure 2 below depicts these sustaining forces, all of which are held within the ancient esoteric and sacred

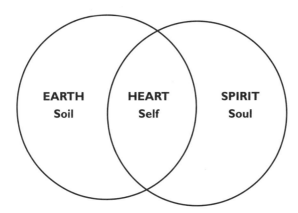

Figure 2. The balance of soil and Soul

geometric symbol known as the vesica piscis, which predates all major religions.

My own magnetic pull has always been to the higher realms, and yet my connection to the Earth is equally as vital to my overall sense of well-being, balance, and fulfillment. I have a strong connection to Spirit and choose to live in the midst of wild and rural Nature so I can regularly commune with the earth; for a healthy body and mind need an equal balance of soil and Soul.

Direct physical contact with the earth is all important and so too is moving through natural landscapes every day and breathing the fresh air of the forests, mountains, countryside, and oceans. What we absorb through our eyes, nose, feet, hands, and the pores of our skin is essential for balancing the body, feelings, and mind and for uplifting the psyche and the Soul. Celebrating the rains and the winds as much as sunshine and blue skies is important too, as these are all Nature's medicines. A lack of physical contact with the elements of the Earth brings (and reflects) imbalance in our lives.

The following quote from the book *Earthing* by Clinton Ober, Stephan T. Sinatra, and Martin Zucker offers an important insight in regard to what I am sharing:

> Beneath our feet is an omnipresent source of natural healing energy that we have become largely disconnected from. By walking barefoot, sitting or lying on the ground we are connecting to Mother Earth and her healing energy, stabilizing electrical signals and protecting the body's delicate bioelectrical circuitry. Walking barefoot also energizes major acupuncture channels and Earthing has been shown to reduce inflammation, chronic pain, stress, and tension, improve sleep and increase energy. It also helps protect against **electromagnetic fields***. If you are standing outside barefoot you are Earthed; your skin and the Earth's surface make a continuous charged surface with the same electrical potential providing a shielding effect, like a protective umbrella, against EMFs.

Similarly, Clemens G. Arvay writes the following in his book *The Biophilia Effect*:

Plants communicate with each other using chemical substances called terpenes which are "understood" by our immune system and lead to a significant increase in the number and activity of our natural killer cells (special white blood cells) as well as the three most important anti-cancer proteins. Natural killer cells are found in our immune system and play an important role in destroying potential cancer cells and removing viruses from our body. It has been shown that spending just one day in woodland will increase the number of natural killer cells for the following seven days. Two or three days will see an increase by more than fifty percent, and the level of natural killer cells remains elevated for another thirty days. Increased activity means that every killer cell is detecting and eliminating viruses and potential cancer cells more efficiently than usual. And all we have to do is to be present and breathe. This important interaction between human and plant is hugely significant for medicine, mental health, and psychotherapy and is just starting to be understood by science.

An Example from My Own Life

I'd like to take a moment to share a story from my own life in regard to the *something missing* that I personally needed to discover in a very specific way. For many years I have meditated on what it is to experience the deepest possible contentment and fulfillment without any form of dependence or attachment. Where, for example, if one wished to, one might live alone in a cave for months or years and remain fulfilled to the core. We have already read about Uther Miraiam's account of living for three years in a simple roundhut that he built himself from the natural materials in the surrounding woodlands and how he experienced this time as a "paradise way of being."

Many years ago, when I moved more deeply into my own journey of psychological integration, conscious evolution, and spiritual awakening, I came across *The Invitation*, a stunning writing by the visionary Oriah Mountain Dreamer. I read this extraordinary Call to Consciousness many times, and my eyes always rested on one particular line: "I want to know what sustains you from the inside when all else falls away." I knew this was set to be one of the greatest teachings of my life and so began to deeply contemplate and meditate on this profound question.

This life has not been an easy one by any means but in 2002 it began to totally crumble. I experienced extreme health challenges, homelessness, financial poverty, a relationship breakdown, and a loss of direction and purpose, the latter continuing until 2009. The line from *The Invitation* remained constantly in my awareness and I knew at a Soul level that I had chosen this experience to find out just what would sustain me if everything did fall away.

When one invites this type of lesson into one's life, the titanium shell of the old identity (which may have originally been constructed many timelines ago) must undergo a total breaking down and this occurs through a series of personal evolutionary wrecking balls. We can be presented with ill health, displacement, homelessness, financial poverty, the severing of key relationships, and the passing (death) of loved ones, along with various other forms of loss, including the loss of direction, meaning, and purpose.

This can be followed by a time of restructuring one's identity, and one's life can be built anew from the *sustaining* factor that has been discovered *when all else has fallen away.* Most people experience at least one of these psychospiritual wrecking balls at some point in their lives, but few will face them all simultaneously.

Life will break us down to the extent that we (at a Soul level) invite it to do so, but of course, the personality may rail against such relentless harsh conditions. Would Saint Francis of Assisi have received the stigmata had he not first renounced all that is worldly in the material sense? Saint Francis lived like a pauper finding strength not only from God but also from Nature, and he believed that nature itself was the mirror of God, calling all creatures his brothers and sisters and even preaching to the birds.

I took this most important life lesson right to the wire in terms of the experiences of being parentless, grandparentless, childless, penniless, and homeless. I suffered an extreme downward spiral regarding my health that took me to death's door as I mentioned earlier, and my homeless status precluded the gift of having pets or even plants. I also detached myself from any culture by purposely choosing to live alone on top of a mountain in rural southern France with only a basic grasp of the language.

This was a necessary step that supported a deep need within me to unhook from cultural conditioning and dependence on or attachment to any form of community. I wished to experience for a period of time (which has transpired to be ten years), stepping outside of cultural entrainment and traditions to release my Consciousness from the overt and covert imprinting of cultural norms. In order to let go into a depth of freedom that anonymity affords, I needed to *disidentify* from it all as much as possible in order to rediscover who I was outside of and beyond any cultural influence. Now, I feel I have experienced enough of this and have arrived at a place within myself where I can choose to re-engage with society on my own terms.

We underestimate just how much we are shaped by the customs and cultures of the countries whose language we speak fluently or well. I needed to immerse myself in a different kind of language in this lifetime—to reconnect to my "native tongue," the language of Love, of Light, the language of the Earth and Sun, the Stars, Constellations, and Cosmos, the Higher Realms.

All of the above scenarios began to unfold in March 2002 when I experienced the total physical collapse that took seven years to recover from (see chapter 1). However, it was not until September 2017 that I came to more fully understand the answer to the question, What sustains you from the inside when all else falls away?, and it was at this point that my life began to turn a corner. What sustains us from the inside when all else falls away is LOVE, and reconnecting to our inborn capacity to love, and love even more.

ONENESS CONSCIOUSNESS

When we live in a state of remembering that we originate from SPIRIT we live in a mode of Oneness. We recognize and experience that we are never separate but are forever connected to LOVE/GOD/CONSCIOUSNESS/SOURCE. Such a state becomes possible when we are anchored in the deepest wisdom, profoundest understanding, and purest expression of human Love. When the life that we live has Love as its foundation, we will never feel separate from the human race, the natural world, or the Higher Dimensions. As long as we are rooted in Love and understand that we are each a spark of the DIVINE experiencing life in this earthly dimension, we will never feel alone.

However, if we remain in any way polarized in separation consciousness, our lives will be beset by a series of experiences that leave us with a sense of emptiness and loneliness, both symptoms of a perceived separation. The key to transcending such a life-denying state is to embrace the fact that we herald from LOVE and that this indeed is the true nature of our very Being. Striving to attain a higher state of Consciousness is what will dissolve the perceived wound of separation. The extent to which we are able to do this will be reflected in the experience we have of our lives, of others, of our community, of society, and of the world as a whole.

A RETURN TO THE FOUR EXISTENTIAL QUESTIONS

At this point, let us return to the four existential questions:

Who are we?
Why are we really here?
Where are we really from?
Where do we go when we "die"?

Following the breakdown of my life in 2002, when everything started to rapidly fall away and I was left with nothing but the question of what sustained me from the inside, I realized then that the answer to all four questions was the same: LOVE. This was not merely a concept but an experiential reality; this, I discovered, was indeed my true identity.

After much searching, seeking, longing, and yearning we arrive at the realization that the only thing that really matters is that we are living LOVE. The highest path a human being can follow is one of purity and devotional love where every response and action arises out of LOVE and from *BE*ing LOVE. When you come to realize such an essential truth at a deep level of gnosis your entire perception and relationship to life changes. When there was nothing outside of myself to hang my identity on and everything had been stripped away, *what sustained me from the inside* was the presence of LOVE—and this will never fall away.

So, who are we? We are Souls incarnate in human form, a vast and coherent system of nearly eight billion vibrating realities experiencing the physical, emotional, mental, psychological, intellectual, psychic, energetic, and spiritual dimensions of existence. It is the quest of each one of us to perfect these levels within ourselves and to evolve along the psychospiritual continuum from self (undifferentiated, adapted, unintegrated, separated love), to Self (integrated, authentic, realized, unified Love), to Higher Self (actualized, enlightened, Self-transcendent LOVE).

Why are we really here? To continue with and complete an aspect of our Soul's journey within the earthly realm of human experience: To heal, integrate, awaken, and evolve into Self-awareness, Self-realization, Self-actualization, and, ultimately, Self-transcendence. To remember the truth of *who we really are* and *why we are really here*. To become enlightened and, as such, cocreate an enlightened world. To transcend third-dimensional consciousness, awaken to a Higher Consciousness state; to embody CONSCIOUSNESS, and cocreate a CONSCIOUS world.

Where are we really from and where do we go when we "die"? We are all from the same mystical origin—SOURCE—the *ultimate* destination of the incarnate human Soul. There are innumerable "spheres" of existence beyond this world that we could say act as stations. The most awakened Souls reside in the upper levels, while those less awakened are located within the lower spheres. A Soul returns to these vast spheres in order to review, contemplate, integrate, learn, evolve, and prepare for its next incarnation, which may not always be on the Earth.

There are numerous "stations," some of which are hosted by non-earthbound Souls who have either transcended the necessity for lives on Earth or have not yet been called to that realm. Many Souls who take leave of the Earth move to other spheres that will better support their evolution. Where they go is determined by the degree to which their Consciousness is awakened. A Soul who has negatively impacted the world may be bound for spheres of a denser vibration, the exception to this being the more evolved Soul whose remit was to seemingly negatively impact the world in service of a higher purpose. Even though a Soul may reside in the upper spheres it is still a long way from the ultimate shorelines of HOME (SOURCE).

Each sphere consists of finer and denser levels that represent the scope and quality of Light being transmitted by a Soul. The most exalted spheres are inhabited by enlightened beings. The more advanced the Soul the greater their radiance. The "peaks" of the spheres in the upper realms are the most heavenly and consist of pure Light, but even the spheres of the denser realms radiate a quality of Light that cannot be found on Earth.

There are many levels in the upper realms and even the densest of these are realms of immense peace and beauty. Souls located within these spheres are more likely to reincarnate on Earth to continue redressing and resolving **karma***. From an earthly perspective, the consciousness of those stationed in the more densely vibrating spheres may take thousands of years to awaken, but awaken they eventually will.

Souls located in the denser levels can evolve and ascend to a higher sphere at any time. Yet, those who continue to exist in a devolved state of consciousness will remain at this level until they have evolved sufficiently to progress to the next ascending sphere.

Souls who are positioned in any sphere within the upper realms may ascend or descend through the levels depending on the status of their c/Consciousness. Enlightened Souls located in the highest peaks of the upper levels rarely reincarnate or incarnate to the Earth; instead they are engaged in the extradimensional support of humanity and the Earth. Such Souls are also continuing their own evolutionary journey and preparing to move closer to SOURCE. All Souls are free to visit others and do so regularly before returning to the community of their own sphere.

Souls reunite in the heavenly realms and share infinite experiences of bliss. They also reconnect with those from their own Soul groups whom they may or may not have encountered in a recent Earthly life. The dimensions that exist beyond the upper realms are solely for beings of the most advanced levels, who only return to the Earthly domain if called upon to urgently assist humanity. Then they may choose a life of "suffering" to be ultimately best equipped to help heal humankind. At the end of such an incarnation, they return back to their sphere and continue to awaken.

On rare occasions, the Earth may experience a visitation by an avatar—a fully enlightened being who has never before taken human form; for example, the energy being/presence referred to as Mahavatar Babaji, also known as "the deathless guru" or the bliss-permeated saint, Anandamayi Ma. Such unprecedented events occur only when there is an urgent need for the evolutionary impact of such a Being, or when the world is in need of a new spiritual template.

As already stated, the spheres *beyond* the upper realms are populated only by the most highly advanced beings. Those previously engaged within the wheel of death and rebirth who have completed its cycle and concluded their Soul contract on Earth, may continue to assist Souls on

Gaia by acting as angelic spirit guides, teachers, and helpers. Many will then join/rejoin the great Councils of Elders in the higher spheres, or, as Luminous Ones, continue to overlight (remain present as forces of pure LIGHT and LOVE) the Souls on Earth. Usually however, Beings of such advanced development remain located within the higher dimensions of the upper realms to teach in the Great Halls of Learning that are present throughout all spheres.

The origins of the human Soul herald from an Infinite and Ultimate Reality, which may be termed SOURCE, EXISTENCE, ALL THAT IS, CREATOR, GOD, THE BELOVED, THE DIVINE, etc. In our continued exploration of *where are we really from* the term SOURCE will encompass all of these. What more can we come to know and understand about this Infinite and Ultimate Reality?

The twenty-six dimensions referred to earlier hold a clue insofar as they represent the sum total of human Consciousness (and experience) for the earthbound Soul. What exists beyond the twenty-sixth dimension remains unknown even to the most Consciously evolved and Spiritually Awakened human mind. Anything pertaining to the mystical, metaphysical, otherworldly, and spiritual has been both explored and open to suggestion for thousands of years. Yet, at the end of all of our searching, exploring, conceiving, and perceiving, we are presented with astonishingly simple answers to the four most fundamental and existential questions of all time:

> *Who Are We?*—We Are LOVE.
> *Why Are We Really Here?*—To BE LOVE.
> *Where Are We Really From?*—We are from LOVE
> *Where do we go when we "die"?*—We Return to LOVE

LOVE is SOURCE/GOD/CONSCIOUSNESS/EXISTENCE ITSELF—a reality that remains unquantifiable, immeasurable, indeterminable, incalculable, and indefinable to the unawakened, or indeed awakened human mind.

A FINAL THOUGHT . . .

What if there are realities *beyond* SOURCE presently inconceivable to the human mind? Could it be that just as primitive human beings had no concept of other countries or continents outside of their own immediate environment, there may well be other SOURCE realities that remain beyond the comprehension of the twenty-first-century human mind? If this were the case, then what beings might inhabit these realities? What would reality look like in their worlds? And, might the Soul itself move beyond what we with our limited human minds consider to be *the* Ultimate Reality (GOD/SOURCE/CONSCIOUSNESS/ SPIRIT/LOVE)?

Could it be that SOURCE/GOD/LOVE is the Sun to the Soul, just as the Sun in our solar system is the source of life on Earth (see figure 3 on the next page)?

To imagine that ours is the only inhabited planet in the Universe and that there is indeed only one Universe is tantamount to primitive thinking. What we term EXISTENCE could be just a part of an even greater incomprehensible ULTIMATE REALITY.

The Soul knows it is LOVE. Yet, is there an ongoing evolutionary trajectory that compels the Soul, and even the *Spirit* as we perceive it, to transcend into another form and reality entirely?

And what of other energies, beings, entities, and life-forms that also exist within and beyond Space and Time that may or may not possess a "Soul"? Are they, too, returning HOME to SOURCE—a HOME somewhere far BEYOND and unknowable to the human mind at this present time?

What is the *ultimate* destination of any Soul, human, or nonhuman or of any nonSoul being or entity, if SOURCE itself amounts to just one of multiple SOURCE REALITIES? Our Universe may be just one of a series of multiverses; a theory also proposed by the late Stephen Hawking and his colleague Thomas Hertog, who together, after decades of research, wrote what would transpire to be Hawking's final research

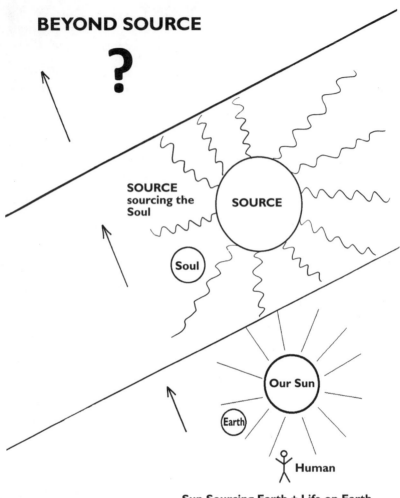

BEYOND SOURCE

Figure 3. Beyond SOURCE?

paper on this subject submitted to the *Journal of High Energy Physics* just ten days before he passed away.

Could there be another reality that exists beyond SOURCE (as we know it)? Black holes are said to be the most powerful sources of energy and life. Even the futurist, seer, and philosopher Nikola Tesla, conceptualized a *baffling, dark spot that the mind cannot conceive, nor mathematics measure, and in which fits the whole Universe.*

So, if a dark spot can contain within it a whole Universe, then could a boundless fathomless incomprehensible N O T H I N G N E S S contain LOVE, GOD, and *EVERYTHING* . . . Soul, Spirit, SOURCE?

Contemplating what may exist beyond SOURCE, is a compelling and fascinating prospect.

5

The Role of Epigenetics in Conscious Evolution

Healing the Historical Wounds of the World

Epigenetics has shaken the foundations of biology and medicine to their core because it reveals that we are not victims but masters of our genes.

BRUCE LIPTON

A few years ago, a colleague spoke to me about an interview he had watched featuring two high-profile speakers who were talking about the reasons for consumerism. As he shared the points that were raised, I found my own thoughts moving in a different direction altogether. Suddenly and quite clearly, the word *epigenetics* sprang into my mind suggesting to me that this is where the current global consumer culture originates from. What I understood in that moment is just how much humanity has become polarized. Historically for many, there has been extreme hardship and deprivation; now we live in a global community of "instant gratification." From a material level, we could say that the majority of citizens living in a westernized society appear to be better off now than at any other time. However, this is only made possible by a consumerism machine that overshadows our world.

What is this phenomenon of epigenetics and just how does it relate to conscious evolution? In Greek *epi* means "besides," so *epigenetics* equates to *something other than* and *beyond* genetics. Studies have revealed that our genes are influenced by the places in which we live, the weather of the country in which we were born (even if we are no longer there), the climate of our present location, the stories of our lives, and our immediate environment, as well as the experiences and environments of our ancestors.

Further research reveals that our DNA is also influenced by our everyday thoughts, actions, words, deeds, emotions, feelings, and intentions. In her book *The Epigenetics Revolution: How Modern Biology Is Rewriting Our Understanding of Genetics, Disease, and Inheritance*, the British biologist, Nessa Carey, describes epigenetics as follows:

> Think of the human lifespan as a very long movie. The cells would be the actors and actresses, essential units that make up the movie. DNA, in turn, would be the script—instructions for all the participants of the movie to perform their roles. Subsequently, the DNA sequence would be the words on the script, and certain blocks of these words that instruct key actions or events to take place would be the genes. The concept of genetics would be like screenwriting. Follow the analogy so far? Great. The concept of epigenetics, then, would be like directing. The script can be the same, but the director can choose to eliminate or tweak certain scenes or dialogue, altering the movie for better or worse. After all, Steven Spielberg's finished product would be drastically different than Woody Allen's for the same movie script, wouldn't it?

THE NEW SCIENCE
OF SELF-EMPOWERMENT

Biologist Bruce Lipton refers to epigenetics as "the new science of self-empowerment" for it brings unparalleled insight and information through scientific research and practical demonstration and affords greater clarity into how we can free ourselves from life-denying ancestral, historical, and cultural stories. Almost five decades ago, Lipton conducted extensive research into cell biology after finally arriving at the realization that it is the environment that fundamentally controls the fate of the cells. In one experiment, he placed a single stem cell into its own petri dish. Within seven days it had divided into fifty thousand genetically identical cells. He then divided these into three separate petri dishes, all of which contained the same culture medium, only with a slightly changed chemistry. Each dish provided a different result. Dish number one produced muscle; dish number two, bone, and dish number three, fat. This experiment proved to him that the environment provides information that influences gene activity.

Environmental signals read by our nervous system are influenced by our perception and the interpretations of our mind. The brain then releases chemicals that match these interpretations, which either enter the blood or travel through the nervous system and into the cells that control behavior and gene activity. As Lipton explains, the brain is controlling the culture medium in our body (blood), which is being used to feed the fifty trillion cells in our bodies. He shares an example of when we are in love and how this facilitates the cells to fulfill their greatest potential and why people in love positively glow. When the chemicals associated with love are added to the petri dish of cells they multiply exuberantly, whereas when the chemicals associated with fear are added to it they stop multiplying. The human body is populated by over fifty trillion cells that respond to the culture medium in our body and our blood and change in accordance with its chemical composition. *Changing chemistry is changing the fate of the cells.*

In a recent communication with Lipton he stated the following:

Only 3 percent of the genome are actual genes: Whereas the remaining 97 percent of the genome, once erroneously referred to as "junk DNA," is perhaps the most important, for it is the DNA that "controls" the readout of the genes [epigenetics]. This is where the power of the mind interfaces with the activity of the genes. The science of epigenetics upends the conventional story of genetics. People are programmed with the belief that genes "control" their lives, and as a consequence see themselves as "victims" of their heredity. In contrast, the science of epigenetics reveals that the environment and our "perception" of it, controls our genes. Since we can change the environment and change our perceptions, we are not victims but *masters* of our genes. This is a revolution in psychology in regard to the question, Are we the "victims" or the "masters" of our lives?

Researchers at the HeartMath Institute in Boulder Creek, California, have also determined that DNA can be influenced by thoughts, feelings, and intention. In an article titled "Modulation of DNA Conformation by Heart-Focused Intention" (2003), the authors McCraty, Atkinson, and Tomasino write that an individual who was holding three DNA samples was directed to generate heart coherence—a beneficial state of mental, emotional and physical balance and harmony—with the aid of a HeartMath technique that utilizes "heart breathing" and intentional positive emotions. The individual managed to intentionally and simultaneously unwind two of the DNA samples to different extents and leave the third unchanged, proving that "aspects of the DNA molecule can be altered through intentionality." The article goes on to state that the data indicates that when individuals are in a heart-focused loving state and in a more coherent mode of physiological functioning, they have a greater ability to alter the conformation of DNA. Individuals capable of generating high ratios of heart coherence were able to alter DNA conformation according to their intention. Control group participants showed low ratios of heart coherence and were unable to intentionally alter the conformation of DNA.

HeartMath founder Doc Childre presented a theory of heart intelligence, hypothesizing that an energetic connection or coupling of information occurs between the DNA in cells and higher-dimensional structures—the Higher Self or Spirit—and that the heart serves as a key access point through which information originating in the higher-dimensional structures is coupled into the physical human system (including DNA), and that states of heart coherence generated through experiencing heartfelt positive emotions increase this coupling. Actual measurements indicate that the heart generates a far stronger electromagnetic force than the brain and so creates an energetic field that is able to unify the higher-dimensional aspects of a human being with the physical systems of the body and DNA. This newly emerging field of epigenetics also proposes the potential for changing the cell status/chemistry by reprograming it through sound, vibration, frequency, meditation, telepathy, the expanded heart field, and an elevated Consciousness.

THE IMPACT OF HUMAN EMOTIONS AND DNA ON THE WORLD

Recently, a group of scientists conducted three experiments to further explore the relationship between human emotions, cells, and DNA. In the first experiment, a group of scientists took leukocytes (white blood cells) from donors, placed them into chambers, and observed their electrical activity. The donor located in a separate room from their cell sample was shown video clips that evoked an array of emotions ranging from happy to sad. While the donor was experiencing these emotional states, the scientists measured the cells' electrical responses. At the exact moments the donor experienced emotional highs and lows, their cells responded with intensified electrical activity and with no recorded time-lapse delay. The same results occurred even when the donor's cells were moved fifty miles away.

In the second experiment, human DNA was placed into a sealed container and the donor situated nearby in another room. The test subject was exposed to various emotional stimuli that affected their sample of DNA: negatively experienced emotions caused the DNA double helix to tighten, positive emotions were shown to relax DNA coils.

In the third experiment, a distance of fifty miles separated donor and sample to ascertain if there could still be a correlation between emotions and DNA. It was discovered that even at a distance the same results were observed: both DNA and donor had identical responses at exactly the same moment. This resulted in the conclusion that an individual and their DNA are able to communicate beyond Space and Time.

In principle, the field of epigenetics reveals the impact of ancestral, historical, psychological, psychospiritual, and environmental influences on human cells and DNA. Experiments revealed that both cells and double-stranded DNA are not only influenced by the inherent traits, conditions, and historical experiences of our biological parents and ancestors but also by the stories of our own lives at a personal and sociological level. The study of human cells and DNA in relation to epigenetics is becoming one of the most prominent, important, and exciting arenas of scientific, psychological, and philosophical exploration.

Research into the field of epigenetics is unfolding at an extraordinary rate and bringing a whole new level of understanding to the theory that our lives and our characters are not set in stone by a predetermined genetic blueprint. Advances in the field of epigenetic research are proving that we have the potential to entirely transcend our historical pasts by reprogramming our genes. For decades, scientists have understood that *genetic determinism* (the concept that all human behavior is determined by genes) is a flawed theory. Science continues to study the epigenetics of biological systems and how these are influenced by events that operate outside of the DNA. It is now understood that the experiences of our ancestors are carried from generation to generation via the epigenetic system.

THE EPIGENETICS OF LOVE AND FEAR

So, what is the role of epigenetics in the context of healing humanity's inherited collective historical wound and shadow? The petri dish experiment conducted by Lipton cited earlier revealed that when the chemicals associated with love were added to cells in a neutral culture medium, the result was an exuberant multiplication of cells. If we imagine the collective human shadow as a culture medium of fear, and ourselves as trillions of stem cells grown with love, then if enough of us infused that culture medium might we be able to totally transform it? Could such an experiment reveal a way to heal the shadow wound of the collective? Once again, we are left contemplating the important question, Which is more powerful, fear or love? Throughout time, the greatest philosophers, mystics, and seers and the most enlightened of ancient civilizations have all shared the same fundamental message: love is the stronger of the two. Lipton's experiment is practical proof of this.

HEALING OUR ANCESTRAL WOUNDS

The following sets out two prime examples of how changing our thoughts changes our world and the role epigenetics can play in this.

Recently, a friend had been advised by a medium to take the bush remedy **baobab*** for the purpose of releasing the burden of health patterns she was carrying through her female ancestral line. It was suggested that doing so would clear and dissolve ancestral imprints that link past and future generations and also help her elderly mother to release these from her own soul memory as she hovered between two worlds. She was advised that this would support them both to become free of an inherited ancestral story. Just days after the friend began to take the remedy, her mother called to say that two of her teeth had fallen out. There was no pain and no dental treatment required. From a psychological-anatomical perspective, teeth represent our ancestry.

"Coincidentally," later that day someone else shared with me that she was intending to launch a public campaign to raise funds for a costly yet critical treatment she needed for a life-threatening condition. She voiced her anticipation at the prospect of becoming "visible on such a scale." Many years earlier she had undergone a powerful past timeline recollection in which she had seen herself as a "leader within a small community." She had called a secret meeting to issue a warning that would save their lives. However, opposing forces stormed the gathering and all present were killed. She explained that she felt as if she had carried the burden of that memory all of her life. As a result, she had mastered the art of remaining invisible within a large group of people.

The campaign she was to launch was no doubt a part of her healing because it meant she would become widely seen. She believed she had taken on the emotions of those who had trusted her. The group, she imagined, must have felt anger, betrayal, fear, and confusion at the time. She did launch her campaign and within a few short weeks she had experienced what her doctors described as a "miracle cure." Could it be that by allowing herself to be so publicly visible she affected her own miracle healing?

Scientific experiments prove again and again that our thoughts and emotional state as well as those of other people can influence our epigenetics. It is possible that those we have shared previous lives with can impact our thoughts and behavior. The more we realize that time is cyclical not linear, and the more we comprehend that the past, present, and future exist in the *now*, the more we are able to heal and clear trauma stories held within our cells. *A healed cell is a healthy cell, and a healthy cell is a happy cell,* vibrating in love. Understanding the role of epigenetics in the context of conscious evolution is the key to clearing and healing **cellular memory*** and the historical stories held at that level.

At this point, I would like to add that from the perspective of conscious evolution, epigenetics is not solely about the influence and presence of historical, psychological, emotional, mental, and physical wounding, at a personal, ancestral, and karmic level, it also includes the joy and happiness experienced by our ancestors, which is of equal influence in terms of the degree to which we can feel these in our day-to-day lives.

TRANSCENDING THE OLD TEMPLATES AND PROGRAMS OF THE OLD PARADIGM

Once upon a very long time ago there existed a Golden Age of peace, harmony, stability, and prosperity in which people did not have to work to feed themselves, for the earth provided food in abundance. The people lived to a very old age with a youthful appearance, and eventually passed on peacefully.

Within many free-spirited and evolved individuals there is an evolutionary impulse to return to such an age by transcending old societal templates and programs of conditioning. These templates and programs operate through what we might call an old paradigm "motherboard" that is wired to entrain human consciousness with corrupt programs and modified blueprints, including templates for age, aging, and gender identification.

For millennia, the collective consciousness has been at the mercy of governing forces that manipulate the messages we receive about life and the world that we live in. As such, the general global population has become mere cogs in a machine that is driven by powers with a vested interest in keeping us physically, emotionally, mentally, and spiritually enslaved. As a result, generation upon generation have lost their true identities, forgotten their true selves, and, instead, become a misrepresentation, distortion, and misinterpretation of the truth of who they really are.

Throughout history, again and again, the brave and the good have sought to free themselves from the agendas of a power over ruling elite, yet, all too often, with devastating consequences. In our present day we find that the same templates and programs are still conditioning us to conform to a dysfunctional system. Our thoughts directly inform our cells, which then influence our emotions and minds and therefore our overall experience of life. So to transcend the control of the ruling elite and improve our lives, we have to change our thoughts. We need to remember, for example, that there is no "us versus them" in actuality for

In the Shadow and Light of LOVE—there is no
separation.
There can, however, be "forgetfulness" . . . shadow
having forgotten its true origin—LIGHT.
And, there is always the enduring Promise
of—Remembrance.
Where Shadow may recall that it too is—LOVE.
At which point it can dissolve into LOVE, surrender
unto LOVE,
Transform fully into Pure LIGHT.

TRANSCENDING THE CONDITIONING OF GENDER AND AGE

We live in a modern culture that is essentially ageist and gender identified. It has no interest in supporting the evolution of a new type of human who reflects inner unification and integration and a more androgynous mind.

The world is flooded with images of age and gender identification through billboards and posters, film and television, magazines and newspapers, and so on. An ageist and sexist media dictates just how we are supposed to look, feel, and act and conditions us to (unconsciously) buy into these old paradigm definitions as if they are perfectly normal. The human cells respond to the instruction they receive and act and age accordingly.

In reality we are not defined by a number (age) or gender; we are each a magnificent Soul who has chosen to be on this Earth for an indefinite but finite time. By nature of our spirit we are eternal, ageless, and androgynous. Awakened individuals are beginning to disassociate from **gender binarism***. Instead, they are aligning more with an experience of identity that is **gender fluid***.

Such terminologies support a psychospiritual shift from *conditioned association* to *liberated disassociation*—a *disidentification* from life-denying patterns to instead an *identification* with a way of living, of BEing, that is more neutral, natural, wholistic, and whole. When we believe or tell ourselves that we are "getting too old for this" or "what more can I expect at my age," the body's cells respond accordingly to such instruction. We need to change our mindset and our belief system because *as we think, so we create.*

We underestimate just how receptive our cells are to instruction, whether it is from ourselves or from the environment. By aligning with societal conditioning on age and gender identification, we limit our quality of life as well as our organic capacity for vibrant well-being.

When we align with societal conditioning, our lives are dictated by a system of control that demands maximum productivity. We need to reform and reinform ourselves at a cellular level, a process I personally began over twenty-five years ago when I started to disidentify from social conditioning. It took years to feel that I was significantly unhooking from a deeply ingrained globally conditioned culture that defines and categorizes people by age and gender, something this independent spirit was not going to accept.

In May 2017, I sent a message to all my friends stating the following:

> For a long time now, I have been deconditioning from numbers around chronological age and from third-dimensional gender definition and identification (the soul is neither male nor female). Our cells take instruction from our feelings and thoughts and from associated cultural social conditioning. For most of my adult life, I have been extricating myself from the old, archaic, power-over system that imposes detrimental and limiting belief systems and blocks the evolutionary psychospiritual trajectory toward androgyny and self-transcendence, which compels us to relinquish all limiting and conditioned stereotypes—"aging" and "gender" amounting to just two of them.

On "new" and "future Earth," the numbers of "years" one has been present on the planet is entirely irrelevant. One is not defined by "age" or "gender." Conditioning has been transcended. Souls walk a regenerative path—the cells are inspired, renewal sourced by a more enlightened mind.

We need to be the cultivators of our own "gardens" and determine how they grow. By reclaiming our identities as ageless and gender fluid beings who cannot, must not, be defined by archaic third-dimensional conditioning, we move one step closer to living the truth of *who we really are:* formless, ageless incarnate souls in a human form.

A NEW STORY

Billions of Souls have come into the world with the individual and collective task of clearing the deeply ingrained old templates and programs of conditioning that exert a staggering influence on the way in which we live and die. The recent phenomenon of epigenetics has presented humanity with a groundbreaking opportunity to free itself from karmic, ancestral, historical, and cultural stories. It is now time to write a different story for humanity; not his-story (patriarchal) or her-story (matriarchal), but OUR NEW STORY, where the personality is aligned with the Soul (not the other way around)—a story that is, primarily, *spirit identified.*

A Shift from an Ego to an Eco-Centric Template
A great wave of awakening is sweeping the world. Millions are beginning to realize that humanity will not survive if we continue to live in the way that we are. Many are starting to recognize their innate roles as guardians or stewards of the Earth, especially in regard to Nature, ecology, and the environment sociologically, politically, and economically.

Securing a peaceful and sustainable future for the world is ultimately dependent on our choices, decisions, and actions and their impact. The abuse of human, animal, environmental, and ecological rights, along with the effect of social injustice, an unethical banking system, consumerism, and an out-of-control pharmaceutical industry, are wreaking havoc across the globe. Yet, an increasing number of people are starting to wake up to this stark reality and act accordingly and responsibly.

Primary Virtual Mediums:
Serve or Sever, Connect or Divide, Unite or Separate

The internet and television influence our modern age for good or ill. There is a remarkable upside to both of these mediums in terms of the evolutionary potential they may afford humanity. However, on a negative note, they can be used to distract and anesthetize the general population and, on a more covert level, they can prevent us from consciously awakening. On a positive note, however, both will greatly facilitate conscious evolution through the dissemination of life-serving and life-enhancing data and information.

These two primary social communication mediums exert the most enormous influence over the collective mind. The internet in particular offers an unparalleled opportunity to evolve and unify and to transcend **duality*** and a mechanistic and separatist culture—something we could only have dreamed of even just twenty years ago. For the Conscious community, this new technobrain is an extraordinary powerhouse for fueling conscious evolution. However, the wireless generated radiation that both television and the internet emit presents a significant problem because of its devastating effect on the physical health of all life.

EPIGENETICS AND THE HEALING
OF THE GENERATIONS

The ancestral lineage into which we are born, along with its predetermined patterns, themes, and stories, is never random. Prior to incarnating, the Soul chooses what it wishes the Self to experience in order to heal and evolve in any particular timelines. In the context of psychospiritual healing and integration, we are never victims, for all the difficulties we undergo are, in fact, perfect-storm scenarios.

Each life brings new opportunities for healing and liberation, and often the circumstances can be immensely challenging. At the moment of conception, we inherit specific genetic and ancestral predispositions that will set the scene for everything we are here to heal and learn. These include certain traits, qualities, restrictions, attributes, gifts, challenges, and virtues. We also bring with us deeply embedded traumas that are held as imprints within the unconscious mind and carried forward from previous generations and timelines.

Our karma begins to unfold at conception in terms of our Soul's choice of parents and then continues in the womb, after our birth, and throughout our lives, until such time it is healed and transcended. An unconscious society is all too quick to label and marginalize those who are especially challenged or deemed to be dysfunctional. Then the focus is solely on judging "symptoms" without seeking to understand their origin or cause. An unconscious society is unable to realize, recognize, validate, support, or understand that a state of crisis is ultimately a healthy condition when viewed from the perspective of the Soul. Those who are able to recognize and heal the origins of trauma emerge mindful in their choices and take full responsibility for the circumstances of their lives. At this point of awareness, we can truly begin to evolve a new life in which fulfillment and liberation are the rich fertile soil from which the authentic Self can grow.

The Epigenetic Healing of Standing Rock

An example of a significant healing of part of a collective wound through epigenetics was demonstrated in December 2016 at Standing Rock, a Native Peoples' reservation in North Dakota and South Dakota. An unequivocal and unconditional apology was made to the First Nation Peoples of Turtle Island (now known as America) by hundreds of U.S. veterans who traveled there to support the cause of the gathered indigenous tribes. In an unprecedented move, they publicly asked the

Native Elders for forgiveness. Wes Clark Jr., who spoke on behalf of the veterans, stated the following:

> We fought you. We took your land. We signed treaties that we broke. We stole minerals from your sacred hills. We blasted the faces of our presidents onto your sacred mountain. We didn't respect you; we polluted your Earth; we've hurt you in so many ways but we've come to say that we are sorry. We are at your service and we beg for your forgiveness.

It is acts such as these that support the fulfillment of the ancient First Nations' prophecy, which says that under the symbol of the rainbow, all of the races and all of the religions of the world will band together. After a great struggle, using only the force of peace, rainbow warriors will finally bring an end to the destruction and desecration of Mother Earth.

The Wounds of Our Ancestors Play Out in Our Lives

History testifies to generation upon generation having endured physical, emotional, mental, and spiritual suffering. We can only wonder about the epigenetic influence of the 90 percent of the indigenous people of the Americas killed during five-hundred years of European colonization or the tens of thousands of people (mostly women) tried and put to death for "witchcraft" in Europe and the American colonies over several hundred years or the millions of innocent civilians (and animals) who have been killed or traumatized throughout all wars, throughout all time. If we take just the latter as an example, we begin to comprehend how the epigenetic influence can pass down through the generations (e.g., the hundreds of millions of innocent men who went to war only to return broken, traumatized, or dehumanized by the experience).

A heavy and often tortured conscience destroyed many a moral and upright man, the consequence of which shattered entire families and communities. Often these fathers, husbands, sons, brothers, uncles, nephews, and lovers were never the same again for how could they be? Prior to being sent to the battlefront, these men would have worked as newsagents, postmen, bakers, grocers, civil servants, lawyers, or bankers, only to return years later with the expectation of carrying on with their lives in the same way as before, even after witnessing and being part of something so unimaginable and still with the feeling of blood on their hands. Many of us reading these words carry the epigenetics of the trauma of our ancestors, most of whom endured extreme hardship in their everyday lives.

In 2016, British television aired a six-part program titled *The Victorian Slum*. This brought into sharp focus the realities of life for the underprivileged of those times. Even though it specifically focused on Victorian London, its retelling of the social history of the times vividly conveyed the incomprehensible conditions that people across the world had to endure.

Arthur Morrison, a London-born nineteenth-century author, journalist, and "slum novelist," described the economically and socially deprived cultural environment caused by poverty as follows:

Black and noisome, the road sticky with slime, and palsied houses, rotten from chimney to cellar, leaning together, apparently by the mere coherence of their ingrained corruption. Dark, silent, uneasy shadows passing and crossing—human vermin in this reeking sink; like goblin exhalations from all that is noxious around. Women with sunken, black-rimmed eyes, whose pallid faces appear and vanish by the light of an occasional gas lamp, and look so like ill-covered skulls that we start at their stare.

The cells of the descendants whose ancestors lived in such inhumane times are encoded with historical trauma. When this cellular memory is activated, it creates within the individual an auto response for related propensities, predispositions, and behavioral traits and impulses. These infiltrate our lives and so it is that we attract people and situations that bring the historical theme of the trauma toward us. We may find ourselves susceptible to inexplicable bouts of depression; we may feel unworthy; we may be stuck in a survival mentality, be prone to self-defeatism and self-sabotage, or feel unable to cope with day-to-day practicalities and life in general. We may feel powerless, impotent, or exhausted, or we may battle a continual array of physical symptoms that blight our lives. We can find ourselves caught in an endless loop of repetitive themes that keep not only ourselves but also our families locked in restrictive and established cycles.

If we consider the ancestral stories carried by the majority of the people in the world, is it any wonder that so many of us have sought respite in addictions, excessive consumerism, and a culture of instant gratification? From an epigenetic perspective, it could be debated that the disconnecting influence of consumerism keeps the majority of humanity from literally re-experiencing their ancestors' stories of physical, emotional, and mental trauma and severe deprivation.

We might also consider if humanity's propensity for "turning a blind eye," which is so prevalent in today's society, is a reaction against an epigenetic history of trauma that is seared into its genetic DNA. For example, when contemplating the lives of our ancestors, we may find ourselves thinking about the suffering they experienced through wars and/or oppressive-aggressive regimes and the impact that these events had on them. Could it be that so many people in the modern world unconsciously or consciously ignore challenging information because they are unconsciously carrying a genetic memory of unspeakable trauma?

In psychotherapeutic terms, there has been a post-generational "splitting off," a disidentification and a disassociation from a history of thousands of years of suffering. Having swung from one extreme to the other, in terms of the severe deprivation of the past and the instant gratification society many of us live in today, might humanity eventually find the middle ground when it has healed epigenetic trauma and become emotionally strong enough to leave excessive consumerism behind?

As far as the conscious evolution of the collective is concerned, the medium of global consumerism may well be serving the overall conscious evolutionary trajectory of humanity. Imagine an archer pulling back the bow to its furthest point of tension before releasing the arrow to fly forward. We might use this analogy for the healing of the wounds of humanity, who must first step back before taking a significant evolutionary leap.

The unhealed stories of our ancestors remain imprinted within our DNA and so continue to play out in our lives until such time that we heal or transcend inherited wounds. This can be achieved by addressing our own karmic wounds, which often carry the theme of those born out by our forebears. In doing so, we not only liberate ourselves but also the generations that have gone and those to come. The fundamental law of cause and effect suggests that everything we experience is the result of our past words, thoughts, or actions. When we are consciously evolved, we are more able to determine the difference between a personal story and an inherited ancestral influence. In the grand scheme of everything, what we experience belongs to us because it is all part of the predestined evolutionary agenda chosen by our Soul. Collectively our ancestors' wounds are our wounds: The stories may be different, but the themes are the same.

CHANGE THE STORY, CHANGE THE WORLD

Until such time as enough of us have resolved, healed, and cleared our karmic and psychological wounds, epigenetic influences will continue to push us toward and into the core of these with the higher purpose of facilitating us to heal not only our own wounds but also those of the collective.

We live in the most critical yet auspicious times. By comparison to our ancestors of even just one hundred years ago, life in Western contemporary society is tantamount to luxurious. Most, no matter how basic, have a roof over their heads, a safe place to stay, three regular meals, weather-appropriate clothing, some kind of income even if only from state benefits, a car or access to transport. This is something our ancestors could only have dreamed of. *We* are their dream come true because by changing the epigenetics, we change the story, and when we Change the Story—Change the World.

6

The Human
and Collective Shadow

*Everyone carries a shadow, and the less it is embodied in
the individual's conscious life, the blacker and denser it is.
At all counts, it forms an unconscious snag, thwarting our
most well-meant intentions.*

CARL JUNG

It was during the last Silver Age that the human shadow emerged.
However, it remained unconscious and so ultimately transpired to
be the primary cause of the downfall of that once great era. When
a split occurs between the personality and the Soul, the ego and the
Self, the human shadow and the Light of who we really are, we project what is held unconsciously within ourselves onto others and into
the world. An example of this can be seen in the contradictory and
dysfunctional behavior of followers of fundamentalist doctrines who
have yet to acknowledge and heal their own shadow wounds. When
a person becomes harmoniously integrated and aligned with their
psychological shadow and Light, their personality and Soul, their ego
and Self, the left and right brain, the heart and mind, and their inner
masculine and feminine, then the emergence of a new Golden Age
becomes possible.

DESCENSION

If our essence is already pure Love, then why would we choose to experience anything other than this original state of Being?

The following analogy might offer insight into this question. Consider the keys on a piano: The dark keys represent the half notes, and the light keys the whole notes. There are just twelve notes on the scale, irrespective of there being eighty-eight keys in total. Each note is influenced by the others, and when played together create either a harmonious or discordant sound. The dark keys depend upon the light, and the light keys depend upon the dark to create any kind of harmony. Psychologically, this analogy illustrates something similar in regard to the integration of the shadow self/ego (dark key) with the Self (light key). Could it be that our descent from light into dark was/is in service of something even greater? Could it be that the human shadow facilitates our capacity to connect with *something even greater* within ourselves as the spiritual beings we truly are?

For millennia the great spiritual Lights of humanity have been teaching us that we are GOD experiencing itself. In this context, perhaps the dark, the shadow, and the unintegrated ego might be compared to the night in relation to the day. Could it be that we are here to learn and grow and evolve and awaken through the human shadow and once it is healed will come to experience the unique and special gifts it has to offer? In the same way the night offers deep peace and stillness and a sense of being closer to the stars and the heavens, will a healed human shadow offer us harmony and contentment and bring us closer to GOD/SOURCE?

Another analogy we might use for the transformation of the unintegrated ego and shadow into the Self is that of a piece of coal and its potential to transform into a diamond. Could our very existence in the world have more of an existential meaning than we might have realized? Imagine a miner descending into the depths and darkness of a mine in search of coal that can be used to create light and energy. Let us ponder this for a moment . . . *coal has the ability to create light and energy and to become a diamond*. In experiencing the human shadow, are we engaged in an ultimate act of altruism? Are we fulfilling a higher objective? In the healing, integrating, and transcending of the psychological, historical, karmic, and ancestral shadow, might we be paving the way for an ultimate future Self and age—the Diamond Self and a Diamond Age?

The Human Shadow

This brings us to the question of what the human-psychological shadow actually is. In a conversation, I had with Richard Spurgeon, a psychosynthesis psychotherapist and a close friend, I learned that the shadow, a term first used by Carl Jung, is all that is not accepted and acceptable to the adapted survival self and is either repressed or remains unintegrated in the unconscious. This might be our anger, rage, judgment, guilt, shame, feelings of inadequacy, and so on.

The shadow is often projected out onto others. This is one way that the psyche attempts to heal and integrate the unowned aspects, for that which is projected is then experienced through the mirror of the recipient of the projection. However, it takes a certain degree of awareness and an ability and willingness to self-reflect for this healing to take place through the recognizing and owning of the projected parts/feelings.

This psychological "shadow work" is one of the most challenging and important aspects of self-healing. It is a central task in our individual journey of self-development, for not only does it lessen the "darkness" held deep within our unconscious and free up others who become caught in our shadow projections, but it also releases the psychological energies that are being used to keep these darker energies contained. These energies then become available in our psyche for growth and life-enhancing activities. Furthermore, we often find that hidden beneath these darker shadow aspects are parts of our Self that have been repressed and prevented from developing by our own fear or shadow energies and all that remains psychologically unintegrated within us.

These aspects may well also be projected onto heroes, teachers, or gurus. When we process and transform our shadow, our inner child is liberated. We are able, once again, to embody and embrace trust, innocence, and wonder.

There is also a collective human shadow that can be experienced at the levels of the group, society, culture, nation, and species. The same dynamics of shadow projection occur at these levels, too, and the consequences can be tragic and catastrophic.

Metaphysical Experiences in My Psychological Work

On one occasion during the five years of OBEs that I experienced between 1997 and 2002, a voice counselled me to: "Never reveal what happens in the room with regard to the Work that you are doing with all those who enter it." And to: "Always lock the door when working." I did work in an unconventional way, which had come to the attention of the tutors where I was training as a psychotherapist. I worked psychospiritually. This eventually led to my having to leave the training after four years having been issued with an ultimatum to either work as a psychotherapist *or* in a mediumistic way, but not combine the two.

My inclusion of metaphysical realities in my therapeutic work had come to light in my psychotherapy supervision group, where students would submit case studies for tutors to assess and advise. One session in particular proved to be the final straw in regard to my training. I had shared the story of a client who had never recovered from her father's tragic passing when she was a young girl. We were working with a psychological model known as **gestalt therapy***, and I was guiding her through that process.

She imagined her deceased father sitting in the chair opposite her for the purpose of talking directly with him. She expressed how "silly" she felt speaking to an empty chair. At that moment, I clearly saw her father sitting opposite her. I hesitated to share what I was seeing, but as her father was encouraging me I broached the subject and began to describe him, including the way he wore his hair, his height, his long legs, the style and color of the clothes he was wearing, his character and manner, and even the pipe he was holding in his hand.

Her face transformed as she listened in astonishment and shared how accurately I had described him. We continued the session and the client was able to express everything she had been suppressing for over five decades. By the time she was ready to leave it was as if I were looking at a different person for she positively glowed and her eyes were sparkling. It was clear to us both that something extraordinary had taken place that morning. Months later, she wrote to thank me for "the session that changed [her] life." This way of working was not acceptable to the training organization however, and as I did not wish to adopt an either/or position, I chose to leave.

Jung believed that the path to enlightenment was to make the darkness conscious. Facing and integrating our own psychospiritual shadow aspects is a major contribution we can all make toward planetary healing, peace, and transformation.

COCREATING A NEW PARADIGM

The transformation of c/Consciousness is either a gradual or accelerated process dependent on our capacity for and commitment to Self-awareness and Self-realization. A new paradigm is one in which we are aligned in greater awareness and understanding and embodying a higher state of BEing. As the prophecies foretold, it will be our personal choices and actions as individuals and as a collective that will ultimately determine if we are to rise or fall.

Humanity's Quest for Peace on Earth

Many of us are aware of an inorganic presence, a dark undercurrent in the world that appears to thwart humanity's quest for peace on Earth. For thousands of years, humans have experienced suppression, repression, and polarization from those they have elected, or those who have ensured they were elected through questionable means.

From a psychological perspective, the unhealed and unconscious human shadow is projected onto the world and acted out by the collective. Whether the global crisis we face is of our own making through the unconscious, unacknowledged, unhealed, and unintegrated historical collective shadow or partially due to other ancestral or karmic influences and/or a darker global agenda, what we do know is that we are on the edge of a tipping point and cannot risk wasting another moment. We need to join together *now* and consciously act. In the words of Martin Luther King Jr.:

> Somebody must have sense enough to meet hate with love. Somebody must have sense enough to meet physical force with Soul force. If we will but try this way, we will be able to change these conditions and yet at the same time win the hearts and Souls of those who have kept these conditions alive—a way as old as the insights of Jesus of Nazareth, as modern as the techniques of Mohandas K. Gandhi. There is another way.

That "somebody" is you and me.

Not Foes, but Allies

We do not need to be Mahatma Gandhi, Mother Teresa, or the Dalai Lama to leave our mark on this world; we only need an open heart and a willingness to learn from, and Consciously let go of, all that may have caused sadness and pain to ourselves or others. You *can* step into a new role and a new you, and by doing so turn your whole life into one that is founded in Love. Strive to forgive and forget—to let go, and let GOD. Recognize that at a Soul level you chose the circumstances of your life in order to learn, heal, and Consciously evolve.

The inner wounds that we each carry rarely originate from this timeline, and the people we may view as being causal to our suffering are often angels in disguise and not the foes we might have believed them to be. At an unconscious level we seek out the ideal people and perfect-storm scenarios that will facilitate our healing; for our deepest wounding is not within our Soul, which remains forever whole and pure, but in our heart.

So, in any suffering you must turn your attention to your heart. It is from this place of release, of opening, and of loving and trusting another, that you can begin to truly receive Love and heal your heart, the place where fulfillment is most needed.

For the heart to heal you need someone who is clear enough to reflect and give affirmation: "I see you are evolving, are growing stronger. I see the beauty of your heart." You need a sensory relationship that reflects your true identity. This could be in the form of a beloved, a friend, a parent, a brother, a sister, a child, a healer, a beloved pet, or even Mother Nature. You need a very specific medicine. Without it you will continue searching.

Fear Has Forgotten It Is Love

Fear expects to be met with fear and when it is met with Love, if it does not retreat, it surrenders. If we rise above fear and center ourselves in Love, we *will* be able to overcome the greatest of challenges. A new Conscious paradigm will not present itself to us but manifest through us. We are of no help to the world when we remain locked in the prison of our own shadow. The consciously evolved individual is a mirror that reflects clarity, neutrality, stability, humanity, and nonduality.

Nothing can deter those who know that they are here to cocreate a visionary new paradigm, but, first, and essentially, we need to heal our own shadow before being sufficiently equipped to heal the world. When we do so, we become effective forces for addressing and resolving the problems of the world because we have made peace with our own. We do not resist challenges but step forward with confidence, able to support the healing of our ailing world. We are able to mindfully respond and bring the light of clarity to issues that beset society. In healing our own psychological shadow, we have transformed ourselves and are therefore able to effect positive change in the world.

7

A New Age of Health, Wellness, and Regeneration

> *It is not to see something first, but to establish solid connections between the previously known and the hitherto unknown that constitutes the essence of scientific discovery. It is this process of tying together, which can best promote true understanding and real progress.*
>
> HANS SELYE

We are about to experience a new epoch of physical well-being and aging. Our move out of the Age of Pisces and into the Age of Aquarius heralds the onset of a highly advanced technological eon in which a new age of medicine and regeneration will be founded upon technologies that prioritize, respect, and protect humanity and Nature (see the appendix for more details). It will produce organic and health-giving solutions by utilizing the harmonious and natural forces of the Earth and the Cosmos. It is a conscious technology that has the ethos of *first do no harm* and *leave no trace* at its heart, and one that will support the human race and all life on this beautiful planet to flourish.

The exploration of a new age of regeneration and healing leads us to an important question: What can we do to create a greater experience of health and well-being in our own lives? Remaining well and living a harmonious life becomes possible when we practice conscious Self-care

112

and understand how to listen to the extraordinary and sophisticated system of intelligence that is the human body. The majority of us have forgotten how to do so and how to trust what we are feeling and sensing in the form of the wise messages we are receiving from our symptoms. Instead, we ignore early warning signs and often leave it until it's too late to heal from the condition that ails us. Another stumbling block along the conventional healing path is the seeking of help from sources that lack sufficient wholistic (whole-person) insight, or the interest to treat disease, or *dis-ease* (meaning a *dis*-connection from *ease*) from a holistic perspective.

Alternative medicine views well-being through an inclusive lens that not only addresses the body but also the emotions, the mind, and the psyche and fundamentally recognizes and respects the influence of each individual Soul. When we approach illness as an "enemy that needs to be beaten," we introduce the energy of separation and lose the potential to engage with it as a messenger and friend.

By not listening to the message illness has to convey, in respect of our deeper healing, integration, evolution, and awakening, we polarize and separate, therefore relinquishing our inborn capacity for self-healing. If we are not aligned at the levels of body, feelings, mind, and Soul, our brain and biochemistry will react to an inner vocabulary of conditioning and fear, which serves only to further exacerbate the symptomology and condition.

Only when we have discovered, uncovered, cleared, and healed the root cause and psychospiritually realigned the physical, emotional, mental, and energetic levels within us will the health challenges that beset us (of the body, emotions, or mind) begin to fully heal and resolve.

What is the ultimate purpose of disease? How does it serve us to experience physical, emotional, and mental imbalance? What does it teach us about ourselves? What is its ultimate gift? If we fail to consider such questions or truly comprehend the meaning of the purpose of disease, we might well find a temporary cure yet sustained wellness might elude us. There is a higher purpose for every experience, and the body understands this well, even if the mind struggles with the concept.

A NEW BODY STORY

A new body story requires us to remain Conscious of how we think, feel, and act toward ourselves and to engage the seven principles for well-being: self-love, conscious nourishment, mindful movement, daily meditation, creative fulfillment, psychospiritual integration, and conscious awakening. It compels us to be mindful of the way we interact with our bodies by wisely choosing the foods and beverages we consume, to take regular beneficial pauses for stillness and sitting in contemplative silence or meditation, and to engage in outdoor pursuits such as walking, moving, and playing in Nature.

MINDFUL MOVEMENT
ON MOTHER EARTH

To oxygenate, strengthen, tone, and relax our body, we need regular and mindful movement and exercise. Moving stimulates our organs and the key systems within the body via reflexology points on the base of our feet, and therefore walking barefoot is especially beneficial because it reconnects us with the Earth. So many of us are disconnected from the Earth energies that are essential for our overall health because of the insulating materials used to make the soles of shoes, especially rubber. This also applies to certain types of flooring, including carpets.

Walking in the midst of Nature where the air is purer is ideal. Fresh air helps us to recycle and release toxins via the breath. Twenty minutes of cardiovascular activity included in a daily walk is highly beneficial. For those who live in polluted towns or cities, ozone therapy is an alternative option for oxygenating the body. Practices such as tai chi, yoga, and qigong all support the movement of *chi* (life force/vital force/energy flow), and this is especially important for those who cannot easily access clean air when walking. Acupuncture, reflexology, and Thai massage are also effective ways of stimulating the energy in the body, releasing emotions, and relaxing and expanding the mind.

The lymphatic system, which is part of the vascular system and an important part of the immune system and comprises a large network of lymphatic vessels that carry a clear fluid called lymph toward the heart, has no pumping action and therefore needs aerobic movement to keep it flowing healthily and to support it to efficiently eliminate toxins through the skin, urine, and feces. Exercise also improves the efficiency of the cardiovascular system by absorbing and transporting oxygen. Swimming, dancing, and brisk walking are extremely beneficial aerobic options, as are garden swings or home-based mini trampolines.

LOVE AS MEDICINE

Two of the greatest gifts we can experience in life are love and well-being. Many of us have an overall sense of well-being yet feel bereft of love. Conversely, the opposite holds true for those who are surrounded by love but struggle with day-to-day health. Most of us would opt for a life of love in the absence of wellness, rather than the other way around, because the beauty and purity of love can transcend anything. Love is not limited to physical experience for it is of the Soul. *Love is free* as the saying goes and, indeed, it is. No matter what our karmic or physical situation, love lives within and beyond us, infuses and surrounds us, and is prized even beyond physical wellness.

Our state of mind can dramatically influence our health and well-being, for *it is not the situation itself that causes our suffering but what the mind does with it.* We may live with the most debilitating physical conditions, yet how we respond (or react) to these determines our day-to-day experience and even the degree to which our symptoms abate or exacerbate. And where love prevails the greatest happiness and joy are to be found regardless of circumstances.

EPIGENETICS AND FOOD AS MEDICINE

Epigenetics also has a role to play in the new body story. For example, molecules that are referred to as MicroRNAs bind to the chromosomes and alter the readout of the genes. The foods we eat release these molecules, which are then picked up by the digestive system and transferred to the cells regulating our genetics. The potential to alter the genetic readout by way of the foods we ingest has been scientifically proven.

Understanding this is fundamental when we consider the influence of consuming organic and natural produce versus the impact of eating processed, treated, or genetically altered foods, the last of which release unknown and unrecognized microRNA molecules into our bloodstream, affecting our genetics. Inorganic and unnatural substances containing genetically modified organisms (GMOs), chemicals, pesticides, petrochemicals, and a plethora of other toxins and poisons impose a misreadout, which negatively affects the entire physical, emotional, mental, psychological, and energetic system.

The organic ecology that is inherent within the human body is intricately balanced, complex, sophisticated, and intelligent. Introducing "alien" microRNA molecules genetically modifies this ecosystem and produces incoherent and reactive symptomology. Ideally, it is important that the inner workings of the systems of the body respond harmoniously to organic and natural microRNA molecular readouts. We can surmise therefore that the produce and beverages we ingest have a major impact on our overall health, biology, and genetics.

An organic diet free of GMOs is fundamental for supporting, attaining, and maintaining well-being. Yet sourcing entirely organic produce is a modern-day dilemma because of the issues of air, soil, and water pollution. The devastating impact of soil depletion, GMOs, fracking, chemtrails, animal pharmaceuticals, ozone pollution, acid rain, pesticides, chemical crop spraying, and poisoning of the soil and water tables through animal urine and feces continue to call into question the safety of our food and compromise its nutritional quality. Nevertheless, living organically is less harmful and helps to bring and maintain balance to our physical, emotional, and mental health.

The Ecosystems of Nature and the Human Body

The foods we eat and the substances we put in and on our bodies are without question of the greatest importance to our overall health. They not only impact the innately intelligent and delicately balanced ecosystem that is the human body but also the intricate and finely tuned ecosystem of the natural world. Eating and applying inorganic and bio-altered products is counterproductive when we are trying to unhook physically, emotionally, and mentally from the old paradigm.

Seek to live a life that *leaves no trace,* not only in relation to food but in all lifestyle choices. Most of us have been raised within a consumer culture that permeates almost every aspect of our lives. Eliminating processed, synthetic, manufactured, inorganic, and unnatural products is of the utmost importance if we are going to support ourselves, the ecology, and the environmental health of our planet.

"Let Food Be Thy Medicine and Medicine Thy Food"

As the Hippocrates quote above suggests, Nature provides everything we need for the health of our bodies, feelings, and minds. Many of her plants, flowers, trees, grasses, fruits, vegetables, resins, oils, seeds and nuts are medicinal and are in harmony with the human biological system. How we consume these foods is a matter of choice. Some people find that a totally raw diet is the healthiest option, whereas others prefer a combination of raw and cooked foods to support their overall health needs. For many, a diet composed of warm foods is more suitable. There is no right or wrong or better or worse when we are conscious and mindful of our body. For example, both Ayurveda and acupuncture promote the consumption of warm foods, whereas many contemporary spiritual nutritionists are inclined toward prescribing a raw diet.

Attaining and maintaining an acid-to-alkaline ratio within the body is important; however, this cannot be medically or scientifically measured with accuracy. Yet, what can be ascertained is that too much acidity or alkalinity creates imbalance and disease. For example, a few alkaline foods are spinach, lemon, almonds, and millet and a few acid forming foods are corn, lentils, oats, cheese, and coffee. It has been suggested that a ratio of seventy-five percent alkaline to twenty-five percent acid is ideal. Scientists have determined that the body fluids of people who are well incline toward a healthy alkaline pH, whereas a highly acidic internal environment is often more prone to disease.

PHENOMENOLOGICAL ABSORPTION

It might be insightful to pause here briefly and consider what you are absorbing in your day-to-day life. What frequency and vibration are you ingesting? What are you absorbing, consciously or unconsciously, from the food and beverages you consume, the thoughts of others, your everyday environment, the media, social media, and the stories of those you interact with on a daily basis? What kind of frequency do you feel you attract to yourself through your own thoughts, words, actions, and deeds?

Everything you are exposed to has a frequency that directly influences your biology and energy. It is essential to be vigilant and discerning about what you ingest and to remain mindful of who or what you allow into your energy field. Surround yourself with people, situations, and environments of a harmonious vibration and this, too, can become your own vibrational reality.

Everything we ingest through our senses and energy fields has an impact on our frequency and therefore influences what we attract into our lives. If you wish to live a blessed life, then do the following:

Release all low-vibrational attachments.

Let Love and Consciousness be the guides that enrich and sustain you.

Refine your diet and drink plenty of pure water.

If it is safe for you to do so, fast occasionally.

Remain mindful of the impact of the people you live with . . . what are their stories and how do these influence your own?

Seek to surround yourself with those who are grounded, balanced, respectful, kind, gentle, inspiring, passionate, creative, and heart-centered.

MINDFUL ABSORPTION

In addition to the types of foods we ingest, we are also wise to consider the impact of our state of mind when eating or drinking and how this facilitates or impedes the absorption of nutrients. A relaxed body, a peaceful mind, and a harmonious environment and mindset are the ideal. Chewing slowly and savoring the quality, texture, and flavor of Nature's foods supports our body's ability to be nourished on the atomic and subtler levels. Rushing, talking, or being distracted by other activities such as television, radio, laptops, and phones, prevents us from Consciously and mindfully connected to the process of nourishing ourselves. This in turn can create imbalance and disharmony within the body's finely tuned ecosystem.

Eating mindfully is instrumental to maintaining and supporting our physical health. Consuming food when in a state of agitation or when preoccupied can be a causal factor in the development and/or acceleration of the early stages of physical disease. Also, the postures we adopt when eating or drinking are an important consideration. When we are incorrectly positioned (i.e., the body is slouched or twisted), this can hinder digestion and the ability to fully absorb and assimilate the nutrients and elemental particles in our food. Simple, wholesome, natural, and Sun-infused foods not only support our physical health but our emotional, mental, and psychic states too.

THE TIMELESS MEDICINE OF WATER

The painter, writer, and poet Kahlil Gibran stated that "in one drop of water are found all the secrets of all the oceans; in one aspect of You are found all the aspects of existence."

Water is necessary for the survival of all life on Earth. According to Professor Martin Chaplin, professor emeritus of applied science at London South Bank University, "water profoundly influences all molecular interactions in biological systems. The existence of life depends critically on the capacity of water to dissolve polar molecules that serve as information carriers."

The human body is made up of 60 percent water, which helps regulate temperature as well as transporting essential molecules, particles, and nutrients around the body and eliminating waste products via metabolic processes. In every moment, we are losing water through digestion, breathing, talking, sweating, coughing, sneezing, and moving. To replenish what is lost we need to regularly hydrate ourselves. To this end, eating fresh natural produce is also of great benefit. Juicy fruits, soft vegetables, a variety of salads and leaves all have a high-water content. The intake of water in preventing dehydration and supporting wellness is *crucial*.

For centuries, some of the most famous spas in the world have been developed around places with seemingly miraculous healing waters including Lourdes in France, Karlovy Vary in the Czech Republic, the natural springs in the hills beyond Panama City, and the famous spas that surround Buda and Pest in Hungary. The results of bathing in and drinking these waters are not merely placebo effects but have been found to improve health, wellness, and cellular coherence.

Eminent scientist, the late Masaru Emoto, author of *The Hidden Messages in Water,* found that water from different geographical areas revealed specific crystallization structures when flash frozen and examined under a microscope. He found that the finest-formed crystals were within the water of the great healing spas of the world such as Lourdes.

He also demonstrated that human thought processes and emotions could change the crystallization of the water: positive thoughts, emotions, and words created beautiful crystals, and negative ones resulted in poorly formed or damaged crystal formations. Given that our bodies are believed to be somewhere in the region of 60 percent water, imagine how they are affected by our thoughts, emotions, and words.

THE INVISIBLE POWER WITHIN FOODS

Similar research conducted by Walter Danzer at the Switzerland-based Lifevision Lab of Soyana has afforded startling insight into the differences between organic and nonorganic foods. Over the course of thirty years of research into the life energy, or "order force" of over fifty foods, Danzer has produced thousands of crystallization images that demonstrate the contradistinction between organic and nonorganic. These astonishing photographs (refer to Danzer's book *The Invisible Power within Foods: A Comparison of Organic and Nonorganic*), reveal unequivocally the stark contrast in the life energy between nonorganic/ GMOs and organic wholefoods. Danzer states: "I have discovered that organic foods possess an amazingly beautiful life energy or order force (life design principle), whereas the life energy of non-organic foods is generally weakened, disrupted, or destroyed." Just viewing these photographs presents a compelling argument for avoiding nonorganic and GMO produce and beverages. The research, results, and images that were recorded by Danzer and his team inspired me to write the following, called "The Whole of CREATION":

Our bodies, Mother Nature, the Earth, stars, Cosmos, Universe, and Universes beyond are extraordinary systems of infinite, innate, complex, ordered, and supra-intelligent structures, patterns, and shapes of phenomenal geometric precision and brilliance. Everything that pertains to life, biological or cosmological, is of intricate, unquantifiable, and unfathomable order; all in perfect synchronicity, alignment, and resonance. Nothing is in juxtaposition to anything else. There are no fragments, only the fractal genius of an infinitely intelligent and divinely perfected, chaotic yet divinely ordered, imponderable phenomenon that is SOURCE Reality: an astro-kaleidoscopic Omniverse within which every quantum particle is but a hologram of the Whole of CREATION.

THE STRESS FACTOR

Eating pure organic foods, drinking pristine natural water, and living in an unpolluted environment support the body but do not guarantee good health. Our emotional, mental, intellectual, and psychological states, our need for social and physical contact with others, and our innate need *to belong,* are equally important, as is our ability to handle the stresses of everyday living. Surprisingly, the stress factors of modern times are comparable in many respects to those of thousands of years ago in terms of physical survival and the ability to thrive in any particular environment. Modern day-to-day life still presents many of us with issues of scarcity, lack, loneliness, and isolation. Feeling an integral and valued part of local (family/neighborhood/town/region) or international (global) community is no less a challenge in this age than it was then.

Many are still striving to meet their basic physical survival needs— oxygen, water, food, shelter, and sleep—although this is alleviated to some extent by a welfare system and credit-based culture. Some may argue that to live in such a modern westernized society is perhaps even more of a struggle for no matter where people are located in the world many are still confronted by illness, disease, and social isolation.

Conventional medicine is far too limited in its understanding of the impact of stress on our overall well-being and the stress that arises out of unhealed and unintegrated psychological processes and social pressures. Illness, unmet physical and emotional needs, disconnection, social isolation, loneliness, historical pain and suffering, and the dehumanizing, desensitizing, and destabilizing effect of cultural industrialization and consumerism keep humanity locked in maintaining cycles of stress and literally caught in a devolutionary spiral. Yet a change in the way we can live and experience our lives is on the horizon in the form of Consciously awakened individuals and group collectives who are lighting the path for a new paradigm in health, wellness, and regeneration.

EVERYTHING IS INTERCONNECTED

Wisdom teachings of the past have consistently stated that all life is interrelated and that our lives on Earth are profoundly interconnected with the Cosmos. Even though there are many who recognize this fundamental principle, medical diagnosis and prognosis remain firmly rooted in old and outdated physiological and biological concepts, modes, and theories. Doctors continue to treat illness as a separate and isolated event in a person's life. Such a stance disassociates and disconnects us from the invaluable truth that the purpose of sickness and disease is ultimately in service of our higher good and always originates from and is directed by the Soul.

Regular detoxing and cleansing of the internal systems, resourcing ourselves with essential vitamins, minerals, and other important nutrients, consuming organic and natural whole foods, bathing under the Sun, Moon, and stars, absorbing light and (pure) oxygen into the cells, physically moving and stretching, and getting sufficient restorative sleep all help us to remain well or support a compromised health condition.

Humans are physical beings but have an energetic and spiritual component too. As such they are equipped with a sixth basic survival need that crosses the physical boundary into the energetic and psychic realms. This is akin to a sixth sense through which we experience the mystical. Just as the ecosystem of the Earth is influenced by the Cosmos, so too is the ecosystem of the physical human body. Our thoughts, beliefs, and experiences also impact our health, well-being and aging process, as do environmental conditions in terms of the culture medium of our family, the community, and a wider authority.

A combination of physical, emotional, mental, psychological, energetic, psychic, spiritual, and environmental factors each play a role in well-being and illness. It is through the physical body that psychological processes ultimately heal and clear. The preconditions for sickness and disease are feeling *ill at ease* and *dis-ease*. This can often originate from karmic, ancestral, historical, and psychological blueprints that remain embedded and unresolved within the unintegrated self.

When medicine fails to acknowledge or accept that the cause of illness heralds from nonphysical factors, the evolution of health care remains at a standstill. We cannot be free of disease in this or any other timeline if we do not understand its primary origin. Allopathic medicine may find a possible "cure," but without primarily comprehending the psychospiritual cause, disease will remain present in the energetic bodies as an unresolved karmic/historical/trauma and subsequently will resurface at another time in order to be addressed.

What remains important in the presence of any disease, whether it is terminal or benign, is a determination and commitment to discover its root cause. To do this we need to leave no stone unturned in regard to the psychological and historical dimensions within ourselves. What we experience as a long human life amounts to less than a nanosecond of time in the *no time* reality that is Infinity and Eternity.

Many Souls come to the Earth for just a short period in order to complete a process that may have begun several incarnations ago. Sometimes it seems that there can be an all too brief experience of this side of the veil, as in the case of a miscarriage or a life cut short. There are as many reasons for leaving this physical vehicle or for remaining in the body to endure a challenging physical condition as there are stars in our known universe.

THE BODY AS GUIDE

The impact of our thoughts, words, and actions on our mental, emotional, and physical health cannot be underestimated. People make an endless amount of decisions and choices throughout their lives, all of which will either support or prove detrimental to their overall well-being. The degree to which one is psychologically integrated, consciously evolved, and spiritually awakened, determines the quality or validity of the choices made. Evolving a relationship with yourself that is grounded in an awareness that is experienced at gut level, or *felt-sense* level (see below), enables you to tune in to your body and listen to the innate wisdom it wishes to convey.

The body is our compass and the greatest psychic in the world. It speaks to us constantly and is our mentor, guide, teacher, and counselor. It is also an oracle, sage, visionary, and seer. Every answer we may ever seek will be found in the small quiet voice within that contains the wisdom of the Universe. If we just listen, all we ever need know/gno about our overall health and happiness will be revealed.

When the body and mind (the biological and the psychological) are aligned in harmony and are Consciously communicating with each other, we discover just why it is we have become physically compromised. By understanding the reasons for this, we are able to put into place an intelligent and effective protocol to bring about the level of healing required. At the very least, we can more effectively manage an existing condition.

The human body is profoundly intelligent, sophisticated, and resilient. In terms of psychobiology, the emotional and mental bodies are instrumental in finding the cause of and potential cure for what ails us. Illness does not happen by chance: We are never its victims because there is always a correlating Soul agenda that is seeking to be Consciously recognized and addressed.

The Felt Sense—The Guiding Principle

What is the *felt sense*? Simply put, it is that small inner voice within or the strong hunch we feel at the deepest inner level. It is the gnosis that arises from the core of our being and is entirely instinctual. It is an unquestionable intuition and innate inner knowing often referred to as a "gut instinct."

Because each microscopic atom, cell, and element within us is fine-tuned and finely attuned to the felt sense, this is essentially a *whole-body* experience. The felt sense expresses through the physical body as an energetic contraction or expansion. When we listen to it, it is as if we are holding a supersensitive compass in our hands and are able to guide ourselves through any storm. The felt sense is an innate and intrinsic guide that gifts us with invaluable insight and precognition. In the case of ill health, it is the felt sense that facilitates *integrated neutrality*. When the mind is at peace, and the senses are deeply experienced, we are able to understand the reason for and higher purpose of a physical imbalance.

The felt sense guides us toward harmony and unity within ourselves. The body knows/gnos when the self is in conflict. Discord on an emotional and mental level creates the same in the physical body. The choices and decisions we make and the relationships we engage in are vital influences that affect our overall well-being. Following the felt sense ensures that whatever our experience, it will always be in accord with the higher directive of our Soul and therefore in service of our healing and highest good.

A new paradigm of health, wellness, and regeneration requires us to operate from a higher level of Consciousness. Evolution itself propels us toward balance, integration, awakening, and transcendence. Recognizing and understanding the fundamental cause of ill health and disease, whether it is karmic, ancestral, historical, psychological, or environmental, is vital. Heart-based solutions that serve wellness and regeneration and support the body, feelings, mind, and psyche to remain aligned in love, peace, and harmony, *are* the Call of a new epoch.

8

Ancient Prophecy and
the Current World Trajectory

*For the ancient Incas, our generation, which is fortunate
enough to experience the "end of history" with the Galactic
Alignment of 2012, is poised to become "the bridge people"
tasked with creating Heaven on Earth.*

SOL LUCKMAN, *CONSCIOUS HEALING*

Our journey continues by exploring what some consider to have
been one of the greatest civilizations on Earth: the Classic Maya.
For millennia, these people were residents of the Yucatan Peninsula,
Guatemala, Belize, El Salvador, Honduras, and some parts of Mexico,
and evidence of this great culture is found scattered across Yucatan
jungles and in the highlands of present-day Guatemala. Here there are
remnants of ancient cities and temple sites in addition to intricately
designed plazas, towering stepped pyramids, and centers of ceremony
and worship adorned with the finest sculpted stones and covered in
hieroglyphic inscriptions.

During the period in Mayan history known as the Preclassic period
(2000 BCE to 250 CE), the Maya developed a farming culture. This
was also when the astonishing structures were built in Mesoamerica,
including those at sites such as Copan, Palenque, Chichen Itza, and the
palace of Xpuhil. Many Mayan temples are said to represent gateways

to sacred knowledge with the purpose of integrating and uniting the Cosmos, the Earth, and humanity. This is also true of particular dates within the Mayan time cycles.

The Maya were a civilization believed to be in direct contact with galactic energies, specifically with **Pleiadeans***, who are said to be fifth-dimensional beings from the Pleiades star system and far more advanced than humanity. This may explain the mystery of how the Maya knew of the four hundred stars in the Pleiades, when today it is possible to see only seven with the naked eye. Even with all our modern technology and resources, we are still unable to measure astronomical data more accurately than the Maya did all those centuries ago. According to contemporary Maya daykeeper Hunbatz Men, the Maya believe that the Milky Way is the generator of all life. The late author Jose Arguelles stated that the stars serve as lenses that transmit energies to planets and that our Sun is the lens through which galactic energies are transmitted as light codes to the Earth.

LORD PACAL: AN ENLIGHTENED BEING?

During the peak of the Maya Classic period, from approximately 435 to 830 CE, Lord Pacal (615–683 CE) ruled over the city of Palenque, which is situated in today's state of Chiapas, Mexico) and its empire for over sixty-eight years. It is said that Pacal came to the Mayan people as an enlightened being. His mission on earth was to guide them toward the light of cosmic wisdom, thus allowing human beings to attain enlightenment (liberation from the restrictions of the third dimension) and complete their destiny.

Pacal was a great initiate believed to have been capable of miraculous healings by simply raising his hand or with just a glance. He was said to be a "master of energy," which he could control with his body and mind. He was also known as a "magician of time." One of his messages was that "God is a number." He had an intricate understanding of the complexity of numbers and mathematics and was able to interpret these as a unique language beyond the spoken word. He taught his people about the thirteen dimensions and their associated mysteries, and the thirteen realms in which physical or energetic realities manifest in ascending frequency. His knowledge of great cycles of time allowed him to record this information for future humanity. He is renowned for guiding the inscription of stone monuments with precise astronomical and astrological information, which was part of the Mayan mission. He knew that as a species humanity would become ignorant of the sacred connection to Nature and become disconnected from the laws of the natural world.

THE LONG COUNT CALENDAR

The ancient Mayan civilization was one of the most astronomically advanced in human history and used what is considered to be the most complex calendar system in the world—the **Long Count*** calendar. The origins and pioneers of the Long Count calendar are not fully known, yet evidence suggests that the Maya inherited it from an even more ancient people of Central America, most likely the **Olmec***, and radically advanced this and other existing calendar systems from earlier cultures, taking astronomical understanding to an even higher level. Using a unique and exceptionally simple calculation system, they created calendars for equinoxes, solstices, eclipse cycles, and cycles of Mercury, but out of a total of seventeen calendars, only the Long Count calendar continues to be studied and used by modern-day people. It remains the most accurate on the planet to date.

According to this calendar, which began on 11–08–3114 BCE and ended on the Winter Solstice of 2012 a time span of 5,125.26 years, we were "between worlds" from 1987, when the Mayan fifth world finished, until 2012, when the sixth world began. This period of between worlds foretold of a time of "revealing" or "apocalypse" and of a time when "truth would be revealed." The Mayan sixth world is "blank" and without prophecy, so therefore humanity finds itself in an unprecedented position in which it is able to cocreate a new epoch that is not tethered to the past or dictated by the current state of the world but is free to materialize a new Conscious paradigm of our collective choosing.

THE COLLAPSE OF THE CLASSIC MAYA

The collapse of the Classic Maya occurred around 900 CE when almost an entire civilization, literally, disappeared over a hundred-year period. There has been much speculation as to why this occurred and how this could have happened. Mayan experts have researched the possibilities of drought, pestilence, and internal feuding to find explanations of what may have led to their disappearance. Some theories suggest that they simply abandoned their lands, dispersing throughout the globe, setting up new indigenous cultures including native tribes like the Hopi. No proof of these or any other theories has come to light. Others speak of the Mayan civilization of that time "ascending," that is, ascending from the Earth over a period of one hundred years to return to their cosmic origins in the Pleiades.

Not all of the Maya are believed to have left, but it was not until the tenth century that the Mayan civilization reemerged, a new culture that became known as the new Maya Empire. What is clear is that approximately nine million people disappeared during the course of a century: to where and why remains an ongoing mystery. Spanish missionaries destroyed most of the sacred codices of the Maya, but some were preserved and it has taken three generations of scholars to decipher these, allowing access to some of the primary codes that constitute their cosmic knowledge.

DECEMBER 21, 2012: THE END POINT

The Maya speak of "Five Worlds" or "Suns" each lasting thirteen **baktuns***, or 5,125 years. All five equate to twenty-six thousand years, the time it takes for the completion of one **Grand Cycle*** (**precession of** the equinoxes*). The reason that the cycles of the Mayan calendars are so relevant to us now, thousands of years later, is because these systems described an end point of December 21, 2012. The Maya used stone carvings to preserve the calendar that encoded the vital end date of Earth's current twenty-six-thousand-year evolutionary cycle. It appears that they knew that this moment in evolution would prove to be a critical turning point as the human race would still be far from living harmoniously with each other and the laws of Nature. This information was recorded for posterity as a warning to help humankind avert the catastrophic prophecies that would prove to be the outcome of remaining psychospiritually unintegrated and unawakened.

From a Dark Age into a Golden Age

The mission of the Classic Maya seems to have been the synchronization of the solar system, the Earth, and its future inhabitants with the much larger galactic community. However, their advanced knowledge and visionary ways of living became lost as humanity descended into a dark age. Now their prophecies have reemerged at this most critical time in order to reconnect us to our potential to cocreate a new Golden Age.

Cyclical Time

The Winter Solstice of 2012 was a critical juncture—a time during which an unprecedented grand alignment occurred and when many cycles within cycles converged. In the West, linear time is observed, consisting of the past and future. However, ancient indigenous and shamanic cultures perceived time as *cyclical* so rather than traveling in a straight line, it turns like a wheel. These cycles of time are based on synchronicity and enable us to influence past situations as well as tap into the potential of future destiny. We currently live in a time of enormous uncertainty and change, a time that the Maya, Hopi, Sioux, Egyptians, Kabbalists, Essenes, Q'ero, and Aborigines all described as the Time of Great Purification, the Shift of Ages, the Great Shift, the Great Transition, and various other terminologies.

Once Upon a Golden Age

As mentioned in chapter 3, the world has seen a Golden Age once before. It was the first age, which preceded the Silver, Bronze, and Iron Ages. The Mahabharata (one of two major Sanskrit epics of ancient India), cites the following in regard to this period:

> Men were neither bought nor sold; there were no poor and no rich; there was no need to labor, because all that men required was obtained by the power of will; the chief virtue was the abandonment of all worldly desires. There was no disease; there was no lessening with the years; there was no hatred or vanity, or evil thought whatsoever; no sorrow, no fear. All mankind could attain to supreme blessedness.

In the Mayan spiritual system of belief, the end of a world age is a moment of great opportunity. Each time this occurs humanity finds itself in a position to choose whether to move into a new and more harmonious phase or to continue on its current path and face an apocalyptic ultimate outcome.

Lord Pacal spoke of the closing of a world age at the time of the December 21, 2012 Winter Solstice, which also happens to be the date that the Maya foretold to be *the beginning of a new creation.* As we approached the world of the sixth sun that began in 2012, we were also in the last three years of a twenty-six-thousand-year completion cycle that heralded the commencement of what both the Maya and Inca had prophesied to be a new Golden Age.

Many other ancient civilizations also considered the December 21, 2012 date to be of great importance. These included the wisdom cultures from the Americas, Sumer, and China. In Egypt the pyramids of the Giza plateau appear to have provided both a time marker as well as an optimum-viewing platform for the astronomical phenomena associated with the Winter Solstice of 2012. The Q'ero, direct descendants of the Incas, spoke of an age of conquest and domination coming to an end and of a new human being born. They also spoke of the Earth being restored to her former beauty, calling this process the Turning of the Earth. They specifically identified the year 2012 as the time when this restoration would begin. Evidence has also shown that many modern indigenous peoples of the Americas, most notably the Hopi but also other tribes from the farthest regions of the Amazon jungles in the South to the frozen wastelands of the Canadian North, agree.

The Turning of the Earth

It is important to understand why the Maya were so interested in the period of time surrounding December 21, 2012, as well as that specific day. They recognized it to be a unique date because of the Galactic Alignment, which they understood would occur when the position of the Winter Solstice Sun aligned exactly with where the Ecliptic Plane (the Sun's apparent path) intersected the Galactic Equator of the Milky Way to form a Cosmic Cross. The eye of the needle of this process was a thirty-six-year window of time that began in 1980 and ended in December 2016, although the full closing of the Galactic Alignment window will occur on December 21, 2021.

Humanity has been presented with a once in a twenty-six-thousand-year opportunity to bypass the lengthy process of moving through each preceding age to, once again, return to a Golden Age. We *can* transcend this dark age in which we are still immersed if we apply visionary and empowered action.

FALL OR FLY?

We have arrived at a critical point on the timeline of humankind. In these liminal times we find ourselves straddling two worlds: (1) the current paradigm and its archaic and self-serving systems and structures and (2) a new emerging paradigm built upon the principles and virtues of unity in diversity, equality, humanity, empathy, kindness, and love.

We are in between times, in between worlds, and in between a third-dimensional to fifth-dimensional Consciousness shift. We are in the midst of an evolutionary process during which, as the ancient indigenous wise ones foretold, an extraordinary shift of consciousness will occur, resulting in an acceleration of collective evolution.

We are in the eye of the storm . . . passing through the eye of the needle . . . from what was, to what is, to what is to become. Since 2012, we have stood on the edge of the precipice and now we have stepped off. The degree to which the collective becomes consciously awakened in the remaining months of 2021 will determine if we are to fall or fly.

THE AGE OF AQUARIUS: EVOLVING AN ENLIGHTENED WORLD

The constellation of Aquarius is governed by the planet Uranus, which rules technology and humanitarianism. The future we are moving toward is one in which these will work hand in hand. Aquarius also rules revolutionary thinking and radical social progress. It exerts a people-empowered directive, and it is during this two-thousand-year age that the ultimate breaking down of all dysfunctional and devolutionary systems will occur. Aquarius stands for *freedom* and will not allow anyone or anything to oppress it.

The new age upon us is one in which independence will become harmoniously balanced with autonomous interdependence. It will be an age of free thinkers whose collective efforts will slowly but surely bring an end to any system that seeks to enslave and/or suppress the conscious awakening of the world. It will be an epoch in which humanity finally breaks free of the disempowering systems of the past and instead begins to thrive in true freedom.

The technology that will emerge is barely conceivable to our twenty-first-century minds. Extraordinary advances will transpire to be the norm and will be created within a world that is innately humane and wise. If the prodigious and visionary inventor and futurist Nikola Tesla was to incarnate again, it would be into the Age of Aquarius, for this is where his genius and futuristic mind would have the freedom to transform the world.

The Shadow of an Astrological Age

As is the case with every human being, each astrological age has a shadow side. The Aquarian shadow at its worst points to the detrimental creation and use of malignant and highly dangerous technology. One of the most ominous aspects of this is artificial intelligence, or AI, which will pose the biggest threat that the world has faced so far. Added to this will be an "antihumanitarian" shadow agenda that will not only seek to strip us of our human rights but also the rights of all life forms on Earth.

If left unchecked, the shadow of any age will cause catastrophic devastation on a world-wide scale. We have only to consider the current Age of Pisces and the predominant influence of organized global religions to recognize how these have been and are the origin and cause of billions of deaths (human/animal/plant) throughout the past two thousand years.

Another shadow aspect of Pisces is the condition of suffering, which has also dominated the Piscean Age. This was/is primarily due to the unawakened consciousness of the collective. The shadow of Pisces took the form of power-hungry "leaders" and self-serving warlords, and its true essence of pure spirituality and love was hijacked and distorted to serve their own ends. The shadow of Pisces is all too prone to self-sacrifice and victimization, and the powers that be took advantage of this in order to control and condition the masses, who, for the most part, yielded in order to survive.

The Light of a Piscean Age

For two millennia, the world has lived out the shadow of a Piscean Age in which polarity, duality, victimization, and separation have dominated. Yet, the Light of Pisces has still been present but to a lesser extent. This can be seen in the purer expression of spirituality, especially in recent times when it has begun to move beyond the fringes of society and into mainstream culture. The great works of art, the prolific philosophical writings, the musical compositions inspired by the Soul, as well as natural medicines, energy healing, empathy and compassion, kindness and care, creativity, design and crafts, are all the gifts of Pisces, as is our connection with the Higher Realms.

The spiritual remit of the Age of Pisces was to balance the metaphysical with the physical and to create harmony between these *seeming* polarities. By consciously acknowledging that we have not lived the full Light of this astrological epoch, we can consciously choose to position ourselves in the Light, not the shadow, of the new Aquarian Age. Aquarius is the rebel *with* a cause and will not allow its wings of freedom and autonomy to be clipped.

LIMINAL TIMES

In these liminal times, humanity is afforded a rare opportunity to take an evolutionary leap into a future that offers unimaginable promise. Yet, this will only prove possible if the predominance of duality consciousness, i.e., "us and them," is recognized as a separating force and is ultimately reconciled. By becoming informed and repeatedly asking questions about *just what is going on in the world,* we will find the answers we are looking for and a way through these critical times.

The Age of Aquarius will compel us to bring an end to destructive "leadership" and transcend prejudice, suffering, oppression, control, manipulation, and a power-over system of rule that is a dangerous threat to all life. We stand between two sweeping eons of time—in a liminal space or transitional phase between what was and what is to come. We are feeling the Call of evolution urging us to unhook from an old, outmoded, and devolutionary past and to step into a future of infinite potential.

As mentioned earlier, the Hopi and the Classic Maya spoke of a world that would enter "A Thousand Years of Peace," which was predicted to begin to unfold at this time. The Classic Maya also referred to this moment, *now,* as heralding a Great Shift into a New Golden Age. But they warned us, too, of the need to stand *together,* aligned in heart, mind, and Soul, if we were to have any chance of fulfilling their vision of peace and prosperity for ALL.

We are the effective macrocosm, and only we and we alone can extricate ourselves from the dark agendas that pervade our world. Those in power are aware that without the obedience of the masses their destructive plans will fail. We need to say no to war, to disempowerment, to being treated as mere pawns in a game of chess played out in top-secret boardrooms behind closed doors. We need to stop fighting each other and instead join *together* as an empowered force of Light. We need to say yes to wellness, joy, harmony, and abundance for ALL. We need to reclaim our autonomy and sovereignty. And we need to cocreate a new story for the world—one that is inspired by the Soul and determined by the heart.

NEW SYSTEMS
OF GLOBAL STEWARDSHIP

So, how do we effectively respond to the upsurge of global crises that proliferate in our world given that we have now tipped over the tipping point?

Energy follows thought, so what we focus on becomes our reality. Fear begets fear and Love begets Love. Both the elements of karma and the wounding of our ancestors need to be taken into account. In these unprecedented times, we *can* transcend karma and liberate ourselves and past generations from the stories of suffering that have been all-pervading in the shadow of a two-thousand-year Piscean Age.

We *can* manifest lives in which safety, creativity, tranquility, and fulfillment are as natural as breathing, where the healing of the world becomes possible if enough of us wake up. New systems of global stewardship can replace the existing and archaic political ones, and these systems can be modeled on the planetary ecosystem itself and the innate and profound intelligence of the human body, where everything works in harmony and is governed by sacred design and homeostasis.

What we essentially think and feel creates our world in every moment, and this world is a direct reflection of our collective inner state. Evolution affords us miraculous opportunities for purification at cellular and "Soulular" levels and for liberation from historical stories that may not even be our own but instead belong to past generations or other timelines. Nearly eight billion people living as LOVE will propel the world beyond the liminal level into the superliminal realm of a new conscious and awakened era.

LIVING THE LIGHT OF THE AQUARIAN AGE

Living the Light of the Aquarian Age is to align ourselves, individually and collectively, with the superlative and all-perceiving, all-knowing intelligence of the heart and Soul. Focusing kindness, goodness, and generosity toward ourselves and each other; applying empathy and compassion as our first line of defense; BEing sensitive, considerate, mindful, and unconditionally loving in every thought, word, and action is the way to live the Light of an Aquarian Age and propel ourselves along the evolutionary spiral of Life.

The Aquarian Age is depicted as a Water Bearer—a mystical healer who pours a ceaseless flow of water (LOVE) into the world energetically and spiritually. Aquarius is "electric" and profoundly futuristic; it is inspirationally progressive and associated with enlightenment. If we choose to live its highest expression, we can LIGHT UP the world with miraculous technologies borne of intuition and sourced by Nature and the Cosmos. The Light of the Aquarian Age will bless us with an eon in which the quantum mind is inspired by Soul. It will be an epoch that is motivated not by profit but by the greater good of all.

THE PROMISE OF
THE NEW AQUARIAN AGE

And here we stand on the threshold of a new epoch of inspired and genius intelligence. It is an epoch that invites us to free ourselves from the chains of the past and start anew, to rise like the lotus from the mud and the phoenix from the ashes into the extraordinary peace of a consciously awakened world that no longer teeters on the edge of extinction because of having stood too long in the shadow of the Piscean Age but is instead awakening to the reality of the freedom that comes through living the Light of a new Aquarian Age in which regeneration flourishes and the world-weary masses experience what it means to feel *truly alive*.

As we begin taking the first steps into the Aquarian Age, it calls on us all to "WAKE UP" and step out of all shadows, not the least of which is our own. If the Age of Pisces has taught us anything, it is that we must BE autonomous beings in our own right. As we prepare to move forward into two sweeping new epochs, we can take the hard-won lessons and heart-won gifts of the Age of Pisces with us.

The Light of Pisces opened the door into the Sacred Realms of the Mystical, Mysticism and Union, the Psychology of the Self, the Philosophy of the Soul, and the *Reality* of Spirit and SOURCE. The Light of Aquarius will open the doorway to an Enlightened Era in which freedom, autonomy, sovereignty, and our innate humanity will reign. This is its promise. However, it is up to us if we, as a collective, choose to live its shadow or Light.

We must prepare if we wish to live the Light of the Age of Aquarius. Our roles have never been more critical than they are now, and never will so much have been achieved by so few for so many. How do we move forward in this liminal time? With Consciousness, Heart, Truth, and Courage: the four principal directives on the evolutionary compass we hold in our hands.

9

The Great Shift of Ages

Never before in the history of humankind has your contribution to the world been more needed. Humanity stands on the very threshold of an ultimate choice: either remain on the current path of destruction or step onto a new consciously awakened path and rise like the phoenix from the ashes.

NICOLYA CHRISTI

Our sacred voyage into the phenomenon we are exploring throughout this book takes us back to the instrumental date of December 21, 2012 and its Call to humanity to consciously WAKE UP. This chapter also recounts the rare cosmic events that took place on and around this unprecedented date and lists the extraordinary cosmic occurrences that carried an instrumental message for humanity from the planets and stars.

As the great ancient civilizations predicted, humanity is confronted by two fundamental options: continue on the present path at our peril or step onto a new enlightened path that will lead to the fulfillment of the prophecies that speak of a new Golden Age and a thousand years of peace for humankind. The latter leads us into a new Conscious paradigm founded on love, truth, freedom, and unity. The former however, keeps us locked into a world of fear, suffering, darkness, control, manipulation, conditioning, and separation. One is the path of Love and the other the path of fear. Which one do you Consciously choose? Each decision is crucial to the outcome. Now more than ever, we need to unify and dedicate ourselves to the Great Work to ensure that humanity takes its next evolutionary step into a new Golden Age. We are being supported in this quest by legions of multidimensional beings, some who overlight the Earth, and others who walk among us.

RARE AND PROFOUND COSMOLOGICAL EVENTS FOR 2012 AND OUR TIMES

To gain a greater perspective of the significance and meaning of the times in which we are living, consider the following cosmological events and theories, many of which took place in the extraordinary year of 2012:

> **Ages shift**—The Western astrological system reveals the shifts of ages, when one great astrological age moves into another. As described in chapter 7, we are currently leaving the Age of Pisces and heading into the Age of Aquarius. It is not possible to pinpoint when exactly this occurs although astronomers and astrologers predict several different timelines for this to happen. What they do all agree on is that the current timeline of humanity is *the* moment when the shift between these two grand epochs is set to unfold. However, it takes hundreds of years to shift fully from one great astrological Age into another.
>
> **The orbit of our galaxy* around the Sun is completed**— It is believed that we are now at the completion point of a multimillion-year circular orbit of our galaxy around the great central Sun. (One orbit of the galaxy takes 225 to 250 million years, and it is understood to have completed between twenty and twenty-five orbits since it began.) Our galaxy moves through space in the form of continuous connecting circles like a great cosmic spiral. As it completes this multimillion-year orbit it is connecting

diagonally to the next ring in the spiral. When this happens all of the planets, solar systems, and their inhabitants simultaneously take an initiatory step into a new evolutionary cycle.

A twenty-six-thousand-year cycle ends—As mentioned in chapter 8, we are at the end of a twenty-six-thousand-year Earth/Sun/Galactic Plane cycle. From our perspective on Earth, the December Solstice Sun moves across the Galactic Plane every twenty-six thousand years. This results in an attunement of consciousness to higher frequencies. The December Solstice of 1998 was the midway point of the thirty-six-year window of time in the galactic alignment process. Because the Sun is so large, it did not complete its journey across the galactic equator until 2016. This process was predicted to induce extraordinary transformations in human Consciousness and will not be fully completed until December 21, 2021.

The end date of December 21, 2012—This end date was written as 13.0.0.0.0 in Mayan Long Count notation. It marked the end of the current era and the commencement of the next era in the Long Count calendar. The start of the current era in 3114 BCE is also written as 13.0.0.0.0. In the Maya philosophy of time, the end of a cycle is also the beginning of the next one, although some people referred to December 22, 2012 as the first day of the new cycle because it equated to 0.0.0.0.1.

A rare astrological formation appears—On December 21, 2012, Jupiter, Pluto, and Saturn were involved in an astrological formation known as a Yod (finger of God). This translated as a higher vision (Jupiter) being projected onto the physical plane (Saturn) and the aligning of the personal will with the Spiritual Will (Pluto).

A thirteen-year window closes—The year 2012 marked the completion of an instrumentally important phase of global awakening that accelerated exponentially in 1999 at the time of the Solar Eclipse. The ancient Maya referred to this thirteen-year window as the Quickening.

Field effect energy reversal—The widest part of the Milky Way is known as the dark rift, which corresponds to the direction of the center of the galaxy. The late John Major Jenkins, researcher of Mayan cosmology and philosophy and author of several books explains that "as the 2012 Winter Solstice Sun aligns with the dark rift and the solstice meridian, then passes to the other side of the center of the galactic equator, this will create a field effect energy reversal. As we resonate with the field sourced from the **Galactic Center***, we will be affected by this changing orientation."

Poles shift—The end of the Mayan Long Count calendar was believed to have culminated in a pole shift in the collective consciousness.

A rare Venus transit occurs—On June 6, 2012, there was a transit of Venus to the Sun as it traveled between the Sun and the Earth. This type of transit of Venus (known as pairs) happens twice in every eight years. The first of these pairs occurred on June 8, 2004, and the second on June 6, 2012. This will not be repeated until 2117. Scholars of ancient calendars state that the 2012 transit was rare and ancient metaphysicists revealed that a new world consciousness would be born during this time. The Maya appear to have understood that a Venus transit acted like a "circuit breaker," switching off the sunspot cycle and impacting the Sun, Moon, Earth, and Venus system. Every planet has its own unique frequency or rate of vibration and since ancient times Venus has been connected with divine and unconditional love. During a Venus/Sun transit the rays of the Sun amplify and direct the frequency of Venus toward the Earth bathing it in these energies for several hours.

Venus moves closer to the Pleiades—Venus moved closer to aligning with the Pleiades and was conjunct Alcyone, one of its stars, on April 3, 2012. Some believe that Alcyone holds the Akashic Records of the Earth.

Two rare Solar Eclipses occur—On May 20, 2012, there was a rare Solar Eclipse during which the Sun and the Moon were conjunct the Pleiades. A second Solar Eclipse on November 13, 2012 occurred close to the Serpens (serpent), which is found in Ophiuchus, the thirteenth constellation, and situated between Scorpio and Sagittarius. Ophiuchus is also known as the **shaman***/serpent healer.

THE LAST OF THIRTEEN, THIRTEEN-YEAR CYCLES

According to Maya cosmology, in 1999 humanity entered the last of thirteen, thirteen-year cycles. They prophesied that the start of this ultimate phase would occur at the time of the Solar Eclipse of that same year and would coincide with a rare planetary alignment known as a Grand Cross, which would involve the four fixed signs of the zodiac: Leo, Taurus, Scorpio, and Aquarius. Two thousand years prior to this rare cosmic occurrence the Bible prophesied that an angel with four faces—one of a lion, one of a bull, one of an eagle (another symbol for the sign of Scorpio), and one of a man—would be revealed to humanity.

The Maya foretold of the last thirteen years of the 5,125-year calendar being the final opportunity for modern civilization to embrace the changes that only become possible at a moment of collective spiritual regeneration. They also stated that during this ultimate window of time, an awakening percentage of humanity would undergo thirteen years of accelerated transformation that would raise their consciousness and vibration. Seven years into the thirteen-year phase (2006) humanity would face a time of great darkness and would be forced to confront the consequences of its actions. They spoke of entering the Sacred Hall of Mirrors, where we would need to look at ourselves and consider our conduct toward each other as well as the impact of our actions on the world.

SERPENT OF LIGHT

From 1999 to 2012, the Earth's Kundalini is said to have moved and realigned. Kundalini is the most powerful energy force on the planet. Known as the "serpent energy," it is located at the base of the spine in human beings. Kundalini tends to remain dormant unless activated by some kind of spiritual practice at which point it can be awakened. This sacred force can catalyze extraordinary transformations within the consciousness and energetic systems of an individual.

In his book *Serpent of Light,* author and writer Drunvalo Melchizedek speaks of the Earth as also having Kundalini energy that, unlike that of most humans, *is* active. He explains how this energy remains attached to one location for a 13,000-year period after which it relocates to another where it will remain for the next 13,000 years, a period of time that is based upon the precession of the equinoxes. When the serpent energy changes location, it is believed to herald a new spiritual era for humanity.

Melchizedek speaks of the Earth's Kundalini as having two poles: one at the exact center of the Earth and the other located at a specific point on its surface. He talks of a pulse of 12,920 years at which point the poles reverse. The Earth's own consciousness simultaneously shifts the Kundalini to its next location on its surface. According to Melchizedek, for the past 13,000 years the surface location of the Earth's Kundalini has been in Tibet. The process of relocating the serpent energy began in 1949, and it is now believed to reside in the Chilean Andes Mountains in South America. In *Spontaneous Evolution* Bruce Lipton and Steve Bhaerman cite the following: "The Dalai Lama has also spoken of it: He says he will be the last Dalai Lama from the Himalayas and that the next one will likely be from the other high mountains, the Andes."

HUMANITY'S DESTINY IS
IN OUR HANDS

Nobody could predict just what would unfold beyond the destined 12/21/2012 date, not even the Maya, Hopi, or other indigenous elders of our current times. All that the ancients could share was that a *major* ending of several grand cycles would occur at this time. Prophecies might not have revealed exactly what would happen, but each was emphatic that the destiny of humanity would be in our own hands. What we do know is that we have an unparalleled opportunity to cocreate a new Conscious paradigm. If we continue to support and uphold duality, then we can expect nothing more than the degeneration of the current global situation in terms of destruction and chaos.

The reality is that we have a one-way ticket to disaster unless we transform the way in which we think, act, and treat the Earth and each other. The relationship we have with our planet reflects the relationship we have with ourselves. We are a microcosm of the macrocosm that is our world. We need only look around us to observe the current state of the collective human consciousness. There are places of extraordinary beauty on this Earth just as there are places of heartbreaking destruction. When we look at the world, we are looking into a mirror: Whatever is within us is projected outside of us into the world.

For the Earth to be restored to her full glory we must first become the extraordinarily beautiful beings that we are. By uniting in Oneness, we can cocreate a world that is built upon love, care, and respect for humanity, Nature, all sentient beings, and all life-forms. We each have a spiritual responsibility to protect the world for future generations. If we join together in and as unconditional love and awakened Consciousness, we *can* fulfill the ancient prophecies of a new Golden Age manifesting in our times.

10

Your Soul's Purpose
and Planetary Rebirth

We are praying, many of the medicine people, the spiritual leaders, the elders, are praying for the world. We are praying that humankind does wake up and think about the future, for we haven't just inherited this Earth from our ancestors, but we are borrowing it from our unborn children.

JOSEPH CHASING HORSE

As we have seen in previous chapters, indigenous elders have been sending out a specific message to the world—a *warning* to humanity to change the way we live and how we treat the planet or prepare for the worst. For every 2012 prophecy that spoke of transition and transformation, there was also one that talked of destruction and apocalypse. We are in the window of crisis still, and we can rise or fall. It remains imperative that we unite to support the Earth in order to avert global catastrophe. Will we experience a new era of peace and harmony or continue to break down and destroy? Both potential outcomes are a possibility. We have a responsibility as human beings to contribute to the former if we are ever to manifest the ancient prophecies that foretell of a thousand years of peace.

As communities and as individuals we simply cannot continue in the way that we are. To believe there is nothing to be done *will* result in the worst-case scenario, so it is upon us now to act as empowered and compassionate forces for good and take immediate action if we are to avoid apocalyptic predictions such as those of Nostradamus. Complacency is our greatest hurdle; we cannot afford to remain indifferent to or ignorant of what we are facing, for our attitude and actions will determine a positive or negative outcome. Prophecies that foretell of a "golden millennium" speak of a *potential* outcome and of raising our consciousness and initiating a positive shift within the collective vibration.

Now is the time to take up the reins of our human and planetary destiny and to direct the course of our future instead of being taken for a ride by those *we have allowed* to control our destination. We need to establish a new way forward that serves the higher good of all. It is critical that we listen, take heed, and *act* upon the wisdom of ancient prophecies that speak of these transformative times. We cannot dismiss apocalyptic prophecies as sensationalism, for if we do it will be at our peril. How will we make a successful transition into a new Conscious world if we sit back waiting to see what will unfold?

It is time to take action and create a better world for each other and all life on Earth. It is time for us as a collective to say, "Enough!" For example, we have only to look around us to see the alarming decline of pollinators. If this continues, we may well find ourselves living in a world devoid of many of Nature's abundant and life-giving gifts.

Our compliance with and acceptance of the current world system reduces us to mere cogs in a machine driven by the agendas of global business, governments, consumerism, and industrial powers. It is our passive acceptance that keeps this machine going. We support the continuation of such a dysfunctional system when we expect a better future to manifest of its own accord or believe that a handful of activists will make this possible: We *all* need to "get global." An architect can hand you the design and building plans for a beautiful house but without your input, the house will not be built.

For the first time in human history there are no prophecies relating to our future, as these came to an end in December 2012. We have a blank slate upon which to write a new story for humanity. We are called to live in the *now,* with what *is,* and so re-create our future from moment to moment. Why do you imagine that ancient prophecies did not extend beyond 2012? Could it be that the wise ones of our past simply did not know if we would rise or fall at the time of the Great Shift of Ages? Many of the prophecies spoke of a transformation of human consciousness. By holding a positive intention, we can manifest this transformation and the promise of a visionary and new Conscious paradigm.

YOUR SOUL'S PURPOSE AND PLANETARY REBIRTH

We have each incarnated with a Soul mission, although most people never remember it because they are caught in life-denying patterns that originate from unresolved and unhealed historical, karmic, or ancestral wounding. Yet, these days more and more people are beginning to remember their higher purpose through the various spiritual and psychotherapeutic modalities that are now available to support healing, Self-integration, and Self-realization. Using the analogy of an onion, many have spent decades peeling back the layers to find their true Self: It is when we finally reach this core of our being that we *remember.*

It is possible to express our gifts in the world proactively without the *peeling away of the layers.* Many an accomplished philosopher, artist, writer, musician, poet, pioneer, inventor, healer, medium, or spiritual teacher has done so, and their contributions have been important to the world. This was possible because they *unconsciously* tapped into their higher purpose.

However, many, including great thinkers and creatives such as Wolfgang Amadeus Mozart, Vincent van Gogh, Leo Tolstoy, Howard Hughes, Oskar Schindler, and Rumi, alongside other extraordinary people living what might be deemed to be an ordinary life, remain unfulfilled in their personal lives because they are split off from their psychological shadow. Unless we heal our deepest trauma we will never experience true fulfillment.

When we incarnate, most of us forget our worldly "missions" and the gifts we came to share, and therefore fulfillment remains elusive, no matter how much we achieve by *doing*. We have forgotten how to BE, and this leaves us with an inner vacuum. This void develops in early childhood when our fundamental physical and emotional needs are unmet.

We need to channel our creative energy to re-find and redefine ourselves and so connect to our higher purpose and express this in the world. When we are psychologically integrated, consciously evolved, and spiritually awakened, we come to find ultimate fulfillment. Until that time, we will continue to be out of touch with the heart of living, or living from our hearts.

We can reclaim the lost Self by helping and supporting each other to remember our unique individuality as creators, and by doing so, help cocreate a new world. Embodying and living our glorious, empowered, and unique True Self *is* our important contribution.

As Mahatma Gandhi stated, "even if you are a minority of one, the truth is a truth." We must stand in our truth even if we are a lone voice in the crowd. Instead of investing our time, energy, and resources in trying to fill the insatiable void within, we need to realize that it is never too late to rediscover and embody our true Selves. To do so, we need to appreciate that we are not victims and that our suffering is largely of our own making.

Gandhi was an exceptional role model of passive resistance and demonstrated that change can be achieved through peaceful action. There are many organizations and resources online, in the local community, and in towns and cities that will support us to become empowered positive transformers of the current global system. We are not alone.

Those of us who think that we are not spiritual enough or are too wounded, too angry, too sad, too unworthy, or too unintelligent to align with our Soul's purpose need to liberate ourselves by recognizing that this is a myth we have believed for too long. We live in an era that invites us to *let go* of the past, not unconsciously as in repressing, splitting off, or denying but through acknowledgment, validation, deep understanding, and acceptance.

The higher frequencies associated with these times gift us with many effective therapeutic practices that offer us support to release the old and step into the new. Why hide in the shadow of your wounded self when you can step into the radiant light of your true Being? All too often we hold on to fears, hurts, and resistances like they were precious jewels; afraid to let them go because we have built an entire identity around them. We have forgotten who we truly are and have instead remained enslaved to our historical stories of suffering. If we refuse to let the past dictate the present we will go from strength to strength and our lives will be forever transformed.

We can make more loving choices and strive to maintain inner peace as a priority that we are no longer willing to compromise. With enough mindful practice, we can remain centered and calm and approach our emotional wounding and the healing that we need in a new empowered way. We can choose to respond rather than react to our own life stories and recognize the positive impact that doing so has on the lives of others and the world. In prioritizing inner peace, we walk, talk, think, feel, and act in peace and become beacons of peace radiating across the globe.

Letting go of the old (fear) and daring to step into the new (Love) allows us to experience the beauty of our Soul, and perhaps, for the first time in this life, come to know what peace and fulfillment truly are.

Fear's ultimate fear is to know, to feel, and to BE Love; enduring, adoring and true Love; the essence of unconditional Love; to fully surrender to Love; to remember it is Love; to become utterly consumed and transformed by Love. Anointed by pure and abiding Love, the thorn becomes the rose.

11

The Cosmology, Psychology, and Spirituality of a New Conscious Eon

Imagine living as LOVE; thinking, feeling, sensing, seeing, hearing, and BEing LOVE. This is how we heal and transform ourselves; this is how we heal and transform the world.

NICOLYA CHRISTI

In this chapter, I highlight some of the important astrological events that have influenced and will be influencing our world. These reflect a period of turmoil in service of change, which is already beginning to take place. The impact of the celestial giants of the zodiac is vastly underestimated. To put it simply, humankind may think it is making the rules by which we live, but the predominating factor is the influence of the Earth and the heavens. Many have heard the old adage "never wake a sleeping tiger" as one may be confronted by an insurmountable force of Nature. This is an apt analogy for the antics of an unconscious humanity in terms of the peril of ignoring forces that are way beyond its control.

Mother Nature has been patient and persevering and has tolerated the childish escapades of those who inhabit her up to a point, but the reality is that *she* will have the last word. The Earth and her galactic family are aligning together to shift the balance of "power" away from those who use it to destroy and into the hands of those who will utilize it to empower and inspire.

The Spirit of the Cosmos is indestructible, unlike human life. Do not wake the sleeping tiger but listen to the collective wisdom of the Cosmos and to what needs to be done to save ourselves from a catastrophic scenario of such magnitude it would be nigh impossible to recover from.

THE ASTROLOGY OF A NEW CONSCIOUS PARADIGM: THE GALACTIC ALIGNMENT ZONE (1975–2021)

The human evolutionary process began to exponentially accelerate in 1975 when we entered into a once-in-every-twenty-six-thousand-years cosmic phenomenon known as the Galactic Alignment Zone (GAZ). We moved into the most intense phase of this—the Quickening—in 1980, a window of time that concluded on December 21, 2016. The purpose of this period was to catalyze an unprecedented spiritual awakening and an unparalleled acceleration in the evolution of consciousness. As one might imagine, the lows of this rollercoaster ride brought many to their knees, yet the highs enabled them to soar to new dimensions that were simply beyond comprehension pre-1980.

Can you believe that we made it through an intense and all-consuming thirty-six-year personal evolutionary rite of passage as well as navigated the uncompromising energies of an accelerated global trajectory, which has, quite literally, taken humanity and Nature to the very edge of a tipping point? As the world teeters on the edge of catastrophe, something extraordinary is also occurring: millions of us are in the process of consciously transforming, or have already transformed, in preparation for *what is to come, who we must be,* and *what we must do.*

December 21, 2016, amounted to a momentous date for consciously awakened humanity as it drew a demarcation line between the pre- and post-galactic alignment Self. On that auspicious date, we stepped over a dimensional threshold. Now, in the progressive winds of evolutionary change we find ourselves standing strong and holding true to Love.

The GAZ.can be compared to the conception point when what is imprinted sets the evolutionary imperative and tone for what will unfold as we move out of the Age of Pisces and into the next two-thousand-year cycle that is the Age of Aquarius. It has afforded humanity a rare opportunity to rise out of the old paradigm and anchor into a new one and has offered an unprecedented turning point for those who are awakened and deeply committed to cocreating a new Conscious world. The GAZ has also brought radical and rapid evolution, and the time has now come for the individuals who passed through the eye of its storm to write a new story for the world.

As of this writing, we are still under the auspices and influence of the GAZ and will be until it finally closes on December 21, 2021. We can liken these final moments to a relay race, where the last and fastest sprinter is the one who can get the team over the finishing line. What we achieve by closing date will set the precedent for the decades, indeed centuries, to follow.

EVOLUTIONARY ASTROLOGY AND THE NEW PARADIGM: SETTING THE SCENE

The information presented below demonstrates the synchronicities between powerful astrological events and the instrumental messages these convey to humanity. They offer an indication of what is likely to unfold in terms of the political systems of the world and what significant related events will unfurl around the globe.

Uranus-Pluto Squares—June 24, 2012, to March 16, 2015

For many years, humanity was under the powerful and unpredictable influence of seven Uranus-Pluto **squares***. The objective of these two cosmic masters was to shatter, break down, and break apart the old constructs within us as individuals and also within the collective.

The impact of the Uranus-Pluto squares on our lives and in the world was that of a wrecking ball. Many of us felt the full force of these as our old personal realities were systematically dismantled. Such was the intensity of this evolutionary Call that, for many, life would never again be the same. Uranus and Pluto helped to break down the old constructs (unintegrated ego) within us. Deeply ingrained and detrimental patterns were shattered by the seven squares, which forced us to wake up and evolve. These took us out of our comfort zones by compelling us to explore attachments to the old that needed to be severed, while simultaneously pushing us into entirely new and unknown terrain.

Saturn-Neptune Squares—November 26, 2015, June 18, 2016, September 10, 2016

Near the end of 2015, Saturn and Neptune also formed a series of challenging squares, the first of which occurred on November 26, 2015, the second on June 18, 2016, and the third on September 10, 2016. The specific purpose of these planetary transits was to help us establish a new story for humanity and the world.

From an evolutionary perspective, Saturn represents the reality of living in a third-dimensional world with all the limitations we face within a physical body. Neptune is our connection to our multidimensionality and to SOURCE. The meeting between these planets afforded humanity an opportunity to manifest a higher vision (Neptune) into physical reality (Saturn). These squares mirrored the archetypal Heaven on Earth directive that we each carry within our psyche, our essence, and our Superconscious Mind. Saturn represents the left hemisphere of the brain and our ability to think logically, while Neptune rules the intuitive right brain and abstract thinking. Together they offered humanity the potential to balance these two hemispheres and so begin to move beyond the experience of duality.

The eclectic mix of Neptune and Saturn placed idealism and realism under the spotlight of conscious awareness. These heavenly beings helped bridge the gap between the physical and the spiritual, the earthly and the heavenly, the unintegrated ego and the true Self, materialism and altruism, and the human shadow and our highest ideals. When the psychological shadow remains unintegrated our individual purpose and higher vision for humanity will not fully manifest. With the integrating of these diverse planetary energies, however, we become potent forces for global harmony.

In its role as the celestial taskmaster, Saturn is concerned with strengthening the container of Self so it can receive the vision, insight, and inspiration of Neptune. Throughout the years between December 2012 and December 2021, we have been and are being forced to ask some fundamental questions as events around the globe spiral further out of control. As we reevaluate our own lives and the world around us, we are strengthened by Saturn and inspired by Neptune to make the changes that the evolutionary Call of these times is impressing upon us.

The Uranus-Pluto and Saturn-Neptune squares presented us with unique and transformational challenges and opportunities for refining, defining, and redefining ourselves with respect to who we truly are and why we are really here. Many of us were pushed to a personal evolutionary tipping point that would bring life-changing realizations and rapid inner transformation. The Saturn-Neptune phase was tantamount to a rite of passage; one that could support a new narrative for our lives. This celestial mix left many people unsure about who they really were and unclear about their role in the world; they began to question everything about their lives, including their beliefs.

Saturn-Pluto Dance—2019

The year 2019 was dominated by the influence of Saturn and Pluto, which became exactly aligned in Capricorn on December 1, 2020. The last time that these two met in Capricorn was about five hundred years ago in January 1518.

Saturn represents the structure of society and the objective of this meeting was to bring the full force of Pluto's shadow (destructive) energy to Earth to initiate radical transformation. This notable astrological event heralded a further intensification of both the personal and the collective evolutionary process and has helped to build more solid foundations for the years to come.

Pluto is symbolic of the huge corporations that control our planet, which by 2019 were becoming increasingly accountable for the impact of their devastating policies and actions. This was the beginning of the end of the negative global patriarchy. Many conscious individuals and groups as well as initiatives and movements around the globe were beginning to see the potential for turning the tide from the world-wide authoritarian model of a *love of power* to the light of socioevolutionary progress inspired and led by the *power of Love*. Civil unrest and social rebellion were the key words for 2019 as people across the planet began to more fully awaken to the truth of authoritarian manipulation and the abuse of the collective. It marked a tipping point when an awakening world said "Enough!"

The influence of Pluto in Capricorn (an earth sign) subjected the Earth to extreme weather patterns, some of which were natural but others of which were engineered. These brought disruption to the status quo and facilitated a further wake-up call for the collective in regard to the natural world and its finely tuned ecosystem. The previous Saturn/Pluto **conjunction*** in Capricorn in 1518 brought about the European Reformation that sparked a religious, social, economic, and political revolution. Five hundred years later we were given the opportunity once again to sow the seeds of revolution for the empowerment of humanity.

Chiron Moves into Aries—2018/2019 to 2027

The asteroid Chiron arrived on the astronomical radar in 1977 heralding the birth of a new age of "alternative healing." It opened a channel to the Soul, as its objective is to bridge the physical and the mystical, and its holistic purpose is to bring together the mind, body, emotions, and spirit. The position of Chiron in an astrological chart indicates the origins of our deepest psychospiritual, historical, ancestral and karmic wounds, and the means by which one can heal not only themselves but others as well. One of the main objectives of Chiron throughout the two-thousand-year era of the Piscean Age was to help humanity heal the concept of suffering and separation by forcing us to confront both personally and collectively whatever held us back from moving to the next level of the evolutionary spiral.

In May 2018, Chiron initially entered Aries; it moved back and forth between Pisces and Aries until March 2019 when it became permanently stationed in Aries until May 2027. This major astrological event will bring about an unparalleled phase in personal and global healing and a new age of regeneration. Chiron's passage through Aries initiates a time of exciting, revolutionary, and evolutionary discovery in the fields of healing and "aging." Solutions will be found for many of the illnesses and diseases that are so much a part of the old paradigm. What will emerge is a whole new approach that will be sourced from Nature, the Earth, the Sun, and frequencies emitted from the Galactic Center. Everything we need to organically heal and support our overall health will be accessed through these natural channels.

And when Neptune joins Chiron in Aries in March 2025 we will begin to witness the physical manifestation of the many ideas and ideals that will arise out of the current Neptune transit through Pisces, which began in February 2012.

Jupiter-Saturn Conjunction at 0 Degrees Aquarius— December 21, 2020

The Jupiter-Saturn conjunction that occurred on December 21, 2020, was an important astrological event, for these two planetary heavyweights entered the sign of Aquarius that day. Looking through the planetary tables as far back as 7 BCE, no Jupiter-Saturn conjunction at this degree could be found, revealing what a truly rare phenomenon it was. The meeting of these two celestial bodies not only initiated new beginnings and a new era but was a precursor to the imminent arrival of the astrological great Age of Aquarius.

The Piscean Age we are leaving is symbolized by the words *I believe*. Operating from the level of the emotional body, people have looked outside of themselves for spiritual guidance and an understanding of the world around them. In the Aquarian Age, *I believe* is superseded by *I Know,* and information comes from the mental body of each individual, not from any external source. The focus on personal consciousness will give way to group consciousness and in this new Aquarian Age, we are all ultimately given the opportunity to connect to our **interdimensional selves***.

Pluto Leaves Capricorn—2024

Pluto finally leaves Capricorn to move into Aquarius in January 2024. This can be understood as the true beginning of the Age of Aquarius and signifies the end of the Age of Pisces, an epoch that lasted over two thousand years. Pluto's move into Aquarius heralds the beginning of a new era founded upon a higher Consciousness when we will begin to discover how to live, age, and create in ways that are both revolutionary and evolutionary. The Aquarian Age will introduce an extraordinary new eon of technological revolution and groundbreaking inventions. At this point, Uranus, Aquarius's ruling planet will still be in the Earth sign of Taurus, where it will facilitate and support the anchoring of the evolutionary objective of Pluto.

Neptune Leaves Pisces—2026

In January 2026, Neptune will take leave of Pisces, not to return for another 170 years. Its purpose in this sign, which marks the end point of the zodiac, is to finally dissolve our overattachment to the past. Its departure will herald the end of the Piscean Age, as Neptune moves into Aries—the starting point of the zodiacal system. Those who are consciously awakened at that time will experience a dissolution of their old story.

Pluto in Aquarius: November 2024–January 2044

From 2008, when Pluto entered the sign of Capricorn, the battle for global power exploded exponentially. Pluto's objective is to shatter all organizations, governments, institutions, and huge corporations that seek to manipulate, control, and enslave the collective. The vast majority of people still look to external authority for answers and have forgotten how to think for themselves. As Pluto prepares to enter Aquarius in the next couple of years, this is all set to change.

We are now living in the death throes of the darkness that has overtaken our planet. We are on the brink of leaving servitude behind and the balance of power will shift out of the hands of the few and into the hands of an awakened and empowered collective as Pluto brings with it a new vision for humanity.

Pluto represents transformation and death of the old form. In Aquarius, we will come to understand that we are an intricate part of a much vaster conscious network we call our Galaxy. Ultimately, the balance of power will tip resulting in greater freedom for all human beings. The new agenda will be a humanitarian one, with the focus on groups and communities as we move toward decentralization.

From March 2023 until Pluto fully enters Aquarius in November 2024, the status quo will crumble and we will experience the transition from the old and how things were, to the new and what is waiting to be born. Societies will rapidly transform as new technologies, new science, and new medicine determine how we live in the future. From now until that time however, we will experience a period of dissolution and chaos as corrupt systems and individuals, along with self-serving organizations and corporations, are held to account.

We will bear witness to mass uprisings, resistance, and rebellion as the old establishment is dismantled. The unscrupulous and unprincipled will be exposed and oppressive controlling regimes and hierarchies will fall. We ourselves will need to engage in nonviolent action that will enable a new and more wholistic vision of a global society to emerge under the conscious stewardship of the collective.

Humanity will take an evolutionary leap as Pluto journeys through Aquarius, but, as in any birth, inevitably, the labour may prove to be difficult. Out of necessity we must now rise up to challenge the powers that be and reclaim our freedom. Only then can we come together, and, by working with Nature, instead of against it, restore balance and harmony to our beautiful planet.

2024 marks the beginning of the end of the seismic impact of the Saturn-Pluto conjunction, which took place in January 2020. This major astrological event triggered the world-changing crises we are currently living through.

From 2024 to 2026, something of a rare nature will occur as the three transpersonal outer planets—Pluto, Neptune, and Uranus—all change astrological signs. By 2025, they will be working together to support rapid and extremely positive global shifts that will enable humanity to forge ahead into a brand-new future.

THE EVOLUTIONARY CALL OF OUR TIMES

For the past few decades, those who have been consciously awakening have been deeply engaged in healing and integration, which are both part of the evolutionary Call of a new paradigm.

I first began to write about a new paradigm in March 2009 in my book *2012: A Clarion Call*. In early January 2013, after four years of writing almost every day, I found myself staring at a blank slate with absolutely nothing to share. I knew then that humankind had entered entirely new terrain. I recognized that before we could even begin to write a new story, it was necessary to anchor ourselves in the evolutionary new landscape that was unfolding. As the weeks, months, and years passed by, I realized that the physical reality of arriving in and cocreating a new paradigm was going to take a lot longer than I had first anticipated.

Many people are sensing a fundamental need to radically transform the physical, emotional, mental, psychological, energetic, and spiritual aspects of their lives. Some may experience this through manifesting a serious or life-threatening condition from which a good percentage will eventually recover, and a handful may even astound the medical community by doing so. Sometimes the reason for encountering such a challenge is to help shatter and reset our personal identity and belief systems. In every such case, there is always a specific evolutionary purpose.

The Call of our times is upon us and urging us to wake up, step up, and step into our roles as cocreators of a new Conscious paradigm. In our commitment to embody the truth of who we really are we realize the extent to which the searing heat of the evolutionary burn is transforming us. We live in the most auspicious times that afford a rare opportunity to take a giant leap in our evolutionary development both as individuals and as a collective. Those who are dedicated to personal transformation can also exert a direct influence on global evolution. The more integrated, evolved, awakened, and heart centered we are, the greater the impact of our presence in the world.

INTENTION, VISUALIZATION, MEDITATION, AND PRAYER

In the shadow of a global authoritative machine that is firmly entrenched in duality and separation, we might well wonder how such a system can be positively transformed. To put it simply, the answer is through *Love.* When enough people join together with a unified vision and intention, especially when working through the mediums of prayer, visualization, and meditation, effecting a physically tangible and visible change becomes possible. This is not merely an ideal without any basis in reality; it has been scientifically proven, recorded, and officially documented as shown in the following examples.

In the late 1980s Princeton University in the United States conducted a research program titled the Global Consciousness Project that set about proving that human feelings affect the quantum field. The same principle was applied in recorded experiments that took place during the Israeli-Lebanese war in the mid-1980s. In 1988, the *Journal of Conflict Resolution* wrote about these experiments in an article titled "The International Peace Project of the Middle East" in which it documented the activities and results of a group of peace activists who had been placed in various war-torn locations. Each one of them was working with a mode of prayer in which one feels the feeling of peace as if it had already happened.

During the window of prayer, terrorist activity was observed to have dropped to *zero*. Targeted experiments took place on different days, weeks, and months, at varying times, and still it was scientifically recorded that when people prayed in unison with a single focus of feeling the feeling of peace as if it were already so, the results were always the same: a dramatic reduction or total absence of violence or conflict. It was shown that distance was a nondetermining factor as experiments were conducted across the internet with thousands of participants from all over the world. Statisticians have determined that the exact number of people required to do this successfully equates to the square root of 1 percent of any given target population. There are nearly eight billion people in the world, and it has been cited that just over eight thousand are needed to do this to effect a change.

It is important that the prayer comes from the depths of the heart and is *felt* as a whole-body prayer, so the energy of love and conviction flows through the cells, organs, skin, and blood of the body as well as the mind and the Soul. This is then transmitted into the quantum field. This proven phenomenon is one way that we, together, can create peace. Imagine just one billion people (the total audience that watched the 2018 football World Cup) *feeling the feeling of peace on earth as if it had already happened* . . . this could truly change the world. The challenge is to be able to continue to hold that feeling in almost every moment.

Feeling Is a Prayer

In his book *The Secrets of the Lost Mode of Prayer: The Hidden Power of Beauty, Blessings, Wisdom, and Hurt,* New York Times bestselling author Gregg Braden states the following:

The secret of the lost mode of prayer is to shift our perspective of life by feeling that the miracle has already happened and our prayers have been answered. Now we have the opportunity to bring this wisdom into our lives as prayers of gratitude for what already exists, rather than asking for our prayers to be answered.

Feeling is prayer in its purest and most potent form. Whether we are in love, peace, joy, fear, sadness, or anger, we are praying all of the time because our feelings *are* prayers. Human beings are *feeling beings,* and so life itself is a living prayer. As long as we hold peace, love, and joy in our hearts, our lives on Earth reflect this. All that we most long for—beauty, joy, love, fulfillment, unity, harmony, and peace—are only a *prayer* away. Imagine what life on Earth would be like if nearly eight billion people were all experiencing the same feelings of beauty and love *at the same time*? Transform our feelings, and we transform the world.

The peace centers of the Zen Master Thich Nhat Hanh are examples of where the practice of holding a vision of a world that is thriving in peace and love is alive and strong. A great bell tolls at regular times, calling the entire community to stop whatever they are doing, pause, and mindfully center themselves in peace and love. It *is* possible to feel the *feeling of peace* in every moment. The answer to global peace is to be found within each one of us. *Love is the answer* and we by our very nature are Love: We truly are the change we wish to see in the world.

Deep conviction and an unshakeable belief in an ideal outcome are powerhouses for transformation. As Jesus was reported to have said, you can renew your life with your beliefs. Two thousand years later and quantum physics and cutting-edge science are telling us the same thing. Almost eight billion people are communicating with the quantum field *all of the time,* and this field is a reflection of both the consciousness and unconsciousness of the collective. In observing the world around us, we begin to gain some insight into the physical, emotional, mental, and psychological state of the people who inhabit it.

Love Is a Living Prayer

Humans are fundamentally loving beings and in that we could say that Life and Love are a living prayer. Love, joy, unity, harmony, peace, and fulfillment are only a prayer away. Imagine the square root of 1 percent of the world's population *feeling the feelings* of these beautiful states and radiating Love *all of the time* . . . that would *indeed* be a Golden Age.

Personal and global transformation and the cocreation of Heaven on Earth become real possibilities when we join together as empowered beings bonded in the Consciousness of Oneness. The experiments conducted on the impact of collective intention for transformation demonstrate that trauma and crime are dramatically reduced when a unified group focuses on feeling the feeling as if *it* (whatever is being focused on) has already happened. Yet, the same experiments also revealed that the measurable results were temporary. This is most likely because after the prayer events had concluded, many of the participants would have returned to their everyday lives, which may not have reflected the ideals they had been praying for. Immersed back into the field of a dysfunctional and disharmonious world, on an unconscious level they were, once again, entrained with aspects of it.

The degree to which we are able to maintain a lasting effect is dependent upon the degree to which we are psychologically integrated, consciously evolved, and spiritually awakened. It is not enough to inspire others to champion personal and global peace as a priority, if we ourselves remain caught in duality consciousness that supports a dystopian world. We each need to become Self-aware, Self-responsible, and Self-accountable. It is our unstinting efforts to heal and become integrated at the deepest levels of our own being that will transform us into inspired visionaries and effective cocreators of a peaceful and harmonious world.

The answer to the question, How do we transform a system that is dysfunctional and corrupt? is Love, and joining together in and as Love, in our hundreds, thousands, millions, and billions and feeling the feeling of peace on Earth as if it is already so.

In 2013, I wrote twenty-two contemporary prayers for inner and world peace. The following verse is taken from one that is titled "Sovereign Being I AM":

See only through the eyes of an Exalted Being
Listen only with the ears of an Exalted Being
Respond only with the wisdom of an Exalted Being
Love only with the heart of an Exalted Being

When billions of people are centered in Love and have attained a state of sustained inner peace then world peace automatically follows. Fundamentally, there are two abiding questions we can apply to any situation: What would love do? What would love have me do? These questions take us out of our minds and into our hearts and serve as new paradigm mantras for these transformational times.

A NEW LIFE STORY

The early days of a new life story can be likened to the game of *Snakes* (or *Chutes*) and *Ladders:* many ladders (inspirational new stories) may be climbed before we meet a snake (the dysfunctional part of an old story) and slide a little or a long way back. It may be a while before we are able to move beyond the snakes to maintain our course. Embracing a new story does not mean that every part of our life has to completely transform all at once. In some cases, it can be that extreme, yet, for the majority, it usually involves changing one or two aspects at a time—for example, our job or work, separating from a significant other, a life-changing move, or a totally fresh approach to health, diet, and lifestyle.

When we are ready to fully embrace a new story, we can lift ourselves out of our old reality. What was once tolerated yet failed to bring overall fulfillment may no longer have a place in our lives, as we prioritize a balanced, integrated, and loving relationship with ourselves, with others, and with the world. Embodying a new story can be uncompromising as we are required to transcend our historically charged emotions and enter the more refined arena of our *feelings*. In doing so, we discover that we can free the energy that is still caught up in perpetuating and maintaining old stories.

TRANSPARENT HEART:
TRANSCENDENT WORLD

An unknown source once gifted the world with the following wisdom: "Live in such a way that if someone spoke badly of you no one would believe it." To live transparently is to live with an open and honest heart, to walk a path of integrity, honor, and love. It is to *live Love*. When first committing to such a way of BEing, the effect may be similar to that of a dietary fast, as layer upon layer of energetic, mental, and emotional toxins that have collected around the heart start to clear after a lifetime (or lifetimes) of social conditioning that has sought to suppress truth at all costs. The world has learned to repress and deny truth, barely recognize truth, or be woefully fearful of truth. In whatever way we have hidden our truth, it has always been at the cost of our own heart.

Yet we are afraid to be honest because of the propensity of others to name, shame, polarize, and blame; to judge, compare, separate, and react (not *respond*). Many of us have been taught from the earliest age that to tell the truth, the whole truth, and nothing but the truth would bring about an undesired outcome. Most of us bear witness to dishonesty in all its guises from the subtle to the overt. From an impressionable age we mimic the actions, reactions, and interactions of those around us as well as a world that demonstrates that honesty is not always the best policy. To be transparent is to be courageous (*coeur* in French means "heart").

A transparent heart is a new paradigm heart that is free of deception and leaves no trace of harm in its wake. A transparent heart is a peaceful heart that neither bargains, justifies, or compromises. It follows a pure path and is trustworthy, steadfast, and tender. It is a heart of beauty and harmony and strives to bring these qualities to all it encounters. A transparent heart is a sovereign heart, a noble heart. It is a compassionate, empathic, and healing heart.

A transparent heart is altruistic in its actions and calls forth the transparent heart in others. When we speak from this heart, our intentions are founded in purity, care, sensitivity, and understanding, and this empowers all. The mind alone is unable to translate the language of Love in its purest essence; this is the sovereign domain of a transparent heart.

In 2011, I wrote the following about a transparent heart and posted it on YouTube:

> A transparent heart is a heart that is completely clear.
> If we imagine a crystal heart held up to the light,
> You could see straight through it.
> It would be completely clear.
> No shadow.
> Nothing hiding.
> Nothing lurking.
> Just, completely clear.
> A transparent heart invites us to be completely honest, to express our truth, to speak our truth with compassion and sensitivity and let the chips fall where they may.
> To embody a transparent heart takes courage.
> And we live in a society; are raised in a way where we are taught not to be transparent. However, if we can learn this completely natural way of being, then the world becomes transcendent because seven billion people on the planet living with a completely transparent heart create a transcendent world.
> We are lifted up to a whole new realm of relating—of BEing.

It takes authenticity, strength, integrity, and commitment to adopt a living and breathing practice of transparency in every moment. Living transparently changes lives; however, it is likely to bring challenges to existing routines, relationships, and lifestyles, and elements of these may need to fall away. The deepest psychospiritual wound is said to be that of separation, which is believed to replicate the "original" (perceived) wound of separation from GOD/SOURCE/THE DIVINE. Yet, if the core of this is to be found in the psychological wound of disconnection from another, then its deepest healing is also to be found in connection with another: *our deepest wounds are formed in relationship and therefore our deepest healing is to be found in relationship.* A transparent heart is the greatest force for healing and transformation if one is ready to embrace this extraordinary and most rewarding way of loving and living.

Living from an open heart compels one toward a sensory relationship that mirrors our true identity as LOVE. A line from a song "Trumpets" by Mike Scott and the Waterboys makes reference to the heart as being "like a church with wide open doors." When our heart is incorruptible and ever virtuous we are *living transparency.*

I AM, YOU ARE, WE ARE LOVE

The answer to all of our questions is really very simple: Love. *Love is the answer to everything.* A new Conscious paradigm requires us to see, speak, and listen with our hearts, and to Love unconditionally. I conclude this chapter with another contemporary spiritual prayer for inner and world peace titled "LOVE":

> *Love—All Beings*
> *Love—Everything*
> *Be—Only Love*
> *Surrender—All Fear*
> *Be Love*
> *Speak—Only Light*
> *Surrender—All That Is Darkness Within You*
> *BE—Love*
> *Speak—Only Truth*
> *Hide—No Longer*
> *Live Truth*
> *Know—Who You Truly Are*
> *Trust—Who You Truly Are*
> *Live—Who You Truly Are*
> *BE—Who You Truly Are*

Love Can Never Be Lost
Love Is Never Poor
Love Is Who You Are
Love Is Light
Love Is Pure
You Are Love

12

New Earth and Future Earth

Imagine a future age in which the Actualized Self is the evolutionary phenomenon by which that age is defined.

NICOLYA CHRISTI

In this final chapter, I share a spontaneous and extraordinary channeling* that flowed through me in 2006. In a matter of minutes, the extensive information presented below was set out before me on paper. It had, literally, arrived in one uninterrupted stream. Essentially, the channeling reveals the existence of three separate yet interconnected Earths. It explains how our current third-dimensional world will continue to play host to a third-dimensional consciousness, and how those with a fifth-dimensional Consciousness will inhabit what is being spoken of as the "New Earth." Beings whose Consciousness is beyond fifth-dimensional (mostly off-planet in terms of both the Existing and New Earths) will be located on the Future Earth, and many of these Beings will serve as overlighting Guides and Teachers for humans on both the Existing and New Earths.

EXISTING EARTH, NEW EARTH, AND FUTURE EARTH

Before I share the information I received in the channeling, I shall first offer further clarity on the differences between the Existing Earth,

New Earth, and Future Earth. From the perspective of Consciousness, the human collective on the Existing Earth is predominantly third-dimensional and for the most part exhibits unconscious, unawakened, and unevolved awareness, or consciousness with a small *c*. What we term the New Earth is the Existing Earth but expressed from a higher octave and is host to a fifth- through ninth-dimensional planetary Consciousness, with a capital *C*. The Future Earth is the most highly advanced and supra-evolved of all three, as it hosts a supremely awakened CONSCIOUSNESS that encompasses the ninth to thirteenth dimensions and is an ultimate dimensional destination for a Soul incarnate in human form.

A NOTE ON THE
TWENTY-SIX DIMENSIONS

As mentioned earlier, I propose that there are twenty-six dimensions in total and that these divide into two evolutionary halves: one to thirteen (the aspect of Soul embodied in human form) and thirteen to twenty-six (the transcended Soul expressing as SOURCE CONSCIOUSNESS). The thirteenth dimension is the midpoint and is about to be brought into the awareness of Consciously awakened beings on Existing Earth.

As the thirteenth dimension becomes accessible in a metaphysical sense, the Consciousness of awakened human beings on Existing Earth will begin to rapidly evolve. Receptors within the **Light body***
will begin to activate and so enable individuals to align to a higher-dimensional Consciousness.

At present the mass consciousness of Existing Earth is third dimensional, and is dominated by the left hemisphere of the brain. As humans on Existing Earth begin to align more fully with fifth-dimensional Consciousness, a significant increase in activity will occur within the right brain. This Consciousness is more hemispherically synchronized and will greatly accelerate and facilitate the conscious evolution of humanity. The evolutionary trajectory of the human incarnate Soul compels it toward the thirteenth dimension, while an Enlightened Consciousness is propelled toward the twenty-sixth.

So, New Earth hosts Souls who are journeying between the fifth and ninth dimensions, and Future Earth is the destination of those whose evolution and awakening leads them to the thirteenth. Levels beyond this remain a mystery. The twenty-sixth dimension is where the Soul (not the Consciousness) completes its journey and ultimately dissolves, while the Consciousness (potentially) continues through SOURCE and BEYOND.

The Great Teachers, Councils, Elders, and Guides of higher-dimensional New Earth are themselves barely able to comprehend just what exists beyond the thirteenth dimension. What has been understood is that the thirteenth to twenty-sixth dimensions are the "other side of Soul." So, the first thirteen dimensions relate to the aspect of Soul embodied in human form and its journey on all three Earths.

The thirteenth dimension is the "bridge" and the place where the earthbound Soul attains the state of Self-transcendence. Until the thirteenth dimension, the human and divine blueprint are unfolding in their unique expression as embodied SOURCE in ascending manifestations of human form, i.e., from a physical body to a Light body. The thirteenth through the twenty-sixth dimensions are the realms where pure Consciousness expresses *only* as pure SOURCE.

THE EXISTING EARTH/NEW EARTH/ FUTURE EARTH CHANNELING

The following is the information that was spontaneously channeled through me in 2006.

✳ Existing Earth ✳

On Existing Earth, beings are evolving from a third-dimensional consciousness to a fifth-dimensional Consciousness. Many perceive that Earth is ascending, which, from the perspective of CONSCIOUSNESS, is a reality. As a planetary Consciousness, existing Earth is in the process of rebirthing and, eventually, in the far distant future, will host all dimensions and become a celestial paradise owing to the unique Nature that can only be found there. Existing Earth is a dominion where Souls choose to incarnate in order to continue the clearing and dissolution process of accrued third-dimensional karma, which they also do on behalf of the Collective.

In the old paradigm of Existing Earth individuals are afforded the opportunity to evolve through suffering. It is there that compassion, empathy, understanding, and unconditional love are the greatest of lessons. These are best learned through many challenges. Even the wisest of spiritual teachers have had to experience suffering and overcome this in order to teach and guide humanity. To be alive on Existing Earth and not experience suffering is nigh impossible given her contract with the Higher Intelligences that govern all of life. So, billions of incarnating Souls are predestined to fulfill particular contracts with a planet whose own Consciousness has chosen a very specific role.

Great sacrifices have been made by Existing Earth to support those who inhabit her to heal, grow, and evolve. In her willingness to offer herself as a place for healing through suffering, she has brought suffering to herself. She has given unconditionally in her quest to facilitate the Conscious Evolution of all sentient beings that reside upon her. Yet, with sacrifice there are great rewards, if not in a single lifetime, then in one that is yet to come. Existing Earth is about to reap the benefits for all she has given by ultimately becoming a Cosmic Paradise. This is part of the Greater Plan.

Existing Earth is evolving from a third-dimensional "consciousness" to a fifth-dimensional Consciousness, and may eventually play host to visitors from all dimensions. Her **ascension*** *is the same as that of ascending humans in the respect that all old paradigm imprints of suffering are to be left behind. Think of someone who through a life of suffering has evolved into a highly developed individual. If they are to reincarnate, they can choose to experience far more conducive and harmonious circumstances— and so it is with existing Earth.*

Nearing the completion of her historical life cycle, Existing Earth is close to approaching her own ascension. During her rebirthing, those who are Consciously awakened have sensed her process rapidly accelerating since December 21, 2012.

✳ The New Earth ✳

New Earth has transcended karma. In this higher expression of Existing Earth, Souls learn through Love not through suffering, and the New Earth is a dimension where a Soul choosing to evolve in human form can do so through Love and Love alone.

To once again clarify the differences between New Earth and Future Earth from a dimensional perspective, New Earth hosts the fifth to ninth levels of Consciousness, while Future Earth hosts the ninth to thirteenth dimensions. Awakened beings on New Earth are evolving along a trajectory of fifth to ninth-dimensional Consciousness and therefore experience greater brain entrainment and DNA-strand activation. They operate from a divine blueprint, not the genetic imprint of those within Existing Earth.

Extraordinary feats are possible beyond the sixth and seventh dimensions on New Earth that include teleporting and bilocating, which means they will be able to travel anywhere through thought, both on and off the planet. Highly evolved futuristic systems of communication exist there, and each one is an infinitely advanced version of what is currently in place within Existing Earth.

Cell phones, landline telephones, microwave, digital, or Wi-Fi systems, or any of the old paradigm technologies of Existing Earth are not found beyond the sixth dimension. All communication systems across all dimensions on New Earth are ultrasophisticated, innately intelligent, and work in harmony with the natural waveforms of planetary energies and resonant solar and galactic frequencies, along with the resources to be found in Nature.

New Earth has an interconnecting system termed InfoVision, which informs through vision and the senses. This is a highly evolved communications network sourced by the Outernet that powers all technological devices and is a super-advanced technology that is 100 percent benign and, indeed, emits life-enhancing frequencies as well as life-resourcing electromagnetic waves.

InfoVision is an interactive supremely advanced version of the television to be found on Existing Earth. It exists solely for the purpose of informing, evolving, connecting, enlightening, and illuminating. All that is available to view is for experiencing, inspiring, uplifting, and/or facilitating sublime relaxation. There are neither "celebrity" nor "fantasy" stories providing "escape." Violence, whether verbal, physical, or originating from a thought field, is entirely absent. There are no degenerative subjects of any kind; instead, profound works of art are often depicted through film and convey inspirational realities that span great cycles of "time." Stories that express the extraordinary and the poetic, and prose, art, creativity, and music that transports can be experienced through InfoVision, which serves to raise vibration, open the heart, enlighten the mind, and awaken the Soul.

Communication through telepathy is common due to a greater portion of the brain being active in those on New Earth. One simply thinks of someone they wish to connect with and, if the channel for doing so in another is "open to receive," they can link in. Thought-field communication is central.

On New Earth, basic physiology has upgraded from carbon to crystalline, and this is reflected in what is fundamentally its crystalline-based technology.

Health, Emotions, Sexuality

On New Earth, as one reaches the higher level of fifth-dimensional Consciousness one begins to transcend sickness and aging. From the sixth dimension beyond there is no sickness because there is no suffering. Healing continues within the third, fourth, and lower-dimensional levels of the fifth; yet in the higher levels such patterns, blueprints, and all such residuals dissolve.

On New Earth, there are no private health care systems because there is an absence of illness. Beings do not degenerate as they do on Existing Earth. In the lower fifth dimension, rather than medical centers and clinics there are "wellness" and "attunement" centers where the focus is on maintaining balance with the support of vibrational practices and remedies. These are far advanced by comparison to those on Existing Earth. At this level, it is not so much about healing, but of rebalancing, realigning, and refining one's internal energy system as dissolution of shadow imprints from the third and fourth dimensions is taking place. As a Being evolves into the higher octaves of the fifth dimension, all imbalances dissipate, dissolve, and dematerialize.

Fifth to ninth-dimensional Consciousness is one of unquestionable understanding of one's own eternal nature, and this enables a continual regeneration of the cells; thus the old learning templates of sickness, disease, degeneration, and aging are transcended.

Beings have little preoccupation with their physical appearance for their focus is on the evolution of Consciousness. When gazing upon their own image, or that of another, they see only emanating, amplified Light in various strengths and hues and immense pleasure is gained from absorbing its various layers.

The brilliance of Light radiating from a Being determines the degree to which their Consciousness has awakened. Experiences of insecurity, inadequacy, fear, envy, jealousy, anger, greed, guilt, sadness, shame, or pain are absent because the emotional body has been transcended. Instead, Beings on New Earth are encouraged and inspired by those more luminous than themselves who radiate greater levels of Light. The Light emitted by those on both New and Future Earth renders everyone "beautiful."

Light pours forth from the heart and the eyes and through the skin and the smile. Nothing is enjoyed more than basking in the shining Light of others, which also helps to magnify one's own. The more dazzling the Light, the more advanced the Being. Even the least radiant Light brings joy and beauty to all.

On fifth-dimensional New Earth, sexual energy is still experienced in the physical only in an infinitely refined way. Centered in and expressing *predominantly through the heart and crown chakras, although all chakras are involved, pure, unadulterated love defines sexual union, which is an extraordinary and transcendent phenomenon. Beings are enveloped in and transmit an indescribable array of otherworldly tones and colors, which not only infuse New Earth but can also reach Existing Earth, helping to heal as well as awaken lovers and beloveds to an elevated experience of higher-dimensional Love.*

True Beloveds—Love on New Earth

On Existing Earth, tens of thousands of individuals have awoken to the understanding that the next stage of the evolution of their heart is to reunite with what is known there as the "twin flame." This is very different from the "Soul mate" of which there are many, in the guise of lovers, mothers, fathers, brothers, sisters, children, friends, partners, "foes," and "adversaries."

Various fusing and infusing processes occur throughout many spirals ("time" as measured by Existing Earth standards) in preparation for the transmutation of a single system (one Being) into a dual system (two beings), to be expressed as a unified system of One Being.

When many spirals fully merge, the newly unified One Being has become androgynous. In this state of androgynous Oneness they continue the journey through all remaining dimensions as One awakened, evolving, and transcending Consciousness. Full unification as One is achieved somewhere between the seventh and the ninth dimensions.

Most beings on New Earth are immersed in varying stages of the "blending" process. Those who are not tend to be the off-planet beings, Teachers, Councils, and Collectives who have already fused as One, having completed this process many spirals ago. These Beings visit the New Earth to impart higher wisdom and assist with transformation, transmutation, and transcendence, as well as to prepare those transitioning from the fifth to ninth dimensions. On Future Earth they support beings to evolve from the ninth into the dimensions beyond.

With awareness and consciousness comes Remembrance. The true beloved does indeed exist in the fifth dimension. This is where the divine complement is to be found. A rare few awakened Souls on Existing Earth have already reunited with their twin flame and are in the very early stages of the "reblending" process. Since December 21, 2012, many more have begun to experience this reunion. On Existing Earth some may believe they are already with their twin flame but in fact are actually in an awakened Soul mate relationship.

To reunite with the true twin flame requires that the Consciousness of an individual is resonant with the vibration and frequency of the higher levels of the fifth dimension. When a "reuniting" on Existing Earth is not part of one's immediate reality, it is often because the beloved is already located on the New Earth or may be in the realms of the afterlife, awaiting a future incarnation. Regardless of where each half of a twin flame is situated, hypercommunication continues between them, and these beloveds will eventually reunite in the fifth-dimensional realm.

It is important to note that there are a few special highly advanced Beings on Existing Earth who will immediately ascend to dimensions beyond the fifth upon leaving the physical body. They are already One with their beloved and, as such, are currently the most evolved Beings on Existing Earth and are here in service to her, humanity, and all life.

Beings who are evolving a fifth-dimensional state of Consciousness automatically begin to align with the New Earth. The blending process toward pure androgyny can only begin when one has transcended the fifth dimension. This cannot be achieved on Existing Earth because she is currently unable to sustain the vibration and frequency that is necessary for this to be possible.

On New Earth transcendence to the sixth dimension is an evolutionary impulse, just as is ascension to fifth-dimensional Consciousness on Existing Earth. Where a being is located along the continuum of fifth to ninth-dimensional evolution determines how union with a beloved is experienced. On the fifth-dimensional level, the connection to the physical is still strong, but sexuality is far more refined. However, as ascension unfolds through the higher levels of the fifth and into the sixth, the physical body begins to evolve into a more subtle energetic form. As it does so, sexual energy and union are experienced in less of a physical way. There are no words currently in the language of the third dimension to describe the sacred union of beloveds who have evolved beyond the fifth dimension.

Animals and Plants on New Earth

New Earth is populated with animals familiar to those on Existing Earth and many more besides. Some have become extinct on Existing Earth and others have never incarnated in that particular realm. Because there is no suffering on New or Future Earth, there is no fear, and therefore, animals choose to cohabit with humans as part of their own evolutionary journey.

Animals are not food sources on New or Future Earth for they are recognized as equal sentient Beings that also experience feelings and thoughts and are intelligent and sensitive; therefore to treat them as inferior is simply not a part of that reality. Because of the absence of fear, animals experience no aggression and instead live in harmony with all living beings around them. They have no desire for food of the flesh, having evolved to a finer state of Consciousness to become herbivores.

Animals live in harmony and peace. They play and enjoy being talked to, sung to, guided, massaged, groomed, held, and hugged. They are relaxed and content, and the relationship between animals and the community is one of mutual love, respect, and appreciation.

Animals on fifth-dimensional New Earth are healing from previous third-dimensional experience and beginning to trust, open their hearts, and develop their minds. Through gentle, loving interaction within an atmosphere of reverence they are learning how to love and, through this, how to evolve and grow. As they move into the Higher Dimensions, they discover the wonder of a new way of living, a new type of body, and the joy of developing finer ways of conversing through body language, energy, and sound.

There are highly evolved Guides who oversee the evolutionary journey of the animals. These include the dolphins and whales, both advanced fifth-dimensional Beings incarnate in animal form on Existing Earth. Their true *purpose is yet to be understood by third-dimensional consciousness. On New Earth, however, alongside other highly evolved species, this becomes very clear and can also be fulfilled. Animals learn through telepathy, which is received from various Interspecies Councils and Master Beings. They also learn through daily interaction with the community.*

When animals on New Earth begin to reach the higher octaves of the fifth dimension and the lower of the sixth, their solid earthly bodies begin to transform into higher vibrational Light.

Plants on New and Future Earth are recognized and responded to as Conscious and sentient beings. They also transcend through their own awakening Consciousness from a physical form into one of Light. Information on the plant realm did not come through in the channeling, but by feeling into the subject it is entirely clear to me that this is also part of the New and Future Earth realities.

✳ New Earth—Future Earth ✳

Future Earth accommodates the most evolved beings and is host to only the most advanced Consciousness, which is in the process of ultimately dissolving into pure LIGHT and LOVE. Such Beings are transmuting into LIGHT and undifferentiated ONENESS with ALL THAT IS.

In the upper dimensions (seventh and above) of New Earth, and within Future Earth, all beings are nourished and sustained by etheric, cosmic, and related energy sources that are specific to those dimensions. On New Earth, the practice of eating food is secondary to other energy sources.

Solar and galactic rays, crystalline and diamond frequencies, and pure planetary vibrational energies sustain life on Future Earth. This is partially true for life on New Earth too, but there is also nourishment in the form of certain food substances as the physical form is still present, albeit in a more highly refined state. Vibrational energy flows ceaselessly in waves akin to the winds on Existing Earth and is a main source of sustenance.

A combination of etheric, cosmic, energetic, and natural resources on the New Earth create grasses, leaves, fruits, berries, nuts, and seeds to support the beings of the fifth to the lower sixth dimensions, given the lighter form of their less-dense physical bodies. All of these substances can be ingested and some beings will do so, while others from the upper sixth and beyond will not need to.

The water imbibed is crystalline pure and sourced from the rejuvenating, cleansing, and unadulterated waterfalls, rivers, and streams that are to be found in abundance on both New and Future Earth. Each dimension becomes less solid and more etheric in nature until it evolves into its ultimate state of pure LIGHT and this is all that is required to ingest.

There is no landfill or rubbish because there are no toxic or nonbiodegradable foods, packaging, or any other such materials. Neither are there any processed, unnatural, or artificial food substances. There are no pharmaceuticals, psychotropics, alcohol, drugs, plastics, tins, or other noxious materials that could harm the delicate ecobalance of New Earth and Future Earth and all who reside upon her. There is no need for hard-copy publications or any paper-based/tree-derived documents owing to the supra-advanced crystalline and diamond technologies of both New and Future Earth. All nonverbal communications are expressed via the Outernet through various benign devices. The Outernet serves a dual purpose in that not only does it source all communications, but it also uses technologies that are actually designed to enhance well-being.

There are no hierarchical, matriarchal, patriarchal, or overruling systems of authority; nor are there any wars, politics, taxes, money, or governments. There are no "jobs," only people fulfilling their ultimate potential via personally chosen roles within the community. There is no crime. Karma is not accrued.

All "time lines" have converged into a singular ascending spiral (dimensional time line) that beings can move within and through. It is possible to visit any time line throughout the entire history of Existing Earth, or any other dimension for social or evolutionary activities.

From the sixth dimension upward on New Earth history is no longer an influence. Just like the impermanence of a Tibetan Mandala, history is blown away by the frequencies of higher-dimensional realms. Beings can fully experience a "moment," but this is then released to make way for the creation of a new and more enlightened moment and, in this way, they can evolve through a sequence of moment-to-moment realities. New Earth beings live in the now and are aligned to an evolutionary impulse toward higher states of Consciousness and greater degrees of awakening.

There are beautiful dwellings on New and Future Earth, and the higher-dimensional the being, the more etheric the abode in which they reside. The beings design and craft these abodes by themselves or with the help of artisan friends. Diamond and crystalline technologies along with solar and galactic energies and naturally harnessed wind and water turbines power these sanctuaries, as well as the moving capsules that are used for physical travel in the various dimensions within New Earth. On Future Earth, such capsules do not exist as all "travel" is via energy following thought.

Beings on Future Earth are fully attuned to their multidimensionality and are able to communicate from multilevels within themselves across multiple time lines and dimensions. On both New and Future Earth there are a large number of crystal cities and unity communities where great crystalline halls of learning are to be found. Studies differ from those on Existing Earth, as learning occurs through osmosis and telepathy, and the process is fundamentally creative. Understanding arises from hemispherically synchronized wave-field transmissions; sound, movement, toning, pulsing, sensing, and intuiting are central elements to this. Infinite modulations covering multilevels of information are available for studying and processing by any being at any time.

The Elders from the fifth and sixth dimensions teach higher-dimensional philosophy from the heart and the mind, which is transmitted directly to the hearts and minds of those who are studying. Everything that becomes "known" is first experienced through gnosis and then processed through the heart and integrated into both the mind and higher-mind.

The system of learning on the New and Future Earths is light years ahead of what is currently in place on Existing Earth. Beings gravitate toward certain areas of learning or intuit what is best for their overall evolutionary needs at any given time. Self-responsibility and

Self-awareness are the "norm," and so it is that studies are chosen from a place of integrated awareness. All trust and are trusted to "know thyself" to a greater degree and to make wise and informed choices that will serve their own higher good, as well as the highest good of all.

From the sixth dimension and beyond, magnificent crystal structures of stunningly intelligent aesthetic and technological design adorn New Earth. Known as crystal cities, these "temples of Light" defy adequate description. An extraordinary expansion of Consciousness is experienced when entering these highest of vibrational palaces.

Downloads of SOURCE LOVE pour directly into the heart and light up the Soul. Euphoric transmissions of diamond-wave energy pulsate throughout the entire being for the dual purpose of regeneration and amplification of inner light. This supports preparation for ascension to the diamond frequency that sources the ninth to the thirteenth dimensions. From a cellular perspective, Existing Earth beings are carbon based, New Earth beings are crystalline, and Future Earth beings live from a diamond template.

Crystal cities play host to various events, initiations, ceremonies, and rites of passage, as well as all major celebrations. Highly advanced Soul groups meet within these special palaces to experience becoming One Collective Soul serving the greater good of all throughout all Space and Time. These group energies overlight third- and fourth-dimensional Earth. Unity Community Elders (note the term Elders has nothing to do with chronological age but the advanced evolution of an individual Soul), also act as mentors for new arrivals to fifth-dimensional New Earth.

After visiting a crystal city, a being returns glowing and pulsating with vibrant energy. The vast influxes of Light absorbed are shared with the community at home as well as utilized to power the crystalline hubs that source the sanctuaries (homes) inhabited by individuals, couples, and families.

On New Earth, great emphasis is placed on experiencing joy, and this can be found in creative expression. All are in touch with their genius and all are artisans. Beings also experience euphoria, ecstasy, and bliss when *engaging in Light exchanges with another, during which they temporarily merge for the purpose of sharing and further amplifying their Light.*

New and Future Earth are dimensions for BEing, evolving, learning, teaching, journeying, guiding, supporting, reflecting, singing, chanting, toning, creating, playing, enjoying, merging, blending, loving, connecting, refining, embodying, transforming, transmuting, transcending, and preparing for ascension to Higher Realms.

Beings are guided and overlighted by Elders, Teachers, and Councils who live between the fifth and the ninth dimensions. Deep respect and reverence is felt for all Beings and Councils, who always prioritize the happiness and harmony of each and every being.

Bilocation

Bilocation to Existing Earth is common and is mostly for the purpose of imparting wisdom, knowledge, guidance, and support to those who are awakening to the next stage of their evolutionary journey. Many Guides reside on Existing Earth and New Earth at the same time. Bilocation to New and Future Earth is encouraged and many on Existing Earth have been to these dimensions through out-of-body or near-death experiences, when in a shamanically induced state, naturally during sleep, or when in an altered state of consciousness. Many "travel" to more subtle dimensions to prepare for their own ascension to a higher octave and/or to teach others about life on New and Future Earth.

Both New and Future Earth are bathed in beneficent and harmonious arrays of different color spectrums. During the solar cycle (daytime) subtle tones of gold, violet, platinum, pink, blue, and deep soft magenta create magnificent skyscapes and landscapes. During the lunar cycle (nighttime), pure white, platinum, and deep indigo hues are the background for a spectacular canopy of celestial planets and stars.

New and Future Earth are populated by vast color-spectrum zones (think of the Aurora borealis currently on Existing Earth) in which beings can immerse themselves for the purpose of realignment, sensory attunement, energetic cleansing, health stimulation, and sublime joy.

Every color seen on Existing Earth, and many more, can be found within these zones. Subtle tones and vibrations gently pulsate throughout New and Future Earth to maintain energetic and vibrational equilibrium.

Human Consciousness
to SOURCE CONSCIOUSNESS

On Future Earth, the physiology of a being has evolved from crystalline to diamond, which is reflected in a technology that is able to facilitate direct communication with highly evolved beings that exist in multiverses.

On Future Earth (ninth to thirteenth dimensions), all are united with their one true beloved Soul. As discussed earlier, from the sixth to the thirteenth dimensions, beloveds are engaged in an evolving blending and merging process, so their energies will ultimately fully fuse and reunify as One with each other and as ONE with SOURCE.

Dimensions beyond the thirteenth leading to the twenty-six are where the Ultimate Guides, Councils, and Elders, who teach within the ninth to thirteenth dimensions, reside. The thirteenth dimension is a journey into the GREAT DISSOLUTION, the end point of all perceived separation and the point of Transfiguration into the Nameless and Formless that is THE ABSOLUTE/SOURCE/EXISTENCE/BEYOND THE BEYOND/ ALL THAT IS.

THE FAR DISTANT FUTURE
OF EXISTING EARTH

Ultimately, third-dimensional consciousness will depart if it fails to evolve and Existing Earth will eventually become a "dark zone" for much of the light will have left with those who have ascended to New Earth.

As Existing Earth becomes ever more shrouded, unconscious Souls will be given a final opportunity to acknowledge that they have lost their way. At this point, the Higher Dimensions will be able to directly intervene and awaken within them a fifth-dimensional state of awareness. There will, however, be a percentage of beings that will remain blind to the intervention/opportunity and will turn away from the potential to ascend into a higher state of Consciousness. Instead, they will cling to the old paradigm of duality and separation.

New Earth will assist those who accept support to transition to a temporary fourth-dimensional **astral plane*** or realm—a bridge or station—in preparation for eventual ascension into the lower fifth-dimensional levels. The fifth- and sixth-dimensional frequencies of New Earth are too potent for beings in a state of lower consciousness to enter, so transition to the fourth-dimensional "holding space" (imagine a departure lounge at an international airport) is where these Souls prepare for ascension to a higher dimension.

There is an infinite outpouring of LOVE for Existing Earth from those in the Higher Dimensions for the role she has taken on and is closer to fulfilling. And she has a new role that will unfold in time as part of the Great Plan: she is to evolve into a new expression with a unique new purpose, which only becomes possible when she is unencumbered by the frequency and vibration of third-dimensional consciousness.

First, she will rest, realign, rebalance, and cleanse and clear herself of lower vibrational consciousness and energies. At this stage she will no longer be referred to as Existing Earth and will instead adopt her original and highly advanced vibrational status of Planet Earth. After this occurs a great wave of fifth-dimensional beings from New Earth will take up residence—it will be as if **Lemuria*** has been reborn.

The third-dimensional portal to Existing Earth will initially close but will reopen with a new vibrational status able to host all frequencies from the fifth dimension and beyond. The cleared and cleansed Earth will be frequently visited by highly advanced Beings helping her to prepare for her new role and purpose.

Earth will become a planetary paradise. Nature will thrive and all the natural cycles and rhythms will return. She will become a paradisiacal destination for sixth- to ninth-dimensional Light Beings to visit and walk among fifth-dimensional sisters and brothers, albeit unseen owing to their Light form. However, the energy of their higher Consciousness will be tangibly felt from a sensory perspective. Beings from many dimensions will come to study and enjoy the rare Nature on Earth in all its abundant glory. Fourth-dimensional consciousness will be able to visit but only if accompanied by a higher vibrational Being. Planet Earth will never again host third-dimensional energies.

New and Future Earth equate to dimensions of pure LOVE. Crystalline and diamond filaments act as connectors to facilitate receptors to perceive, receive, decode, and transmit information streaming into the heart. Threads carry and exchange information throughout the entire sensory field of a being, which are picked up by supra-neural highways linking directly to active crystalline networks within the brain.

The fifth/sixth-dimensional brain is a secondary process receptor utilized primarily for structuring, balancing, and organizing. This type of brain is active in a way that the three-dimensional brain is not. Within the fifth/sixth-dimensional brain exists a crystalline-neural center that acts as both transmitter and receiver. Information and data travel along these supra-neural highways enabling hypercommunication, data input/output, transmissions, and information exchanges, all of which are processed and integrated through the heart before being expressed.

The highly advanced systems to be found on New and Future Earth exist because of the interconnection between the crystalline elements within fifth/sixth-dimensional beings, the crystalline core of the New Earth, the diamond activation of the ninth-dimensional brain and core of Future Earth, and the resonant and responsive hypercommunication highways to be found throughout the Universe.

Both New and Future Earth are populated by highly advanced and evolved civilizations living multidimensional realities in the higher octaves. Beings located within the other Earth dimensions live in harmonious alignment with the vast legions of highly advanced **multiuniversals** * inhabiting or frequenting New and Future Earth. Interconnected with multiexistences and through multiverses (including off-planet races, beings, and energies that are so highly advanced they remain beyond third-dimensional comprehension), New and Future Earth are hosts to a supra-luminous collective who are evolving into the fullest and highest potential of a Soul incarnate in human form.

EXISTING EARTH = self • NEW EARTH = Self • FUTURE EARTH = Higher Self

We can see from this channeled information that the c/Consciousness of the world not only coevolves with new expressions of Earth, but that the Earth herself is able to evolve and transcend her own third-dimensional limitations. These three representations of Earth run parallel to the trajectory of human c/Consciousness—Existing Earth = self, New Earth = Self, Future Earth = Higher Self—and in this sense, we might say that the Earth herself is evolving in a similar way. The defining factor for which Earth we inhabit is determined by the level of our c/Consciousness and frequency.

Are there three independent Earths within the Cosmos? Perhaps . . . there have been reports of the discovery of another Earth by space scientists. But as I understand it, the three bodies exist simultaneously in the same space as parallel realities.

The highly evolved and advanced Consciousness and vibration of Future Earth influences the vibration and Consciousness of New Earth, which, in turn, seeks to bring these higher states of awareness and technologies of the future to the current world of Existing Earth. However, the lower consciousness and frequency of Existing Earth continues to manifest fear and therefore cannot influence the New and Future Earths, which manifest LOVE and therefore deflect anything other than this.

The evolutionary remit of both New and Future Earth is to support the third-dimensional population of Existing Earth to evolve, to transcend suffering, and to remember who they really are and where they are really from.

Our abiding purpose is to meet fear with LOVE. This must be our daily practice. It is why we are here.

A Message for Humanity

*This Is Our Moment,
We Were Born for These Times*

> *The secret of living a fulfilling life is to be ready at any moment to give up who you are for who you could become.*
>
> SUFI PROVERB

In this book, I have attempted to explain, among many other things, why and how we now find ourselves at the very edge of an ultimate tipping point—as one Great Age concludes and another is set to begin. Ancient wisdom cultures prophesied that this New Age would herald either catastrophe or regeneration. This moment is aptly summarized in a poem by Christopher Logue:

> *Come to the edge.*
> *We might fall.*
> *Come to the edge.*
> *It's too high!*
> *COME TO THE EDGE!*
> *And they came,*
> *and he pushed,*
> *And they flew.*

In the context of the overall message of this book, the "he" referred to in the poem is LOVE; the ultimate guiding and sustaining force for ALL life on Earth and beyond this mortal realm. We now stand on an evolutionary edge and are being called by LOVE to transcend our fear of stepping off, pushed by the often extremely challenging yet ultimately liberating evolutionary winds of Conscious and spiritual awakening.

In these tumultuous times of change, there are many different perspectives in regard to what is really going on in the world. Every dysfunctional and nefarious system within society is falling under the glaring spotlight of truth; we have reached an evolutionary crossroads, a time for profound questioning and soul searching, as we seek to establish how to navigate the years and decades ahead in such a way that devolutionary systems, structures, and forces are dismantled, dissolved, and transcended. This is something that can only be achieved if we unite and act in the name of Love and Truth; the outcome of which is a consciously empowered people setting a new precedent for the world, a new inspired template for humanity, co-creating and co-establishing a new sweeping epoch in which the *power of love* supersedes everything.

Love is the answer to everything.

Collective Conscious evolution bestows miraculous opportunities and will free us from the ties that bind, the old stories that keep us tethered to the past and an old power over/love of power paradigm. How do we navigate our way through these immensely challenging times? It is through the *power of love*. LOVE is the answer. By simplifying, purifying, and remembering who we truly are, why we are really here, and where we are really from, we strengthen our connection to LOVE (GOD), embodying the LOVE we each are. When our energetic field is strong, in resonance, and consciously entrained with the Higher Dimensions, we heal ourselves, and, collectively, heal the world.

It is LOVE and LOVE alone that will lead us to lasting inner-peace and joy and bring peace and unconditional freedom to the world.

Conscious awakening compels us to Consciously connect with our True Self, our Soul, and to SOURCE/LOVE, to align, so that together we can cocreate a new and enlightened reality.

As the world is held in the grip of uncertainty and chaos, a promising new epoch is pushing to be born. For this to occur, we must take that evolutionary leap, step off the edge of the old story, and experience our wings unfolding, trusting that we will not fall, but *fly*. As crises throughout the world continue to spin out of control we have never been more ideally positioned to birth a new heart-centered humanity, a new Conscious paradigm, and a new enlightened world. Divine timing is the wind in our sails. Just as spots of ink spread across blotting paper, so too is Conscious evolution spreading across the planet. We are Consciously waking up in our millions, and it has taken something of unprecedented proportions, a global event on a scale of such magnitude, to drive collective unconscious fear and ignorance to the surface in order to push us over that evolutionary edge.

Without doubt, the year 2012 was our date with destiny—a wake-up call for humanity—and the subsequent years have served only to affirm the fact that we are in the midst of a Great Shift of Ages. We are called upon to surrender the old stories and embrace a new story for humanity founded on equality, compassion, respect, and harmony; a world in which peace and plenty are experienced by ALL life-forms on this Earth.

It is time to join hands and *remember*: We are a vast and coherent system of nearly eight billion vibrating energies—physical, emotional, mental, psychological, intellectual, psychic, energetic, and spiritual—polarized in either fear or Love. When the majority of us are living, breathing, and BEing Love, the world will be transformed.

Twenty-first-century society is evolving its relationship with "God" to reflect the awakening Consciousness of the times, as we move away from the old religious connotations and interpretations of this phenomenon into a divinely timed true understanding and representation of GOD as LOVE: "God" is, and always has been, LOVE.

✳

We are LOVE.

We are from LOVE.

We are here to LOVE.

And, it is to LOVE we shall return, when we leave this earthly realm.

LOVE really is the answer to everything. It is as simple as that.

Namaste and LOVE,

Nicolya

The Synthesis of Psychology, Biology, and Technology in a New Conscious Epoch

The astrological Age of Aquarius we are just entering into now and that will last approximately twenty-one hundred years, brings with it groundbreaking and exciting new discoveries in the arenas of regenerative medicine (including the growth of new body parts), education, nutrition, technology, and science (especially quantum science). Ancient astrologers cited the visionary and future-oriented Aquarius to be *a sign of all things that are newly invented* and *a sign of the humanitarian*. Social injustice will be undone and people will unite in great numbers in order to deconstruct the outmoded systems of the old paradigm. These will be replaced with philanthropic, beneficent, and enlightened new systems that uphold democracy, sociocracy, and altruism.

This new Conscious epoch of healing and regeneration seeks to align and balance quantum science and spirituality, biology and technology, psychology and physiology, and morphology and ecology. This appendix explores various new technologies and methodologies that bring the aforementioned into a coherent and inspired synthesis.

THE ROLE OF TRAUMA IN ILLNESS

An instrumental part of a new epoch in medicine and healing is the recognition of *trauma* as the fundamental origin of illness that manifests as either responsive (regenerative) or reactionary (degenerative) symptomology. Human beings have evolved the faculty of thought and our ability to think, consider, reflect, and contemplate sets us apart from other sentient beings. We are (consciously or unconsciously) hypersensitive to the environment of our modern world. We are also naturally equipped with an inborn primal-survival protect and defend reaction, which triggers within us a primitive flight or fight response. This renders us susceptible to unnaturally induced stress-related reactions that leave us vulnerable to a plethora of illnesses. It is this adaptive survival-stress reaction that is a causal factor in a seemingly endless list of illnesses besetting a greater proportion of humanity under duress due to the demands of their day-to-day lives and the expectations of a contemporary culture. This impacts us at physical, emotional, mental, psychological, and energetic levels as our unconscious or conscious attempts to adapt to the unnatural and indigestible realities of modern life that continue to dominate our experiences.

Author and bioenergetics and informational health care specialist Richard Flook points to this in a model that he has developed called UDIN, an acronym for an Unexpected, Dramatic, Isolating, No Strategy Event. Flook claims that left untreated, UDIN events cause the body to change, freeze, fight, or defend itself, which in turn brings about illness and disease.

Similarly, German physician Dr. Rykye Geerd Hamer states in his book *Ediciones de la Nueva Medicina* that the underlying cause of illness has its roots in the psychological dimension of the human being. Hamer postulates that sickness and disease are the result of unresolved conflict and shock that register in a particular location within the human brain. His hypothesis is that if left unaddressed, these will eventually manifest as imbalance and disturbance in a correlating site within the physical body.

From 1978 to 1983 Hamer's research led him to discover an intrinsic link, which he terms a "triad" between the *psyche,* the *brain,* and the *body.* He recognized the capacity of the brain to switch on a program of illness as a response/reaction to a significant conflict or shock and, equally, switch off that program when this has been resolved. The theory that active conflict or shock forms the basis of all physical disease also conveys the idea that when treating illness or disease, the main focus must be on treating the *cause* and not merely the symptoms.

Hamer proposes that *no disease really exists.* He believes that what established medicine refers to as a "disease" is, in actuality, a "special meaningful program of nature" to which bacteria, viruses, and fungi belong. His theories claim to explain every disease and treatment. The cure to them all, he states, is always the *resolving of the conflict,* and he considers the use of medical interventions such as chemotherapy or pain-relieving drugs like morphine to be deadly. He proposes that symptomology must be explored from all angles and that certain potential "cures" may be an anathema to that which is currently accepted by the medical profession. In terms of healing treatments and protocols, what is proved to be effective for one may be ineffective for another.

In summary, Hamer's theory is based upon five fundamental biological laws:

1. Biological programs are caused by conflict or shock.
2. Biological programs always run in two phases.
3. All biological programs are controlled by a particular brain area, which determines their progress.
4. All microorganisms serve a useful purpose in symbiosis with humans.
5. All biological programs fulfill a meaningful purpose.

Hamer experienced a high success rate with his therapeutic approach and conducted many trials that yielded positive results. He theorized that all living beings have evolved to the extent that they are able to physically adapt and appropriately respond to a serious or life-threatening challenge. This adaptation process first instructs the body to actively attempt to free itself of an imbalance. Following a natural healing (i.e., discovering the root cause of an illness), he suggests that a release will occur, and that it is this that will return the biology back to homeostasis.

Hamer scientifically authenticated his theories by researching and documenting an extensive range of cases of the progression of disease, all of which he defined as following a natural adaptation process. He collated thousands of CT scans, each one revealing the process of a *ring pattern* taking form in a portion of the brain that correlated to a diagnosed disease. Detailed case histories were taken from all his patients that revealed that the very same diseases corresponded to identical or similar life challenges prior to onset. For instance, bone issues turned out to be related to a lack of self-worth, liver problems indicated a fear of starvation, and thyroid issues resulted from a feeling of powerlessness.

Hamer filed over fifty thousand case studies to substantiate his claims. His research reveals that if the historical-psychological cause of the disease can be resolved, the body will begin to heal and regain and maintain homeostasis. He has achieved a 98 percent success rate with patients who had avoided conventional treatment and pharmaceutical intervention.

CATASTROPHIC DISASSOCIATION

The majority of people have become disconnected from and lost trust and faith in their own biology. With a little insight however, most would be astonished by the innate wisdom of their own body. Physical symptoms are feared because of a failure to understand that both the cause and cure of illness are to be found within the psychoenergetic levels of the Self. Such disconnection from this fundamental reality leads to *catastrophic disassociation* from the body and the true (higher) purpose of disease. Unhealed, unresolved, and unintegrated conflict, shock, and trauma are baseline triggers for much of the ill health experienced by people today.

The evolutionary shift from *physiological (catastrophic) disassociation* to *psychological association and biological integration* is fundamental to a new paradigm of health, healing, and regeneration. We can empower ourselves in regard to illness and disease by seeking to understand the correlation between sickness and original trauma. Only then is it possible to become liberated from predisposed physical conditions.

A NEW ERA IN HEALTH CARE

Since 2009, I have been writing about the phenomenon of the *new human*—a psychologically integrated, consciously evolved, and spiritually awakened human being, who is no longer limited by the effects of trauma, karma, and epigenetics but instead is guided by a visionary and more mystical directive.

The vision of a conscious new epoch in healing, wellness, and regeneration includes the redefining of existing GP surgeries and medical clinics throughout the world. A part of its aim would be to establish Wellness Surgeries and "Retunement" Centers that offer nonpharmaceutical treatments for all our health needs, whether physical, emotional, mental, energetic, or psychic.

These clinics would also support individuals and communities to attain, regain, and maintain a greater experience of overall health and well-being, from the physical to the psychological to the psychospiritual. The focus would be on *education to empower and encourage* visitors to become the primary active participators in their own healing and wellness. The clinics would be extensively upgraded versions of existing GP surgeries located in every village, town, and city, and approaches and technologies profiled throughout this appendix would feature as standard treatments.

A full spectrum of holistic protocols including wave-field therapies, vibrational medicine, bioenergetic medicine, sound healing, frequency technologies, and psychospiritual healing practices are just some of the therapies that would be available. Other protocols would include advanced methodologies in the fields of nutraceuticals, infoceuticals, acupuncture, aromatherapy, hydrotherapy, thermotherapy, acupressure, massage, kinesiology, homeopathy, wholistic dentistry, naturopathy, nutritional therapy, Ayurveda, yoga, tai chi, qi gong, meditation, breathwork and movement, humanistic and transpersonal psychotherapies, creative/creativity therapies, and wholistic dietary based self-care.

These wellness clinics would also serve as "retuning centers" for the body, emotions, mind, energy, and psyche and would be designed to work toward attaining homeostasis. A cure can never be guaranteed because the outcome of an illness is determined not only by the agenda of the Soul but also by one's engagement with it. These futuristic surgeries would serve as primary support systems for patients undergoing necessary surgical procedures and hospital treatments. These centers would also work in conjunction with hospitals and medical consultants to offer pre- and post-operative care. Revolutionary new practices would eventually emerge and work in conjunction with more conventional medical practices.

FREQUENCIES FOR HEALTH, WELLNESS, AND REGENERATION

The work of the brilliant German biophysicist, scientist, and author Dieter Broers has highlighted the effect of weak (nonthermal) electromagnetic fields on biological systems. For over four decades Broers has been developing various wave-field technologies. At the forefront of these are two devices: the MF 150 MHz and the NFS 8.

MF 150 MHz

Broers was the first to discover that the 150 MHz is a carrier frequency of human DNA, and it was this that led him to the MF 150 MHz. After thirty-five years of numerous clinical trials, it was finally approved as a legitimate medical device in 2016. The MF 150 MHz works by emitting electromagnetic waves of 150 MHz, which, according to Broers, act as a Trojan horse for opening a door into the cell. It proceeds to instruct the cell with original core information thus reinforming the DNA of its divine order and so returning it to optimum frequency.

The therapeutic value of the MF 150 MHz has been demonstrated and proven in extensive clinical trials and has an impressive track record for accelerating the healing of arthritis and skin and bone disorders. It rapidly heals wounds, alleviates pain, and has been found by many medical professionals to have a significantly positive effect on a wide range of other conditions from cancer and multiple sclerosis to chronic obstructive pulmonary disease, or COPD. It works for a variety of conditions and also supports those in good health to remain so.

Broers explains that the frequency of 150 MHz opens a transdimensional channel into hyperspace that enables the user to connect with aspects of the Higher Self and so receive information directly from the Soul that might otherwise be inaccessible. The device appears to facilitate a connection with the Higher Self because its frequency activates the pineal gland and this then transforms melatonin into **DMT***. In this context the device has been tested on thousands of patients, most of whom were able to connect with, explore, and come to understand the deeper reason and purpose for their specific physical challenge. In many cases spontaneous healing or a significant relief of symptoms occurred.

Broers also discovered that the MF 150 MHz not only supported and brought about healing and regeneration but also catalyzed experiences of expanded consciousness among its users who, at that time, were mostly patients of doctor colleagues or control groups of healthy individuals.

Broers talks of the capacity of the MF 150 MHz to enable access to the subtle layers of "time" and to pierce the veils of awareness. In ideal conditions, the frequency can induce a hypnogogic state in which an individual can view their historical story, a past timeline, or an ancestral influence that may disclose the root cause of a current physical imbalance or disease. This was affirmed at a symposium organized by the work group for alternative medicine in October 2016. Fifty medical doctors and natural health practitioners convened to share the results of clinical trials, research, and experience. The oncologist and researcher Dr. Frank Daudert also gave a lecture at the event on the hypnotherapeutic aspects of the usage of the MF 150 AH and reported on the results of an empiric study that verified the "hypnotherapeutic effects" on patients who had used it.

Broers personally observed the expansion of Consciousness in individuals using the MF 150 MHz, which had also been scientifically measured with magnetic and electrochemical methods. A patient using the device experiences an expanded perspective similar to one who undergoes an NDE.

NFS 8

The deterioration of our chronobiological rhythms is a result of the sea of electroradiation that most of humanity now swims in. Dieter Broers's second groundbreaking device is the NFS (natural field simulator) 8, which works with the frequency of 8 Hz and has been proven to act as a counter deterrent against electrostress and electropollution.

The NFS 8, which is worn against the thymus gland in the form of a pendant, affords protection against electric and magnetic fields (EMFs), electromagnetic radiation (EMR), and other artificial and electronegative energies. This device serves another important purpose in that it supports the function of the pineal gland and the role it plays in spiritual awakening. It acts as a magnet to draw life enhancing fields toward us from Nature and the Cosmos so that we can surround ourselves with them. Broers's empirical research and experiments into the 8 Hz frequency led him to the realization that it propagates spherically, so when wearing the device around the neck, one is in a near field area that stabilizes our own energy field and deflects harmful frequencies.

Professor Karl Hecht, an eminent physiologist who was involved in the Russian space program's medical division, invited Broers to accompany him on a visit to the space program laboratories in Moscow. Together they attended meetings with Russian scientists and officials who shared what they were working on and their discoveries after observing returning cosmonauts. Broers duly noted that upon arriving back from their space missions, the cosmonauts had subsequently experienced varying levels of physical and mental imbalance after having spent prolonged periods of time removed from the Earth's magnetic field. He realized the importance of strengthening and fortifying this field in humans, especially since the magnetic field of the Earth has significantly decreased, and there is a potential now for humanity to experience similar imbalances.

When attending a meeting at IMBP Moscow with the Russian scientists involved in the space program, Professor Hecht concluded the following in regard to the geomagnetic field: the magnetosphere is necessary for humans, animals, and plants, and was discovered by Russian space medicine after the first cosmic flights revealed that the weakness of the magnetosphere in space had negative effects on the cosmonauts. The second twenty-four-hour flight with cosmonaut Gherman Titov, in contrast to Yuri Gagarin's first one-hundred-minute flight, resulted in significant disturbances of well-being, including vomiting. Given the spacecraft flew over 300 km from the Earth, the crews were without the protection of the magnetosphere. By making use of the NFS 8 technology these issues were resolved.

Other documented experiments of the NFS 8 include tests conducted with children. Broers cites one example of a mother placing the unit under the pillow of her hyperactive child who, for the first time in months, slept through the entire night. The device continued to be so effective that the previously prescribed pharmaceuticals were no longer required. Stock exchange supervisors reported resounding success when using the NFS 8, finding that it so improved their concentration levels that they were able to avoid burnout and remain at their jobs for much longer. In another experiment a friend of Broers wore the device to meetings he was to attend including a visit to the spiritual teacher Mother Meera. Upon seeing him she immediately enquired about the energy she was able to perceive all around him.

The NFS 8 pulses to 8 Hz, which is the same frequency as the

Schumann resonances—a set of spectrum peaks in the extremely low frequency (ELF) portion of the Earth's electromagnetic field spectrum that carry the 8 Hz waves to the pineal gland and maintain us in a field of this specific frequency. Broers describes the NFS 8 as a nature field stabilizer and a carrier and producer of this natural frequency of the Earth. For billions of years, all living creatures have grown within this field, this "womb of the Earth," and without it life is simply not possible. If shielded from this frequency for extended periods of time, symptoms of biological deterioration and degeneration begin to occur.

The Earth's magnetic field is decreasing faster than geophysicists had first anticipated. This is not a new anomaly and has been discussed for several years in the scientific and physics communities. Yet only now is their hypothesis, along with evidence produced by volcanologists, being proven to be the case.

The Earth's magnetic poles are said to be shifting. A pole shift originates from the core of the Earth and as this is subject to change so, too, is the Earth's magnetic field, a fact that is gradually filtering into the wider public domain. Broers has been following and studying this data for several years and has also observed that it is decreasing. The result of this is a negative impact on health and well-being, yet, conversely, it also allows for the 150 MHz rays from the Sun to reach us in greater intensity leading to naturally induced access to the spiritual realms and to our biological blueprint.

Scientific studies are now proving that a weaker magnetic field can catalyze increased telepathic and psychic abilities within human beings. The frequency of 150 MHz creates a balance between the right and left hemispheres of the brain, and it is this that facilitates telepathy and psychic states. The changes occurring with the Earth's magnetic field particularly impact those who are sensitive, and, as a result, unusual metaphysical phenomena are being reported across the world.

Both the MF 150 MHz and the NFS 8 offer far-reaching potential for countering (and remaining protected from) a spectrum of physical, psychological, and energetic imbalances induced by negative frequencies.

Both units have been shown to radically improve, and, in many cases "cure" the biopsychospiritual stressors caused by discordant electromagnetic frequencies and electromagnetic radiation.

Whether clearing epigenetic blueprints, historical imprints, ancestral wounds, or struggling with the harmful effects of electromagnetic toxicity, Broers's devices are validated technologies that entrain physiology, biology, psychology, energy, spirit, and Soul. Both devices are scientifically and legally verified as playing a significant role in regaining and/or maintaining overall health and are an instrumental "medicine" for a new age of health.

RADIONICS

In October 2019, I felt compelled to write a fiction novel based on fact that contains a deep message for humanity. It alternates between three timelines: WW2, the present day, and a potential dystopian world of the near future. For the first fourteen months, I was immersed in the WW2 story, and reentering that time frame triggered a powerful reaction in my body, as layer after layer of deeply held cellular Soul memory began to release in a never-ending array of extreme physical symptoms.

In March 2021, a good friend recommended that I see a practitioner of radionics. I had heard of this healing modality in my late teens and now it had come back to me. Desperate for some relief from the ongoing physical bombardment I was experiencing, I contacted the practitioner—Linda Kinsella—and we began to work together. Within just four weeks, most of the symptoms I had endured for over seventeen months, disappeared. Nothing I had tried previously had yielded such results. Having personally experienced radionics, I believe wholeheartedly that it needs to become a central part of mainstream medicine and the new GP offices I have written about in this book.

Radionics originated in the work of the neurologist Dr. Albert Abrams (1863–1924), who claimed that his diagnostic system— Electronic Reactions of Abrams—enabled disease to be detected before it was clinically identifiable in any orthodox way. He postulated that disease was an imbalance of the electrons of the atoms of the body and theorized that it was a form of radiating energy that could be detected by the electronic reactions, which could be measured by devices he invented.

Today radionics is a vitally important modality that incorporates and addresses thought fields, epigenetics, emotions, cellular memory, Western science, esoteric healing, astrology, geometry and patterns, consciousness, telepathy, and more. It unifies Western science with the Eastern philosophies and quantum sciences. It is a vast and complex subject but its fundamental principles are simple: it has a sound and practical basis, with repeatable positive results, encouraging the natural self-healing ability of the patient.

Linda Kinsella has over twenty years of experience in natural healing modalities and is interested in the transformative, empowering, and natural healing power of the life force. She is of the mind that radionics applications detect and treat the underlying causes of physical and energetic blockages and imbalance within this vital life force. Radionics, like ageless wisdom and the science of epigenetics, addresses the importance and right use of thought power and how an individual or group can heal by positive thought and a loving heart, aided by the creative mind and an ability to understand and work with energies.

Linda says that radionics sees organs, diseases, and remedies as having their own particular frequency or vibration. These vibrational frequencies are expressed in numerical rates, and used with radionics instruments or patterns, together with a "hair witness" from the client, to both evaluate and treat and reach behind the patient's given symptoms. Congestion, overstimulation, lack of coordination, injury, shock, geopathic stress, latent viruses, parasitic infection, the embedded vibrational patterns of toxins and poisons, and many other factors causing severe disruption may be transformed by well-selected radionics remedies.

Radionics invites us to reorient our ideas with its supersensory force that also taps into the healing power of Nature and the Cosmos. This vital force is the way to a new integration in which medicine will be equally scientific, philosophical, and spiritual.

MOLECULAR RESONANCE EFFECT TECHNOLOGY

The catastrophic radiation leak at the nuclear plant in Chernobyl, Ukraine, in 1986 caused more than six hundred thousand cancer-related deaths. Some researchers cite figures closer to three million yet no official statistics exist. Scientist and physicist Dr. Igor Smirnov, along with his scientific team, were sent to investigate the effects of the radiation on a village within the one-thousand-mile exclusion zone. Once there, the team discovered an anomaly within the affected perimeter: One group of individuals who were living within the thousand-mile radiation zone were found to be free of related symptoms and illness, while the majority of others also living within the zone were discovered to be suffering from the effects of radiation. After much on-site research it was found that the reason the former group had remained unaffected was due to the mountain spring water that sourced their village.

The subsequent discovery of unique characteristics in the spring water compelled Smirnov to find a way to effect molecular alignment so that the structure and frequency of water could become similar to that found within human cells. He also modified its electrical properties to the more ideal ion exchange (proton pump) across the cellular membrane. This resulted in decreased physiological viscosity and surface tension and a mechanism to deliver nutrients *into* and expel intracellular toxins *out of* the body.

This discovery ultimately led to his invention of Molecular Resonance Effect Technology (MRET), which was tested in the laboratories of several leading universities around the globe. These tests revealed that when water was activated with this technology the beneficial properties discovered confirmed its potential to help counter a multitude of negative environmental effects experienced by the physical body. MRET water has been shown to support wound healing as well as suppress growth of harmful bacteria such as staph and E. coli. When consumed on a regular basis, it also helps the body to resist the harmful effect of EMRs/EMFs.

MRET-activated water is produced within a thirty-minute time frame and at the single push of a button. This technology has since demonstrated how the single-file molecular alignment of water—and that of many other water-based liquids—can be modified in order to become coherent. This results in low entropy of the human biological system, which, in turn, supports stability and the body's natural ability to resist environmental challenges.

Smirnov's breakthrough in water activation led him to develop *another* polymer, which is also part of the patented MRET polymer family. This highly protective innovation was designed to combat the damaging effects of EMR emitted by wireless devices such as cell phones, wireless routers, Bluetooth devices, cordless phones, and other smart technologies people use on a daily basis. Due to the unique flexibility of his patented polymer material, Smirnov's invention has found its way into a variety of consumer-friendly radiation protection devices that can be worn on the body or used in a number of environments including homes, offices, and vehicles.

Fundamentally, Smirnov's patented radiation protection technology uses randomized frequencies to provide normalizing effects on the body in order to protect it from the impact that wireless and wired radiation has on living cells. It adds coherence to man-made electromagnetic signals by aligning them to natural electromagnetic fields—the same fields in which humans, plants, and animals had until recently coexisted peacefully.

LIVING IN HARMONY: A LIFESPACE HOME

The majority of humanity is living in an increasingly highly toxic electropolluted environment and a wireless world and whether we use

Wi-Fi or not, this imposes a significant danger to our overall health and well-being. Even if we purposely avoid cell phones, satellite navigation systems, smart meters, laptops, computers, headsets, and digital devices such as televisions, music systems, and radios, we are still impacted by the use of these technologies in the general community and the larger public domains such as shopping malls, public transport, stations, airports, hospitals, and our working environments. In particular, the imminent roll out of the 5G technology, which utilizes many untested frequencies of the electromagnetic spectrum including the millimeter wave, could initiate a potentially devastating effect on all cell-based organisms including plants, trees, bacteria, insects, animals, and human beings. The so-called evolutionary step that took us from analogue to digital and from wireless to smart poses a great threat to our health and well-being. If the general public had any idea of the real dangers they are being exposed to, protests would be taking place across the world.

Being an "electrosensitive," I have always struggled with the impact of electrostress on my mind and body. This has been the case whether the source is the television, electric plugs, remote controls, refrigerators, radios, washing machines, telephones, mobile phones, overhead and fluorescent lighting, or even the dashboard of a car. The bottom line is that if it is electrical, or digital, it will have a negative impact my physical health. One day, after years of suffering, I followed a link online and found a possible solution to my electrostress problem in the form of a "life-resonant" technology invented by Simon Fox

Fox, an electrosensitive himself, has easily made the connection between wireless radiation and its overarching impact. He finds it "frightening" to witness how man-made EMFs override and distort the life-giving frequencies we naturally receive from our environment, especially at this critical time when as a species we need to evolve beyond what we are now subjected to in our world. He remains extremely concerned that the flow of inspiration that he has grown accustomed to nurturing within himself is severely reduced in so many others who spend most or all of their time in incoherent and dangerous fields of radiation.

Over the course of several enlightening conversations, Fox explained that he has observed that when in an unhealthy environment, he is able to restore harmony in his body by connecting to the Earth. He states that "it is perfectly possible, when entrained with patterns found in nature, to remain significantly unaffected by electromagnetic pollution." This view has ultimately led to the development of a unique technology designed specifically to support us to stay in balance within an electrohostile environment.

Nature's Solutions

The ideal scenario for combating the effects of electrostress is to spend extended periods of time in the forest or to live and work primarily in Nature. Given the fact that this is not possible for most individuals, Fox has been researching potential solutions for over twelve years resulting in the development of Lifespace technology, which effectively brings the forest and Nature into the home and workplace. While the actual Lifespace technology is too complex and multilayered to go into here, Fox summarizes it as follows:

> Lifespace technology is not the solution to all the problems associated with life-damaging frequencies, and sometimes there is a misunderstanding that it is capable of "blocking" every form of undesirable energy. Rather, the device has been developed to try and bring more balance to the situation by using the Earth's natural life-affirming frequencies to induce a more biosupportive field into our homes and workspaces in order to enhance our well-being. By constantly repatterning our biofield with natural elements we gradually build up more resistance to unnatural, i.e., harmful, EMF frequencies. And whilst for anyone who suffers from electrosensitivity (approximately 10 percent of the population) this can be a life saver, the effects are also tangible for many who are not.

The Lifespace home unit is a small device that plugs into the main electricity supply within a building. Described simply, it holds "patterns of information" that become active and energized when plugged in, creating a harmonious environment for the body and encouraging it to remember its natural harmonic state. Fox explains that harmony is not something that can be forced upon the body but says that the body will return to harmony when it is located in an environment that contains the right contextual clues for it to literally feel at home. Those clues or reference points are found within the natural frequencies of the planet itself, within Nature, and within vital cosmic fields of information that are often drowned out and distorted by electromagnetic pollution. When they are present and undistorted, the body immediately recognizes, entrains, and harmonizes with them.

The Proof of the Pudding

After several informative discussions, Fox arranged to send me a set of his devices. They were very easy to set up; one simply plugs them in, and they are good to go. I found the impact of the units to be immediate. Straight away, an air of calm energy permeated the room. The air felt clean, bright, and somehow purer. I sat at my laptop anticipating nothing other than the usual unmanageable burning sensations, painful eyes, instant exhaustion, and nausea but, to my astonishment, all of these symptoms had diminished by 90 percent. It was unbelievable. I experienced almost no pain or burning, and this has continued to be the case.

We may not be able to change the situation as it is right now, but we can establish protective measures that will go some way to negating the harmful effects of current technology. There are leading-edge scientists and modern-day visionaries, some of whom are mentioned in this book, who have workable and proven solutions that can support people to remain well in a wireless world. *Our health is in our own hands.* The world as it is may present a danger zone with its electropollution, harmful frequencies, and radiation, but there are counter solutions available that at least present us with a choice.

MOLECULAR BIOLOGY AND (DISRUPTIVE) REGENERATIVE MEDICINE TECHNOLOGY

Carlo Ventura, M.D., Ph.D., is a revolutionary and pioneering biologist and a full professor of molecular biology at the University of Bologna, Italy, whose work includes cellular and regenerative cellular biology. His research into stem-cell programming is groundbreaking and reveals how it is possible to achieve cellular regeneration through exposure to extremely low frequency signals in electromagnetic fields similar to those produced by the human heart and the Earth.

Many of his contemporaries recognize his work as having the potential for affecting an evolutionary leap in regenerative medicine. Ventura is one of a handful of pioneers exploring a relatively new field of research he calls disruptive regenerative medicine technology.

Ventura discovered that ELF magnetic fields and radioelectric fields could enhance stem-cell pluripotency, allowing the direct reprogramming of human dermal skin fibroblasts into myocardial, neuronal, and skeletal muscle lineages. The cellular ability to generate and handle electromagnetic patterning is also the foundation for considering the possibility that cellular fate can be directed with physical energies. He proposes that cells and stem cells entail bioelectronic circuits and are able to produce physical energies like electromagnetic fields, nano-mechanical vibrations (including sounds), and light.

Ventura explained the following to me: While producing these "waves," a transpiring "nano world" unfolds in a sequence of wonderful oscillatory patterns. These exhibit features of connectedness and synchronization, the major form of recognition and even bimolecular recognition, without the necessity for the signaling molecules to touch each other. He suggested that stem cells sense these energies and transform that sensing into an ability to reprogram, because they are able to differentiate in all of the most complex of lineages, i.e., cardiac, neural, skeletal, muscular, and vascular. They produce trophic molecules capable of priming regenerative circuits within the tissues. Based upon the diffusive features of these energies, we are now able to target the stem cells at their origin. This affords a new path in regenerative and precision medicine because we can regenerate tissues without the need for cell or tissue transplantation.

The regenerative technologies deployed by Ventura and his team will allow the reprogramming in situ of the stem cells in all our tissues without resorting to cell or tissue transplantation and will boost our inherent ability for self-healing.

REJUVENATION AND REGENERATION THROUGH SOUND/TONE/MUSIC

This appendix would not be complete without including the vastly underestimated and overlooked role that sound, tone, and music play in health and well-being. Modern science now acknowledges this as a fundamental fact because all matter is composed of vibration and sound. Specific sound frequencies can be used not only for therapeutic healing but also to act as a catalyst for conscious evolution, spiritual awakening, and extradimensional experiences.

PINEAL TONING FOR HEALING AND SPIRITUAL AWAKENING

The extraordinary sound vibration of pineal toning stimulates a part of the parasympathetic nervous system known as the vagus nerve, resulting in deep relaxation and a significant reduction of stress. It also induces a sense of equilibrium, wellness, and radiance along with a peaceful and centered state. There are twenty-four toning levels in total amounting to the structure of a choral symphony. Pineal toning creates enhanced states of awareness and extraordinary experiences of healing and metaphysical insights. The biological impact of toning is reflected in studies on plant growth. For example, research affiliated with the Monterrey

Institute of Technology of Mexico studied the effects of music on plant physiology, growth, and yield productivity and concluded that classical music is the most beneficial and that certain pieces referred to as "the best of Mozart" set the benchmark for effectiveness. When the twenty-four individual tones were played in their numeric sequence, it was observed to be as much as 33 percent more beneficial than the best of Mozart.

THE HIGH VIBRATIONAL MEDICINE OF MUSIC

Human beings have an intimate relationship with music, and its healing power has been recognized for millennia. Beautiful music directed toward the womb can reassure the fetus. It is also able to reach all tissues and cells within the human body. Long-term research has shown that certain sounds and audio frequencies can help to synchronize our internal rhythms, harmonize and support brain activity, and regulate breathing, heartbeat, and blood pressure.

Vera Brandes is head of the Research Program for Music Medicine at the Paracelsus Medical University in Salzburg. The philosophy of her work is based upon the theory that everything in the physical body is a specific compaction of a collection of vibrating particles. From this, it can be deduced that by using a specific corresponding vibration, matter can be returned to its correct function. Brandes explained to me that the new science of music medicine uses this possibility by studying how the vibrations of music relate to the physical body as well as impact the subtle bodies and other levels that extend into the etheric realms. She teaches how this can be achieved with special forms of sound and by the influence of thought.

Brandes is a pioneer in the branch of vibrational medicine that proves music exists beyond the linguistic space and is more concrete than language because it can precisely determine emotional connotation. At the same time music transports highly complex vibrational information in a compressed form to every cell of the body and informs every thought and feeling. It can affect the body, mind, and Consciousness with mathematical precision.

Brandes began her research work at the University Mozarteum where she gathered a team of dedicated experts. Together they designed and formulated a range of studies that led to a number of scientific breakthroughs in the emerging field of *music effect research*. Dr. Roland Haas, then Dean of the University Mozarteum, paved the way for Brandes's ambitious goal of discovering exactly how and why we are affected by music through an interdisciplinary approach that combined physiology, chronobiology, and morphological psychology.

Brandes was convinced that many psychosomatic disorders could be significantly improved with the application of the correct auditory stimulation and vibration. She designed programs for specific diagnoses and tested these in large clinically controlled trials that included placebos. The trials were designed and conducted by a team of leading researchers in the field of psychosomatic medicine, psychiatry, public health, and heart-rate variability. The results unequivocally proved that the method invented by Brandes was more effective than any other of that time.

In her study on depression, which to this day remains the largest of its kind, Brandes treated outpatients suffering from various types and degrees of the condition over a period of five weeks. Participants were recruited through articles in daily newspapers and from public radio programs. This suggested that it was only sufferers of depression with an affinity for music that contacted the study team to express interest in joining the trial. Yet, interviews revealed their prime motivation was the fact that they had tried all other known methods without success. Interestingly, the music-medicine programs she initially and specifically developed for the treatment of depression worked equally well for patients suffering from both the acute and chronic condition. The duration of treatments of between five and ten weeks also helped to heal chronic pain, as more than 90 percent of patients experiencing it also suffered from depression.

According to Brandes, the most remarkable finding was that the heart-rate variability of the people treated with her method increased by a factor equal to the naturally occurring loss accompanying normal aging in healthy individuals in a period of a decade, suggesting that her method has the ability to rejuvenate the heart by ten years in just four weeks. This result is even more important because many of those who took part were patients suffering from hypertension who were under various forms of medication, including beta-blockers.

The analysis of the high frequency spectrum of the heart-rate variability in the study participants clearly demonstrated that the balance between the sympathetic and parasympathetic nervous systems was restored. Furthermore, this continued to improve steadily even when the patients had stopped listening to the prescribed programs during the week-long trial. Brandes and her team were delighted that their study subjects had regained the ability to restore healthy function. It had been their vision from the beginning to create a method that would preclude the necessity for lifelong dependency but one that would work quickly and effectively in remedying the cause of the disease rather than just the symptoms.

The Instrumental Medicine for Quality Sleep

In 2003, Brandes began to research the effect of insufficient sleep on human beings and how this can alter the activity and structure of the genes that are responsible for biological rhythms. It is now known that the desynchronization of the human circadian clock can cause and trigger a wide range of health disturbances. Early studies have already pointed to the negative effects and havoc that a lack of sleep can wreak on our genes. These epigenetic changes were found among shift and night workers whose internal rhythms are constantly disrupted.

Disrupted sleep blocks the ability of the body to self-regulate, self-repair, and self-heal. Improving the quality of sleep strengthens the immune system and therefore minimizes the risk of becoming unwell. It also enhances our performance capacity and overall well-being.

Coherence of the heart and brain state optimizes our ability to fall asleep easily and to sleep well, helping us to recharge and regenerate. In 2015, Brandes devised a system for sleep founded on her philosophy and discoveries that use music medicine as a natural transformer to harmonically attune the body, mind, and Soul. This "medicine" directs the systems of the body toward regeneration and healing and enables them to support and activate all the necessary mechanisms specific to each sleep cycle—an important prerequisite for physical and mental well-being.

The music used is created especially for its rhythmic, aesthetic, and tonal qualities and produces a comforting and easy-listening experience. At the same time, it addresses the senses in a variety of ways, while transmitting specific sound sequences that have a beneficial neurological effect. These are embedded in highly complex sound images that precisely match human chronobiology. These special mechanisms were developed after twenty years of research and have been tested in large clinical trials as well as statistically validated. The end result is something unique and entirely different from music routinely used for relaxation and sleep.

Brandes attaches great importance to working exclusively with new compositions in order to avoid any unintended associations or adverse memories that might otherwise be triggered. Studies have shown that brain-heart coherence is directly connected with brain function and performance, especially when under stress. During sleep, this coherence prevents stress-related bodily or mental disturbances and positively supports healing processes.

Science has proved that Brandes's devices are effective. Multiple comprehensive studies have shown that they synchronize inner rhythms and heart-brain coherence. The optimum function of the sympathetic nervous system is important for maintaining ideal heart-rate variability. At the same time, music medicine has a significant effect on alpha, theta, and delta brain activity. Her sleep system was found to directly impact parasympathetic regulation, which itself promotes heart-brain coherence. This in turn positively affects sleep quality and many other necessary healing processes.

With the cooperation of other scientists, Brandes was able to enrich and complete music effect research through many findings from a variety of disciplines. Results were integrated into her patented method of music medicine, which is specifically effective in protecting health. It is also used in conjunction with other treatments for patients suffering from serious diseases such as cancer and neurological or developmental disorders.

The sleep device developed by Brandes and her technical team is exclusive to her music medicine system. Specifically, composed music programs have been recorded with Sympathetic Resonance Technology (SRT). The SRT format has been especially adapted to meet her exacting standards and is based on the scientific insight that each physical system is penetrated and surrounded by energetic fields. When a system oscillates within the spectrum of its optimal frequency it functions far better and allows for higher levels of human potential and performance. The system uses high digital audio playback without data losses, which results in the specific psychoacoustic effects necessary for audio stimulation. A direct current from an AccuBattery pack is used so that no forms of potentially harmful alternating electrical fields occur that could disturb sleep. Brandes's work offers an exciting insight into the vast potential of music medicine and reveals greater possibilities for its practical application.

THE RECOLLECTION AND EMBODIMENT OF NEW TEMPLATES FOR REGENERATION, WELL-BEING, AND INSPIRATION

From the moment of conception, Nature is guiding us to move through the cycle of energetic phases—alternating phases of, for example, day and night, the four seasons, and, ultimately, the cycle of life and death—preparing us for a continuum of inner adaptation to the constancy of outer changes.

Depending on individual qualities and social and environmental conditions, we are naturally able to change our personal, physiological, and emotional state. Our feelings are influenced by the cycles of life—the morning and evening and the spring, summer, autumn, and winter—and the forces of Nature, including the Sun, Moon, wind, rain, hail, sleet, and snow. Similar influences exist in the macrocosm, within Nature around us, from quiet and peaceful lagoons and lakes to flowing rivers and majestic waterfalls, from deep forests to vast lowlands and dry deserts, from massive mountain ranges to the mystical above and beyond them, a kaleidoscopic bountiful energetic spectrum.

We can find the whole spectrum of the macrocosm existent within the singular interconnected human microcosm. The inner reflects the outer and vice-versa; as above so below. The fixed and often rigid rules of so-called modern society are juxtaposed to Nature's intricate variability. Overreliance on intellectual answers to life's broad scale of subtleties and multidimensional/multipolar nature is diminishing our ability to connect more fully with the world around us, other people, and other beings and tap into the deeper mysteries of life. Our capacity to wonder and to be fascinated, enchanted, enthused, inspired, astonished, and amazed also loses its aliveness. For instance, when dwelling too much in the past, our inability to surrender, let go, and forgive can also prove to be an obstacle, minimizing our inborn capacity for receiving something that supersedes rationale and mental projection and transcends and gifts us with something "new" and unknown, expressed through and beyond perception.

AOUM: A NEW HOLISTIC STORY OF PHYSICAL-ENERGETIC MOVEMENT

Within the "old" structures, overly rigid templates, repetitive postures, prescriptive movements, disciplined workouts, hierarchical structures, and advanced systems within systems are predominantly intellectual approaches, often with a colloquial axiom of "no pain, no gain." Many such models create addictive tendencies; for example, a person experiences suffering if they miss a session. In an untrained and dualistic mind, such practices can ultimately confine and impose strict boundaries that are often difficult to define, and therefore hard to liberate ourselves from.

In these changing times, however, new free-flowing templates, practices, and qualities are coming to the foreground that can expand our personal amplitude (physical, emotional, mental, energetic) and potential for opening to and integrating new forms of movement that can free us from those that overly engage the mind.

AOUM is one such unique practice that Jano Stefanik, a Europe-based Talgar practitioner and facilitator, has developed. Symbolically, AOUM is founded on the principle of the four seasons and is a mantric expression of the four basic bioenergetic phases of a human microcosm. The main two phases are opening/inhalation, or Tao (connecting with the outer world/the environment), and closing/exhalation, or Chum (connecting with the inner world/the organism). In addition, the fundamental states of Tao and Chum each have two phases—active and passive. All four phases in their energetic potential are equal to each other.

Each of the four bioenergetic phases corresponds with a specific emotional coloring, our physiology, and our mindset, as well as subtler aspects including bioenergetic frequencies. Our prevalent energetic phase plays an integral role in how we react (close down) or respond (open up) to life, how we manage "conflicts," how we maintain health, and, indeed, how we engage with life in general. Below is a more detailed look at each phase.

Tao A: Active Phase of Opening

In the morning, active stretching with warm alive feelings brings vibrancy, life, and feelings of joy back into our being as well as optimism, enthusiasm, playfulness, lightness, and an openness to new impulses. This is a recognition of the start of a new cycle with its active potential. In Nature, we find parallels in springtime, the phase of active growth and preparation for the next phase.

Tao O: Passive Phase of Opening

A conducive time to experience this phase is before the first meal of the day. However, most people have busy lifestyles and may not have/make the time to engage at such a time. This is the phase of realization; we can experience it fully only after the quality active phase of opening—preparation. It can also be a meditative state aligned with the opening phase, when our senses, eyes, minds, and posture are open. We look for stillness, silence, and the practice of opening in our connection with the outer world. Dynamics are no longer desired. This natural desire or impulse is something that develops gradually, an impulse to move on for instance, or an impulse to simply pause, stop.

This phase corresponds to summer, blossoms and sunshine, and the peak of opening. It is a relaxed, youthful, abundant, and vibrant state. We can find/generate feelings (frequencies) of unity, freedom, and measureless joy with the loss of hierarchies and authorities.

Ideally, we practice phases A–O in a sequence. After an active phase of preparation, a deserved phase of realization follows. A short morning session of a Tao practice might only take three to five minutes, but qualitatively it has a potential to enrich the rest of our day with additional energy and an overall different "tone."

Chum U: Active Phase of Closing

This is the dynamic and active phase of our intellectual work. Most of our daily social activities—our work or business activities, reaching our aims and goals, our social interactions, driving, eating, talking, and laughing—require us to remain in this phase. Our expectations of success and recognition, our aspirations for prestige and for winning, our determination and will power, all of these are experienced by this phase. In Nature, this phase corresponds to autumn, the active process of ripening, and preparations for the next phase.

Chum M: Passive Phase of Closing

This is the phase of relaxation, the finalization of the cycle and the phase of sleep. It is the time for inner reorganization, regeneration, meditative inward states, and disconnection from the outer world and a feeling of nostalgia and inner-harmony softness. This phase corresponds to winter, when Nature closes in and various species move into hibernation.

Balancing Tao and Chum

In the modern world, Chum processes prevail in all aspects of our lives. Most of our health issues originate from the imbalance (and blocking) of natural transitions between these various phases. If we are seeking more overall balance within ourselves and our lives, we need to acknowledge how far removed we have come from Tao. The current challenging times are just one example of this, as spontaneity, freedom, joy, happiness, unconditional ways, and a sense of connection are at best compromised and at worst denied. And so major asymmetries are the daily reality for most of us as we battle through the maze of disconnectivity and constrictive/restrictive patterns and themes that underpin modern life.

Once we lose connection, we no longer remember the eternal youthfulness of our Souls, and we begin to lose enthusiasm for the new and unknown, for inspiration and the miracle that is life and natural living. We lose contact with our personal rhythm, which results in a lack of natural joy. We become disconnected, depriving ourselves of the profound universal potential that exists within each one of us. The divine spark within is what connects us to our essential selves, to Source, and without this, we remain less than fully alive. Part of our daily quest is to attain and maintain the balance between body, feelings, mind, heart and Soul.

The inner world has been largely considered to be fixed or given, and the outer world regarded as the primary focus of our interest and development. We have been deeply conditioned to seek guidance outside of ourselves, to look up to authorities in health, education, and religion, instead of looking up to the stars, the Cosmos, and Mother Earth, to Nature Herself. We have been taught to seek help from "out there" when we are feeling unwell, to turn to pharmaceuticals and allopathic medicines, instead of tapping into the extrasensory wisdom, guidance, potentialities, and miraculous healing powers of our own bodies and Souls.

AOUM opens up practical, profound, and transformational potentialities through the simplified practice and methodology of realigning various aspects of our being, tuning into our own bioenergetic rhythm, and opening to our inner guidance—the inner wisdom of our being. Our incredible self-regulatory capacity, yet to be fully comprehended, can guide us through new levels of understanding of our organism as a whole. Its qualitative scope is difficult to assess from the perspective of more traditional linear and structured disciplines. But this holistic practice, which cares for body, mind, and Soul, affords a return to wholeness, authenticity, simplicity, purity, and grace.

SHINING LIGHTS FOR OUR TIMES

AOUM is a simple practice for Self-discovery, Self-awareness, and Self-realization. It encourages us to open to the new that is more reflective of our evolving needs in these transformational times. It offers us tools to dissolve old limiting patterns and experience the sensation of letting go of that which no longer serves us with our whole being, as we open to the new. It honors the importance of struggle and loss, actively transforming these into beautiful opportunities for new beginnings that lead us out of the predicament of a predominant intellect and overidentified mind, the security/prison of the known, and into fulfillment, the felt-sense, body, feelings, heart wisdom, the freedom of the unknown. It calls on us to cultivate right relationship with ourselves and balance our inner worlds, which brings a more balanced relationship with the outer world. It compels us to disentangle from the insatiable demands of the overly dominant intellect, confining structures, and the "shoulds" and "oughts" of the overstimulated and over-conditioned mind.

In essence, AOUM—and all the other new psychological, biological, and technological findings and advancements—are shining lights for our times, here to guide us to reconnect with our own innate capacity and deep-down desire for simplicity and purity—the quality of peace that arises when we declutter our minds. They afford us the possibility to create new and liberating foundations and support our entire organism to maximize its incredible regulatory ability and therefore function at its fullest potential, thus supporting us to live in harmony with ourselves and each other, while compelling us to cocreate a simpler, purer, and deeply organic and harmonious world.

Glossary

AKASHIC FIELD—A nonphysical compendium of all experiences and expressions; all thoughts, feelings, words, actions, deeds, and intents to have ever existed throughout all time, by any being, human or otherwise

Akashic Records—Information of our past, present, and future lives said to be stored on Alcyone, one of the stars of the Pleiades.

ascension—When the physical and energetic bodies reach higher dimensions without going through the death process. The highest level of ascension is when the cells of the physical body increase their vibration to such a degree they can no longer remain in a carbon state.

astral body—A subtle energy body beyond the physical made up of prana (life force) and attached to the physical form that survives after "death."

astral plane—The fourth-dimensional nonphysical realm of Consciousness, which corresponds to the physical world but is not of it. The plane through which a Soul passes upon physical death from the third dimension into a higher one.

astral travel—Intentional out-of-body experience (OBE) where an aspect of soul transcends the physical-material plane and travels across multiverses and through multitimelines.

avatar—A highly advanced Being who has never had a previous life on Earth visits the world for a single lifetime and takes on a human form with the purpose of awakening humanity.

baktun—A period of 394 years in the Mayan calendar, thirteen of which make up the Long Count calendar.

baobab—One of the most powerful of all flower/bush remedies that comes from the baobab tree found only in the Kimberley region of northwest Australia.

cellular memory—Memories of all experiences that are held in our cells.

chakras—In Sanskrit *chakra* means "disk" or "wheel" and refers to vortexes or energy centers within the body. There are seven primary centers.

channeling—Acting as a conduit for messages from the spirit world and the Cosmos.

collective consciousness—The entrained consciousness of the collective human race.

conjunction (in astrology)—Two planets within a 0 degree orb of each other.

Conscious Dying Experience (CDE)—An event where a person physically and consciously experiences the dying process before returning fully to a state of being alive in the human body.

Consciously awakened—The ability to be guided by Higher Intelligences, including higher levels of the Self. Being aware of and/ or connected to the multidimensional Self (the multiple aspects of the incarnate Soul that reside in different dimensions).

Conscious Mind—Self, Psychospiritually Awake Self, Psychospiritually Aware Self.

consciousness—The psychospiritually and consciously unawakened, socially conditioned, third-dimensional expression of self.

Consciousness—The Psychospiritually Awakened, Connected, and Integrated, Consciously Aware, fifth-dimensional expression of Self.

CONSCIOUSNESS—GOD/SOURCE/EXISTENCE/ALL THAT IS/LOVE/SPIRIT.

dimensions—Multifacets of perceived reality, and Reality Itself, from a metaphysical and spiritual perspective. Multimetaphysical levels where multitudes of souls reside in between incarnations, the levels they are stationed at are determined by the remit and stage of the journey of the soul.

DMT (dimethyltryptamine)—A chemical substance that is found throughout Nature including the human brain and is responsible for altering and expanding human Consciousness. It is a natural psychedelic and is active in the brain particularly in transitory stages like birth and death.

duality—Polarization, separation, opposition; divisive thoughts, feelings, and actions.

electromagnetic field—Invisible electric and magnetic force fields, often referred to as EMFs, which are accelerated when particles are charged (e.g., electrons).

enlightenment—The process of becoming fully consciously and spiritually awake in human form.

epigenetics—Changes within organisms and environmental factors that modify gene expression but not the genetic code itself.

etheric—Closest of the energy bodies to the physical body, the etheric body acts as a filter between the physical and all other energetic bodies.

existential—An exploration of the meaning of life, what pertains to life, and what exists beyond life. A crisis of meaning, when life, the universe, and all things have no meaning except for that which an individual defines for themselves.

fifth dimension—A higher-dimension beyond the current third-dimensional world.

fifth-dimensional Consciousness—A Higher Consciousness entrained and aligned with a more evolved and awakened state of being and connected to higher dimensional realities.

frequency—The metaphysical tone of an individual. The degree to which the Light is active within and around one, dependent on the degree to which one is consciously and spiritually awakened.

Galactic Center—The centermost point of the galaxy.

Galactic Plane—The plane in which the majority of our disc-shaped galaxy mass lies.

galaxy—A vast formation of plasma clouds that contains a large system of stars.

gateway—See "portal."

gender binarism—The classification of gender into two distinct, opposite, and disconnected forms of masculine and feminine.

gender fluidity—The identification of gender that is not fixed but fluid, e.g., at times the individual is more identified with the inner male and at others, the inner female but always experiences these complementary modes of being as perfectly balanced and organic.

gestalt therapy—A person-centered psychotherapy practice developed by Fritz Perls, Laura Perls, and Paul Goodman in the 1940s and 1950s, first described in the 1951 book *Gestalt Therapy*. It includes chair work, where one talks to an imagined other in an opposite chair and engages in psychotherapeutically healing dialogue with the "other."

gnosis—The ability to "know" without any evidence or proof. To know, but not know how we know; we just *know.*

Grand Cycle—A complete sweeping era of "time" from beginning to end.

Great Mystery—That which is beyond conscious comprehension, the vast, unfathomable, unknowable, barely perceivable infinite BEYOND, where the soul's journey continues as we pass from this world. The origin of the soul, and beyond the soul.

Higher Self—An extended part of the Self, vibrating in a higher dimension.

HOME—The origin of the Soul, where we come from and where we return after leaving the human vessel.

hypercommunication—Hyperdimensional highways of communication—physical to metaphysical to physical communication—in which crown, brow, throat, and heart chakras are especially active.

interdimensional selves—As multidimensional beings we are travelling across multitimelines through multiportals and gateways through multidimensional reality.

karma—The law of cause and effect—usually redressed long-term across multiple timelines (past timelines). The more integrated, awakened, and evolved one becomes, the more one is prone to instant karma, where the "misdeed" is resolved in the short term/immediate life/ same timeline.

Lemuria—An ancient/original civilization believed to have existed on earth some 80,000 years ago. A highly advanced, conscious, and awakened collective of spiritually connected Beings of Light. A blueprint for the future Diamond Age.

Light—LOVE/GOD made manifest in the form of LIGHT.

Light body—An energy body that exists at a higher level and closer to the Soul. It opens portals to the Higher Realms of light and connects us with the universal mind.

Light Workers—Souls who have incarnated on the Earth to assist with the ascension of humanity and the planet.

Long Count—Period of 5,125 years of the Mayan calendar. It began August 11, 3114 BCE and ended on December 21, 2012.

lucid dream—A dream in which the dreamer is aware that they are dreaming.

Luminous Ones—Higher-Dimensional Beings of Light; Highest spiritual Teachers of humanity; Supra-Advanced Intelligences overlighting humanity and working in service of human and planetary evolution.

matrix—The psychospiritually unconscious and unawakened human world.

Mayan calendar—A calendar with an end date of 2012 believed to have been given to the Mayan people by the Pleiadeans.

metaphysics—The branch of philosophy concerned with the nature of reality and existence.

Milky Way—Our spiral-shaped galaxy and home to billions of stars, including our Sun.

multiuniversals—Highly evolved super-intelligent beings and energy forms that exist and travel between universes.

near-death experience (NDE)—An event where an individual momentarily "dies" but returns fully to a state of being alive in the human body.

Olmec—The "mother culture" of the Mayan civilization.

out-of-body experience (OBE)—When the Consciousness leaves the confines of the physical body.

paradigm—An aeon or Grand Cycle of time. The beginning and end of a world-defining, sweeping era of time. Old world = old paradigm and new world = new paradigm.

Pleiadeans—Fifth-dimensional beings said to hail from the Pleiades star system.

portal—Cosmic gateway for travelling through multidimensions. An opening to another reality, past and future timelines, and beyond the world. A vortex swirl energy created geomagnetic forces with a magnetic pulling force

precession—The circular movement of the Earth's axis.

precession of the equinoxes—Axial precession imparts a "wobbling" motion to the rotational axis of an astronomical body causing the axis to slowly trace out a "cone." The Earth goes through one such complete cycle lasting a period of approximately twenty-six thousand years, during which the positions of stars slowly change.

psychic attack—An energetic attack from otherworldly or low-vibrational worldly energies that are not your own. Ill intent from conscious or subconscious sources to harm an individual.

psychospiritual—The integration of the psychological and the spiritual.

self—The third-dimensional ego/self or "personality" living in the physical world of duality and separated from the Self or Higher Self.

Self—Authentic, True, psychospiritually healed and integrated personality.

Self-transcendence—A fully manifested state of being in but not of the world.

shaman—A person with the ability to contact and see other worlds and dimensions; a tribal "medicine" person with extraordinary abilities to heal.

sociocracy—A system of governance that seeks to achieve solutions that create harmonious social environments and productive organizations.

Soul—The immortal part of ourselves.

SOURCE—THE ETERNAL FORCE; GOD/THE DIVINE/THE BELOVED/THE ALMIGHTY/CONSCIOUSNESS/LIGHT/ LOVE.

square (in astrology)—A 90° angle between two planets. The tension point within an astrological chart, which reveals challenges in service of healing and growth. A motivating, compelling, and magnetic force that serves an ultimate higher good.

Superconscious Mind—Higher Self, Soul Communion, the bridge between Self and Soul.

sweat lodge—A mud, dome-shaped hut heated by steam from water poured onto hot stones. They are central to First Nations Peoples' traditions for purifying and sacred ritual.

third dimension—The physical world anchored in linear Space-Time reality.

third-dimensional consciousness—A consciously unawakened state, psychospiritually asleep.

Unconscious—The vast compendium of the sum total of all personal experience throughout all timelines; an encyclopedia of all collective experience on Earth.

unconscious mind—self, psychospiritually asleep self, psychospiritually unaware self.

vibration—The oscillation and movement of a particle. All creation manifests from divine energy, and everything that is physically manifested vibrates within certain ranges of frequency. The density or consciousness of a living organism governs how slowly or quickly the energy vibrates physically.

yuga—In Hinduism yuga is an epoch or era within a four-age cycle.

Index

About the Author

Nicolya Christi is a visionary, futurist, and author. Her first book, *2012: A Clarion Call—Your Soul's Purpose in Conscious Evolution,* was placed in the top ten book reviews by *Publishers Weekly* in spring 2011. Professor Ervin Laszlo, twice nominated for the Nobel Peace Prize, endorsed it as "the most remarkable spiritual book on this or any other subject I have ever read." Satish Kumar described her as "a great visionary and thinker whose work in articulating and promoting conscious evolution is outstanding." Barbara Marx Hubbard referred to her as "our guide through this evolutionary global shift, and one of the best I have encountered."

She is also the author of *Contemporary Spirituality for an Evolving World: A Handbook for Conscious Evolution* and a slimline series she launched in late 2020, *Four Fundamentals: A Pocket Book for Self-Healing, Self-Awakening, and Self Liberation.*

She recently completed her debut novel, an epic fiction-based-on-fact story for our times, the first of a trilogy of books interweaving defining historical timelines.

Nicolya's Work is founded on spirituality, metaphysics, philosophy, and psychology. She has developed various psychospiritual maps and models for evolving consciousness and brings unique new theories to the psychological and spiritual domains, all of which are inspired by extensive personal experience in these fields.

Between June 1997 and November 2002, she underwent multiple out-of-body experiences, which included mystical encounters, a life-changing experience of conscious dying in March 2002, and a consciousness-transforming experience of enlightenment in October 2009.

Her Work is founded upon three fundamental principles: psychological integration, conscious evolution, and spiritual awakening. Its trajectory spans the conscious evolution of the individual and the world itself—from Conscious Awareness to Conscious Integration, to Self and Collective Realization, to Self and Collective Actualization, and, ultimately, Self and Collective Transcendence.